The Apartisan American

The Apartisan American

Dealignment and Changing Electoral Politics

Russell J. Dalton

University of California, Irvine

Los Angeles | London | New Delhi
Singapore | Washington DC

Los Angeles | London | New Delhi
Singapore | Washington DC

FOR INFORMATION:

CQ Press
An Imprint of SAGE Publications, Inc.
2455 Teller Road
Thousand Oaks, California 91320
E-mail: order@sagepub.com

SAGE Publications Ltd.
1 Oliver's Yard
55 City Road
London, EC1Y 1SP
United Kingdom

SAGE Publications India Pvt. Ltd.
B 1/I 1 Mohan Cooperative Industrial Area
Mathura Road, New Delhi 110 044
India

SAGE Publications Asia-Pacific Pte. Ltd.
33 Pekin Street #02-01
Far East Square
Singapore 048763

Acquisitions Editor: Charisse Kiino
Production Editor: Elizabeth Kline
Copy Editor: Shannon Kelly
Typesetter: C&M Digitals (P) Ltd.
Proofreader: Emily Bakely
Indexer: Jean Casalegno
Cover Designer: Matthew Simmons,
                www.MyselfIncluded.com
Marketing Manager: Christopher O'Brien

Printed in the United States of America

Library of Congress Cataloging-in-Publication Data

Dalton, Russell J.

The apartisan American : dealignment and changing electoral politics / Russell J. Dalton.

p. cm.
Includes bibliographical references and index.

ISBN 978-1-4522-1694-2 (alk. paper)
1. Party affiliation—United States—History—20th century.
2. Party affiliation—United States—History—21st century.
3. Elections—United States—History—20th century.
4. Elections—United States—History—21st century. I. Title.

JK2271.D36 2013
324.0973—dc23   2011051359

This book is printed on acid-free paper.

12 13 14 15 16 10 9 8 7 6 5 4 3 2 1

To the memory of

my three BFFs

TABLE OF CONTENTS

TABLES AND FIGURES

TABLES

FIGURES

PREFACE

After the 2000 elections, Matthew Dowd advised the George W. Bush administration that the percentage of independents was small and decreasing, so Republicans could ignore them and focus on mobilizing their ideological base. At almost the same time, other political strategists were saying that election trends predominately depend on independent swing voters, and the campaign that wins independents wins elections. As the 2012 election approaches, these same debates continue: some campaign strategists claim that the independent vote will determine the election outcome, while others stress the need to mobilize a party's base voters. Academic researchers are also divided on these same points. Even more striking, many of these debaters use the same public opinion polls and election evidence but reach quite different conclusions.

These are starkly different images of American electoral politics, with fundamental implications on how an administration governs, that administration's policy priorities, and how politicians campaign for elections. Would the Bush administration have pursued more centrist policies if it believed moderate voters would determine its reelection chances or results in the House and Senate? Would President Bill Clinton have followed his famous triangulation policies if he believed he could win reelection by focusing on the Democrats' liberal base? To what extent have the policies of the Barack Obama administration (or the Republican majority in the U.S. House of Representatives since 2010) been linked to the administration's perceptions of this debate (and of Obama's likely supporters in 2012)?

This book engages in this ongoing debate and tracks the growth of independents who have rejected party identities over the past sixty years. In 2010–2011, independents represented the largest single share of the public, outnumbering Democratic Party or Republican Party identifiers. Yet some skeptics argue that the dealignment is an illusion. Even more important, I maintain that independents' social and political characteristics have changed over time. Instead of the politically disengaged independents of the 1950s, today's independents are mostly interested in politics and are highly educated. These new apartisans are altering the dynamics of electoral politics and thereby the workings of the democratic process. I describe these patterns in this book, compare the American experience to that of other Western democracies, and consider the implications for American politics in the future.

Of the many people who helped with this project, I owe an exceptional debt to Marty Wattenberg. Marty and I collaborated on research studying party dealignment in Western democracies (*Parties without Partisans*, 2000), which built on Marty's research on dealignment in the United States (*The Decline of American Political Parties*, 1998; *The Rise of Candidate Centered Politics*, 2002) and my cross national research (*Electoral Change in Advanced Industrial Democracies*, 1984). As I began this study of the U.S. experience, updating past evidence through the 2010 election, Wattenberg's research was often my starting point. Throughout the analysis and writing process, he generously shared suggestions, new data, and his vast knowledge of American politics. While we differ in some of our interpretations of youth and politics, we broadly agree about the extent and implications of dealignment in America. If imitation is the greatest form of flattery, you can find lots of flattery for Marty's earlier research in this book.

The American National Election Studies (ANES) deserves equal credit. Since 1952 this project has tracked the political opinions and behavior of the American electorate. The majority of evidence in this book is based on the ANES. The founders of this project—Angus Campbell, Philip Converse, Warren Miller, and Donald Stokes—gave voice to the average citizen and created the theoretical and empirical model that underlies the research presented here. I took courses from Converse, Miller, and Stokes while at Michigan, and I am sure each of them would be amazed and proud of how the ANES has developed. Their scholarship once defined the agenda of electoral research in America. Now the project depends on others to do the research.

I would like to thank the scholars who reviewed this book—Alexandra Cole, California State University, Northridge; William Field, Rutgers University; Barbara Norrander, University of Arizona; and Karen Shafer, Arizona State University—for their helpful comments and reflections. I also benefitted from the advice and assistance of Natalie Cook, Marc Howard, Ian McAllister, Helmut Norpoth, Henrik Ekengren Oscarsson, Kelly Rivera, Robert Rohschneider, and Bernhard Wessels at various stages of this project. I discussed many of these ideas with students in my classes at the University of California, Irvine and learned from these exchanges. Finally, Charisse Kiino, Elizabeth Kline, Shannon Kelly, and the production team at CQ Press have been wonderful to work with; they are an author's dream of a supportive publisher. Thank you to all these people.

I wrote this book to be accessible to all those who study parties and elections: students, faculty, and practitioners. The goal is to raise important questions for electoral politics and marshal the best available evidence to address these questions in an accessible way for a broad array of readers. Electoral politics is one of the most important aspects of the democratic process, so I hope this work adds to our understanding of how citizens and parties are changing and the implications of such change for the democratic process.

Russell J. Dalton
Irvine, California

AUTHOR BIOGRAPHY

RUSSELL J. DALTON is professor of political science at the University of California, Irvine, and was the founding director of the Center for the Study of Democracy at UC Irvine. He has received a Fulbright Professorship at the University of Mannheim, a Barbra Streisand Center Fellowship, a German Marshall Research Fellowship, and a POSCO Fellowship at the East/West Center in Hawaii. His recent publications include *Patterns of Party Government* (2011), *The Good Citizen* (2009), *Citizen Politics* (2008), and *Democratic Challenges, Democratic Choices* (2004). He is co-editor of *Citizens, Context and Choice* (2011), *Party Politics in East Asia* (2008), *The Oxford Handbook of Political Behavior* (2007), *Citizens, Democracy and Markets around the Pacific Rim* (2006), *Democracy Transformed?* (2003), and *Parties without Partisans* (2001). Dalton's scholarly interests include comparative public opinion, political parties, and political participation.

THE APARTISAN AMERICAN

> Why would you want to be nonpartisan? If
> you're a partisan, you know what you stand for.
> People know what the Democrats stand for (tax
> and spend), they know what Republicans stand for
> (which is America), and then you can decide which
> one you want to support.
>
> Stephen Colbert
> *The Colbert Report* (August 10, 2011)

Lyse first heard Barack Obama speak at the Harkin Steak Fry in the summer of 2007, and she was immediately impressed by the candidate. She became deeply engaged in the Obama campaign, working for it throughout the fall, organizing a group of Obama supporters in her high school (Barackstars), and ultimately serving as an Obama precinct captain at the January 2008 Iowa caucuses. Lyse repeated this involvement in the fall presidential election and celebrated Obama's victory in November. A picture of her with Obama at an Iowa campaign event graces her Facebook page.

After the election Lyse enrolled at the University of Iowa and became a political science major. This led to an internship working in the state legislature. Lyse seemed on course to become a Democratic politico. However, after the internship experience she returned home and changed her voter registration from Democrat to independent (even though she remains a staunch supporter of President Obama).

What led Lyse to reject party affiliation and become an independent? Her story, and the story of millions like her, is the focus of this book. At the time of John F. Kennedy's election in 1960, only a quarter of the American public claimed to be independent, but this number has grown over the following decades. Since 2004 about 40 percent of the public call themselves independent, outnumbering both Democrats (about one-third of the public) and Republicans (just over a quarter of the public). The largest group of Americans today is independent of party identities.

The growing importance of independents can be seen in recent elections. Although parties and candidates necessarily cater to their base voters, increasing attention is being paid to the increasing number of independents, who are more likely to shift votes between elections. If parties seek to increase their vote share since the last poll, independents are often where they search for these new voters. For instance, the vote swing to George W. Bush in 2000 came largely from independents, just as Obama's victory in 2008 depended on winning disproportionate support from independents. The Republican gains in 2010 also benefitted from independents swinging back toward that party. Moreover, if new political movements—groups as different as Ralph Nader's supporters in 2000 or the Tea Party movement in 2010—seek voters, they are most likely to find support among independents.

Furthermore, many of these new independents are like Lyse. They are young. Instead of the disengaged independents of the past, these new independents are often better educated and more interested in politics. However, despite their political interest they have not developed the partisan allegiances of their parents' generation. In addition, they are often cynical about both political parties and the current system of party competition. These are the new independents—the *apartisan Americans*—who give this book its title.

This book describes the growing number of Americans who are independent of partisan identities and the factors contributing to their growth. Even if political elites remain wedded to their partisan identities, the citizens themselves are changing. Our goal is to document these changes and their implications for American electoral politics.

THE CONCEPT OF PARTY IDENTIFICATION

Several years ago, I was a beginning political science professor at Florida State University in Tallahassee. On the day of the presidential election, I went to the polls to cast my ballot. While standing in the inevitable line, I started talking with the older woman standing in front of me. She told me about her experiences in a long series of election campaigns that began before I was born. Interesting stuff for a political science professor who studies elections. When she talked about the current election, she made an observation I'll never forget. She said, "I always vote for the best candidate in the election regardless of the political party. But it just seems that in every election the best candidate is a Democrat."

This woman is representative of a traditional pattern of partisan loyalties in American electoral politics. She had distinct political interests, but our conversation suggested that these interests were partially shaped by her initial partisan orientations. Being a Democrat was often a family tradition in Florida at the time. It was common to hear people say that they voted for the Democrats, as did their parents, their grandparents, and so forth back to the post–Civil War reconstruction of the South. And nationally most Americans identified with either the Democratic or Republican Party.

A generation or more ago, such partisan attachments were widespread among Americans. People did not just vote for the Republican or the Democratic candidate, they considered themselves to be a Republican or a Democrat. *The American Voter* describes such a partisan identity as *a long-term, affective psychological attachment to a preferred political party*.[1] Stating a party identification was viewed as similar to identifying with a religious denomination or social class.[2] These orientations were formed early in life, often before young people fully understood the content of these labels, and they largely endured through life even as the politicians and parties changed.[3] Even if one temporarily voted for a candidate of a different party, there was a strong tendency to return "home" at the next election or even the next office listed on the ballot. Partisanship also was at the core of individuals' political beliefs, affecting how they thought of themselves and politics.

After reviewing four decades of electoral research on partisanship, Herbert Weisberg and Steve Greene concluded that "Party identification is the linchpin of our modern understanding of electoral democracy, and it is likely to retain that crucial theoretical position."[4] Similarly, I have stated that a "strong case can be made that the concept of partisan identification is the most important development in modern electoral behavior research."[5]

So what makes party identification so important? The concept of party identification has reached such prominence because these orientations affect many different aspects of political behavior. The developers of the concept stressed its functional importance:

> *Few factors are of greater importance for our national elections than the lasting attachment of tens of millions of Americans to one of the parties. These loyalties establish a basic division of electoral strength within which the competition of particular campaigns takes place. And they are an important factor in ensuring the stability of the party system itself. . . . The strength and direction of party identification are of central importance in accounting for attitudes and behavior.*[6]

Partisan identities serve as an organizing device for the voters' political evaluations and judgments.[7] For instance, once a person becomes psychologically attached to a party, he or she tends to see politics from a partisan perspective. Being a Democratic identifier makes one more likely to be sympathetic to Democratic Party leaders and the policies they advocate and skeptical of the leaders and policies of the Republican Party. Faced with a new issue or political controversy, the knowledge of what position is favored by one's party is a valuable cue in developing one's own position. The authors of *The American Voter* thus described partisanship as a "perceptual screen"—through it one sees what supports one's partisan orientation while filtering out dissonant information. The stronger the party bond, the more likely is the selection and distortion processes of information.

Moreover, in comparison to other potential political cues, such as class or religion, party attachments are relevant across a much broader range of political phenomena because parties are so central to the political process. Issues and events frequently are presented to the public in partisan terms, and nearly all politicians are affiliated with a political party. When an elected official appears on television, it is almost always with a "D" or an "R" following his or her name. Furthermore, as researchers have studied the information shortcuts that voters use to orient themselves to politics, partisanship has emerged as the ultimate cost-saving device.[8] Partisan cues are an efficient decisional shortcut because people can use their partisan identities to decide what policies to support and oppose.

This cue-giving function of partisanship is strongest for voting behavior, because it is here that citizens make explicit partisan choices. Philip Converse described partisanship as the basis for a "normal vote", that is, the voting outcome expected if voter decisions were based solely on standing partisan commitments.[9] If issues or candidate images come into play, their influence can be measured by their ability to cause significant defections from normal partisan predispositions. For the unsophisticated voter, long-term partisan loyalty and repeated experience with one's preferred party provide a clear and low-cost cue for voting. Even for the sophisticated citizen, a candidate's party affiliation normally signifies a policy program that can serve as the basis for reasonable electoral choice. Like the Tallahassee resident at the beginning of this section, people say that they vote for the best person regardless of party, it just happens that their party routinely nominates the best candidate.

Similarly, partisanship gives party leaders an expected base of popular support that generally (within limits) supports them at the next election. Each election does not begin as a blank slate. Republicans and Democrats start campaigns with standing commitments from their core supporters, and partisan ties encourage a stability and continuity in electoral results. This is another consequence of Converse's notion of a normal vote. Electoral change normally occurs at the margins of these partisan coalitions, especially among independents.

Partisan ties also mobilize people to become politically engaged. Just like a sports loyalty, an attachment to a political party draws an individual into the political process to support his or her side. Participation in campaign activities is generally more common among strong partisan identifiers.[10] Political parties can more easily mobilize partisans to turn out at the polls, and partisans feel a stronger personal motivation to support their party and its candidates. Partisans often think of elections as a contest between "my party" and the "other guy's."

Finally, partisanship encompasses a set of normative attitudes regarding the role that political parties should play in the democratic system. Herbert Weisberg expressed the formal theory for this view, arguing that party identification is multidimensional—tapping evaluations of specific parties, independence from parties, and support for the *institution* of the party system in general.[11]

In summary, partisanship is a central element in the functioning of citizens' political behavior and party systems. Partisan ties:

- bind individuals to their preferred political party, as well as the system of party democracy;
- help orient the individual to the complexities of politics;
- provide a framework for assimilating political information and understanding political issues;
- act as a guide in making political judgments;
- mobilize individuals to participate in parties, elections, and the processes of representative government;
- provide a source of political stability for the individual and the party system; and
- shape images of partisan politics, elections, and the process of representative democracy.

Thus, the extent of partisanship is an important political variable, and changes in these feelings over time may affect the functioning of party-based democracy. In broad terms I agree with the above descriptions and believe party identification is the most important single question to ask in an election survey because it has such broad effects on individual electoral behavior.

THE IMPLICATIONS OF PARTISAN DEALIGNMENT

Because party identification is so important for political behavior, the initial signs of eroding partisanship in the 1960s generated substantial scholarly and political attention.[12] Party support normally ebbs and flows between elections, but after the 1964 election the number of Americans who expressed a partisan identity began a substantial decline. There was a partial respite from this in the 1980s, but the downward slide started again in the 1990s.[13] Today, fewer Americans express a party identification than at any time in modern electoral history.

Despite these trends, another scholarly perspective claims that evidence of declining partisan attachments overstates the problem. One argument holds that a changing political climate stimulates people to say they are independent of any party while simultaneously feeling an enduring attachment to one party. For example, Bruce Keith and his colleagues claimed that the decrease in the percentage of party identifiers through the 1980s was a myth—many partisans were supposedly hiding under the cloak of independence while actually favoring a specific party.[14] A recent reassessment repeats this claim: "As things stand today [2011], much of the speculation about Independents, and indeed some from academia, perpetuate a myth."[15] Other research emphasizes the continuing partisan ties among the majority of Americans and the continuing impact of partisanship on political behavior.[16] A skeptic might suggest that this is similar to arguing that people who go to church are still religious and perhaps becoming even more religious while ignoring the fact that fewer pews are full every Sunday.

Chapter 2 takes up this debate by presenting the evidence of Americans' weakening partisanship. Furthermore, voters aren't simply shedding their party attachments in the United States; there is an erosion in partisan loyalties across a wide set of nations. The pattern of weakening partisanship is thus not unique to the United States or due to the specific institutional or political conditions of American politics.[17]

The key to judging the significance of dealignment is to understand the factors contributing to partisan voters becoming independents. Chapter 3 examines alternative explanations of why the distribution of mobilization types has changed over time. Chapter 4 describes who comprises this new group of independents.

Based on the initial theory of, and empirical research on, party identification, one should predict that weakening party ties among the public would have a negative consequence for democracy. Decreasing partisanship should reverse all the beneficial functions described above. For example, turnout should decrease (it has), people should become more fluid in their political views and voting choices (they have), and skepticism about the process and institutions of representative democracies should increase (it has). Indeed, the first evidence of American dealignment was greeted by a chorus of academic angst.

However, contemporary electoral researchers are divided on the significance of partisan dealignment, which justifies the additional research presented here. The classic party identification model predicts that nonpartisans are less knowledgeable and less involved in politics, so dealignment should erode the bases of electoral politics and representative democracy. Indeed, in the 1950s and 1960s, most independents fit this characterization.[18] This empirical finding led to a normative argument that partisanship was good for democracy and independence was bad.

However, many of the new independents follow a different course, earning the apartisan label described earlier in this chapter. Apartisans are interested in politics and are often politically sophisticated, but they lack a partisan identity. Indeed, there is a deep philosophical tradition that sees independence from political parties as a benefit to democracy.[19] These new independents may come closer to the model of the rational citizen that is lionized in democratic theory but seldom found in the early empirical studies of public opinion. A sophisticated independent might be politically engaged and even vote but lack firm commitments to a specific party. Such an independent might actually judge the candidates and sometimes pick the best candidate regardless of party.

The second half of this book focuses on the implications of partisan dealignment. Chapter 5 investigates the participation patterns of partisans and apartisans and how these have changed over time. Partisans should understandably focus on electoral politics because of their partisan loyalties. Apartisans may be more likely to adopt different forms of political participation that are more direct and less partisan. Thus, changes in party identification may coexist with changes in patterns of political participation.

The next three chapters examine how changing patterns of political identity are affecting electoral politics. Chapter 6 discusses differences in how apartisans and party identifiers perceive political parties and how these perceptions have changed over time. Chapter 7 analyses the voting choices of Americans and how apartisans differ significantly from the traditional image of independents by introducing more issue-based voting into the electoral process. Chapter 8 considers how changing patterns of political mobilization contribute to a more volatile electorate that is more willing to split the ticket.

Finally, I am a strong believer that we better understand contemporary American politics through comparison—either to politics of another time or in other democracies. Much of this book looks at changes over time in the nature of partisanship and independence in the United States and the consequences of these changes. Chapter 9 expands these comparisons to look at the United States in a cross-national context. The major lesson is that "we are not alone"—many of the changes in American politics described in this volume are occurring in other Western democracies. This suggests the explanations for change and their implications don't lie in the specifics of American political history or political institutions, but in broader forces affecting other modern democracies.

PLUS ÇA CHANGE, OR REAL CHANGE?

As the percentage of independents has grown in public opinion surveys, this has generated substantial debate on the implications of this trend for American politics. Some experts claim that this change is ephemeral and little has really altered. These experts say that people are acting the same as ever and perhaps just expressing themselves in different ways.

The answer to this debate has real political implications. One of the most prominent examples came from George W. Bush's campaign strategist, Matthew Dowd. In 2000 Dowd argued that the percentage of truly independent voters was small and decreasing, and therefore the Bush administration could ignore them and focus on mobilizing its base among strong Republicans.[20]

Others have seen the dealignment trend as altering the content and dynamics of American politics. Both Democratic and Republican candidates try to mobilize their core supporters, and most Americans still have an attachment to one of those parties. But at the same time, candidates now campaign more consciously for the support of independents to increase their electoral base. As *Washington Post* columnist David

Broder observed in 2009, "Independent voters make up the swing vote in almost every contested election—including the presidential race."[21] Apartisan independents are too large a group to ignore in elections, and their preferences can and do often shift election outcomes.

Some political observers go even further. For instance, Arnold Schwarzenegger reacted to the changing nature of the California electorate by advocating the development of "postpartisanship" politics at his 2007 inauguration as governor of California, declaring that "All of our most deeply held dreams and aspirations require us to build on our common bonds rather than keep resorting to the tired battle cries of partisan politics that divides and demoralizes us."[22] Similarly, Barack Obama has repeatedly called for deemphasizing partisanship as a means to improve political processes and outcomes. In articulating his political philosophy in *The Audacity of Hope,* Obama stated, "Perhaps more than any other time in our recent history, we need a new kind of politics, one that can excavate and build upon those shared understandings that pull us together as Americans."[23] Obama's inability to actually develop postpartisan politics and the continuing bitterness of political discourse has stimulated other attempts to echo concerns about the mischief of excessive partisanship, including New York mayor Michael Bloomberg's "No Labels" rejection of partisanship and Jon Stewart's "Restore Sanity" rally.[24]

I believe the contemporary electorate is different in many important ways from the electorate of the 1950s that provided the basis for the classic *The American Voter.* Many of the basic relationships between partisan attitudes and behaviors persist, but the characteristics of the electorate have changed in ways that affect the outcomes of these relationships. However, I also recognize that electoral researchers disagree on whether basic partisan identities are changing and on the implications if they indeed are.

Thus, this book seeks to systematically consider these contrasting images of partisan stability and change in order to better understand the political identities of the American electorate. And if these partisan identities *have* changed significantly over the past several decades, what are the implications for democracy?

THE TWO SIDES OF
THE DEALIGNMENT DEBATE

When Angus Campbell and his colleagues surveyed the American public in 1952, they found that the large majority expressed clear attachments to a preferred political party. The depth of these attachments was often striking, bordering on multigenerational family traditions as seen in the following two examples from their interviews:[1]

> All my ancestors all the way up have always voted Democratic and I felt like it would have made my poor old daddy turn over in his grave if I voted any other way. He fought in the Civil War and went through too much.

> I'm a borned Republican, sister. We're Republicans from the start to the finish, clear back on the family tree. Hot Republicans all along. I'm not so much in favor of Eisenhower as the party he is on. I won't weaken my party by voting for a Democrat.

Most people today still have partisan attachments, although perhaps not ones as intense as in the two examples above. However, chapter 1 noted that public opinion surveys beginning in the mid- to late 1960s show a decline in the percentage of party identifiers. Although there have been ebbs and flows in this trend, Americans today appear to be much less partisan than people in the mid-twentieth century.

In both the 2008 and 2010 elections, for example, politicians and political analysts paid close attention to independents regarding them as the swing voters who would decide the elections. Indeed, in responding to the Democratic losses in 2010, White House advisers emphasized the shift of independents toward the Republicans as a major reason for the outcome, and they placed a priority on winning back independents in Obama's 2012 campaign.[2]

Yet some experts assert that claims of weakening partisanship are an artifact of measurement or interpretation. Even the Democrats' November 2010 call to win back independents in 2012 was greeted with skepticism by some who cited academic electoral research to argue that dealignment is a myth.[3] Elections are still largely a contest between Republicans and Democrats, and most people routinely vote for the same party. Partisanship also remains the strongest predictor of voting choice.

This chapter begins by briefly outlining the debate on weakening party ties in America. I then trace the levels of partisanship across the past half century using evidence from the American National Election Studies (ANES) and other sources. In addition, I examine other evidence of partisan dealignment in the stability of partisanship across elections and the trends in voter registration patterns. Research shows that the decline of partisanship is generally occurring in other democracies and not just in the United States. The results, I believe, provide strong evidence that party loyalties have been weakening across most other advanced industrial democracies.

TWO VIEWS OF PARTISAN CHANGE

In their initial study of the 1952 election, the researchers at the University of Michigan introduced the concept of "party identification" to capture a pattern of partisan loyalty that they observed among their survey respondents.[4] They conceived of party identification as a long-term, affective, psychological attachment to a preferred political party. Indeed, in many instances it seemed like an inherited family trait, much like a religious attachment or other social identity. Partisanship was relatively stable over time, and the strength of party ties tended to increase with age and the repeated electoral experience of voting for one's preferred party.

As noted in chapter 1, the concept of partisanship has become a central aspect of electoral research. The existence of enduring partisan identities helps researchers explain how many people deal with the complexities of politics, especially when they have limited knowledge of or interest in politics. Partisanship is the ultimate cue to how "people like me" think about candidates and issues and to which party in an election is likely to best represent an individual's views. Partisanship also mobilizes people to show up at the polls to support "their party" and prevent the opposition from gaining office. These multiple effects are why partisanship is widely cited as the most important concept developed in political behavior research.

Consequently, when party loyalties appeared to weaken in the late 1960s, this evoked substantial concern among electoral researchers and politicians.[5] Moreover, this trend has subsequently appeared in most other established democracies.[6] In most advanced industrial democracies, fewer people today express party attachments than they did in the first election surveys done in each nation. Thus, some researchers argue that the nature of contemporary politics has changed to produce *partisan dealignment*, which is a persisting pattern of weaker public attachments to political parties.[7]

There are several alternative explanations for this dealignment trend—a topic discussed more in chapter 3.[8] Perhaps the most prominent explanations link dealignment to the specific issues and political events of recent American political history. For instance, the civil rights movement and the Vietnam War undoubtedly eroded some peoples' ties to their traditionally preferred party.[9] Political elites' decreasing emphasis on partisanship during this period was another potential source of dealignment, although weak partisanship continued even after party polarization revived in the 1990s.[10] Social modernization has also generally eroded bonds to social groups and hierarchic organizations of various types, and political parties may suffer as part of this spreading disenchantment with organizations. Other researchers suggest that dealignment reflects the growing political sophistication of contemporary publics, which diminishes the need for habitual party cues as citizens make their own political choices.[11] These explanations differ in the consequences they project as a result of weakened partisanship, but their proponents all agree that mass partisanship has weakened significantly in America. These analysts see the electorate of today as different from that described in the pages of *The American Voter*.

In contrast, other experts question the existence of a dealignment trend. For example, Bruce Keith and his colleagues doubt that the decrease in the percentage of party identifiers is a meaningful change— many partisans are supposedly "hiding" under the cloak of independents but nevertheless lean toward a specific party.[12] Donald Green, Bradley Palmquist, and Eric Schickler examined a broad array of partisan behaviors in the American public and concluded that "Partisanship is alive and well, and as far as we can tell, it is as influential for us as it was for our parents and grandparents."[13] Karen Kaufmann, John Petrocik, and Daron Shaw echo these comments in describing dealignment as a major myth about American voters, stating that "The often-reported decline in identification with parties and the increase in negativity toward parties are greatly overemphasized."[14] A recent replication of the early study by Keith and his colleagues argues that little has changed through 2008.[15] In short, these experts doubt that partisan ties are really weakening.

If the concept of partisanship is the linchpin of our understanding of modern electoral behavior, then the debate over whether partisan ties are actually weakening is important for understanding the American public and electoral politics. Therefore, this chapter marshals evidence from multiple sources to map how the levels of partisanship have changed over the past six decades.

HOW TO MEASURE PARTISANSHIP

If you are talking with your friends about politics, it is natural for you to think about some friends as Republicans and others as Democrats. Some may even seem independent of a firm partisan label. When researchers started studying voters through systematic public opinion studies, they noted the same patterns in people's opinions and voting choices. Angus Campbell, one of the directors of the University of Michigan election studies in the 1950s, was a social psychologist who brought knowledge of reference group theory and attitude formation to the project. In their initial study of the 1952 election, the Michigan researchers introduced the concept of "party identification" that became central to their social-psychological model of voting choice.[16]

The surveys by the Michigan researchers—Angus Campbell, Philip Converse, Warren Miller, and Donald Stokes—eventually became the ANES, which are the major resource for academic research on American electoral behavior.[17] This project has surveyed the American public in every presidential election since 1952.

For respondents in these surveys during the 1950s and 1960s, their participation typically began with a middle-aged woman knocking on their door and saying the household had been selected to participate in this national survey. During these decades, public opinion surveys were still quite rare, especially ones that came from the far-off University of Michigan. After introductions the interviewer asked a long series of questions about images of the candidates and parties, positions on the issues of the day, and involvement in politics. Interviews frequently lasted an hour or more. Even though the methodology and commonality of surveys has changed since the 1950s, the content of surveys still involves a long list of questions about politics.

One of the standard ANES questions is the focus of this book. It simply asks: "Generally speaking, do you think of yourself as a Republican, a Democrat, an Independent, or what?" If a respondent claims to be a Republican or a Democrat, that person is asked if he or she would call himself or herself a strong Republican or Democrat or a not-very-strong Republican or Democrat. If a respondent claims to be independent, that person is asked if he or she thinks of himself or herself as closer to the Republican or Democratic Party. I invite the reader to stop for a second and think of how you would answer this set of questions if the ANES interviewer was sitting across the room from you on your living room couch.

These two questions measure the direction of partisanship—Republicans and Democrats—and the strength of partisanship from independent to strong partisans. This yields a seven-category description of the partisan orientations of Americans, ranging from strong Democrats on the left to strong Republicans on the right. The two pie charts in Figure 2.1 show the distribution of partisanship when comparing the first ANES survey of 1952 to the most recent presidential election in 2008.

FIGURE 2.1 Party Identification in 1952 and 2008

▶ *The distribution of partisans and independents has changed substantially over the past half century.*

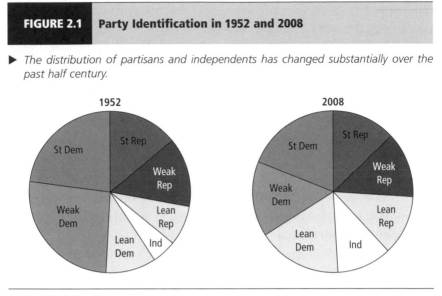

1952

2008

Source: ANES, 1952 and 2008.

In 1952 only a small share of the public (23 percent) claimed to be independent, and in the follow-up question most of these individuals said they leaned either toward the Democrats (10 percent) or the Republicans (8 percent). Consequently, more than three-quarters of the public stated a partisan identity, and that number is even higher if one includes "leaners." Nearly half (49 percent) of the public expressed either a weak or strong identification with the Democratic Party. This was the legacy of the Democrats' ascendance under Franklin Roosevelt and the New Deal era. In contrast, barely a quarter of the public identified with the Republican Party (28 percent). Illustrating the separation that can exist between party identities and immediate voting preferences, however, despite this large partisan imbalance favoring the Democrats in 1952, Dwight Eisenhower won a majority of the popular vote (55.2 percent) as the Republican presidential candidate. The Republicans also won majorities in both the House of Representatives and the Senate. Many Americans thought of themselves as Democrats in 1952, but they voted Republican in the national elections.

The second pie chart in the figure shows how the distribution of partisan types changed by 2008. Most Americans still identify with a political party, and thus partisanship remains a central aspect of political behavior. However, this time comparison shows a substantial growth in independents, from 23 percent of the public in 1952 to 40 percent in 2008! Independents outnumber both Democratic identifiers (34 percent) and Republicans (26 percent). This means that elections should be more competitive between the parties, since the gap between Democratic and Republican identifiers has narrowed considerably. The new reality of electoral politics is that neither party begins with a core base of voters sufficient to dominate election outcomes. Obama's electoral majority in 2008 could not be based solely on the minority of Democratic identifiers; it required substantial support from independents. Similarly, the Republican wave in 2010 required that many of these same independents swing toward the Republicans. This volatility is indicative of a dealigned electorate.

If we focus on independents, the percentage of "pure independents"— those who initially state they are independents and say they don't lean toward either party—doubled over this time span. The percentages of independents that lean to the Democrats or to the Republicans have also increased by half or more over time. In short, independents of all types grew substantially more common between these two elections, and the percentage of Democratic identifiers declined by about the same amount. These two pie charts present the crux of the evidence for partisan dealignment in America.

THE GROWTH OF INDEPENDENTS

Tracking the percentage of independents over the elections since 1952 provides more evidence of how partisan identities have changed. For simplicity's sake, I ignore the partisan balance between Republicans and Democrats and describe the percentage of independents within the public.

Figure 2.2 displays the percentage of pure and leaning independents separately across elections, since there is debate on the differing nature of both groups. The start point and end point in the figure are the same as the two pie charts in Figure 2.1, now with all the intervening presidential elections included.

FIGURE 2.2	Independents Increase

▶ *The percentage of independents has grown substantially over time.*

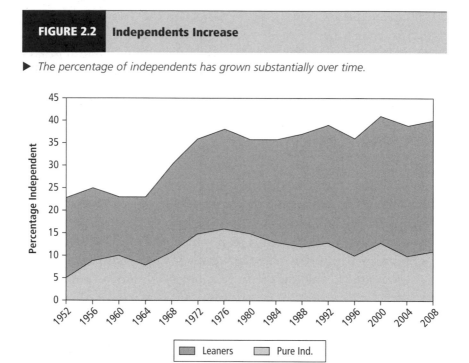

Source: ANES 1952–2008 cumulative file.

In broad terms, the trends among independents fall into four periods. First, 1952 through 1964 is often called the "stable state" period of partisanship. Even with the shift from Eisenhower's Republican victories in 1952 and 1956 to the John F. Kennedy and Lyndon B. Johnson Democratic victories in 1960 and 1964, partisan loyalties proved highly stable. About three-quarters of the public identified with a party and a quarter lacked party attachments.[18] A second period spans the years 1964–1976. This was an exceptional time in American politics. Most accounts of these years stress the political conflict over the Vietnam War, the civil rights movement, and the Watergate scandal as eroding public trust in politics and partisan loyalties.[19] This was also a period of partisan realignment in the South, as Democratic identities among many white voters conflicted with the policies of the Democratic Party nationally. In the midst of this tumult, the number of independents grew to comprise 38 percent of the public in 1976. Aware of these opinion trends, the Ronald Reagan administration tried to restore public faith in politics, and both parties tried to rejuvenate their support. Partisanship seemed to hold steady during this third period (1980 to about 1992–1996), with no increase or decrease in the percentage of independents. Finally, since 1996 the percentage of independents has grown slightly, although the percentage of pure independents seems to be dropping slightly and the percentage of leaning independents increasing slightly.

If one probes more deeply, these historical events leave their traces in partisanship trends. For instance, in the 1950s up to one-fifth of African Americans gave apolitical responses to the party identification question largely because of their exclusion from politics in the South and marginalization in northern states.[20] By the end of the 1960s, this apolitical segment dropped to levels found in the rest of the electorate as African Americans followed a pattern of strengthening ties to the Democratic Party. In contrast, white southerners were heavily partisan in the 1950s, and the events of the 1960s and 1970s eroded these party loyalties. By the last several elections, the levels of independence among southern whites rivaled that of the entire electorate—so dealignment since the 1950s has actually been stronger among this group.

The Gallup Poll has measured American partisanship for even longer than the ANES.[21] Although Gallup doesn't use the same wording of the partisanship question or the same scientific sampling methods as the ANES, the longitudinal trends are quite similar. Independents comprised less than a quarter of the public from 1944 until 1964, but then there was a marked increase in the percentage of independents until the 1976 election. The Gallup trend shows the same plateauing pattern after 1976, with increasing numbers of independents in the last decade. Gallup reported that 41 percent of Americans were independents at the time of the 2010 elections. Trend data from the General Social Survey follow the same general trajectory, with the percentage of nonpartisans growing from 26 percent in 1972 to a full 45 percent in the 2010 survey.

Because many electoral researchers claim that there has been a recent resurgence of partisanship, I decided to take a closer look at patterns over the last decade. I turned to the surveys collected in the ABC News polls.[22]

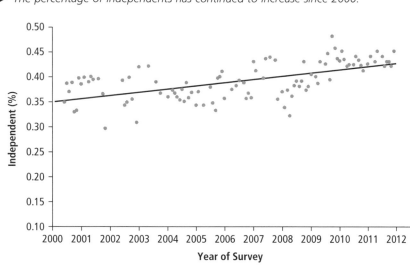

FIGURE 2.3   **Dealignment over the Last Decade**

▶ *The percentage of independents has continued to increase since 2000.*

Source: ABC News polls from the iPOLL database at the Roper Center, University of Connecticut; additional *Washington Post* polls in 2009–2011.

ABC uses a simple version of the ANES party identification question and surveys Americans on a nearly monthly basis. Figure 2.3 shows the percentage of independents for nearly one hundred separate surveys conducted from January 2000 until fall 2011. Over the last decade, the percentage of independents has clearly increased—from around 35 percent in the early 2000s to about 45 percent in 2010–2011.[23] So, regardless of methodologies, the dealignment trend is clear.

The political socialization panel conducted by M. Kent Jennings and his colleagues gives us further insights into the longer-term trends over time.[24] This unique study tracked a group of people who were high school seniors in 1965, interviewing the same people in 1965 and then again in 1973, 1982, and 1997. In the 1965 interview, 37 percent of the students said they were independents. After the next eight politically tumultuous years, 47 percent claimed to be independents in 1973. Then partisanship strengthened over the rest of their lives, so that by 1997 only

36 percent still claimed to be independent—although this is much higher than for their own parents at the same ages. Furthermore, when the offspring of the 1965 generation were themselves interviewed in 1997, more of them said they were independents (43 percent) than their parents had at the same age. In short, there was a sharp antipartisan climate during the late 1960s and early 1970s, and even though that time has passed, future generations are continuing this nonpartisan trend.

If partisanship is the framework that structures the political behavior of average Americans, then the evidence from the ANES and other surveys indicate that these orientations have substantially weakened across the last several decades. Significantly fewer Americans now approach politics with a fixed party loyalty—although most people do still have party allegiances. The potential to reshape electoral behavior and the nature of citizen politics exists when a plurality of citizens lacks party identities.

A Closer Look at Independents

The most common skepticism of dealignment focuses on the two categories of independents. The critics argue that only the "pure independents" truly lack partisan attachments. This group has grown by only 5 to 6 percent in the past five decades. Most of the overall growth in independents comes from among those who say they lean toward the Democrats or Republicans. The critics claim that because it has become more fashionable to say one is independent, some partisans claim to be independent and then display their true party loyalties when asked if they lean toward a particular party. John Petrocik, for example, states that "A reluctance to confess a party preference is nothing more than a reflection of the inclination of Americans to prefer to think of themselves as independent-minded and inclined to judge things on the merit."[25] He then concludes that leaners aren't true independents. Thus, various analyses show that leaning independents often look more like weak partisans than like pure independents.

This behavioral contrast between leaning and pure independents is addressed in many of the chapters that follow. But we should first think about how people might be answering the partisanship question in order to guide our analyses and interpretation.

The stem of the partisanship question is phrased to elicit an identity with a party: "Do you consider yourself a Republican, a Democrat, an Independent, or what?" The separation of pure independents and leaners comes from a second question that is more ambiguous: "Do you think of yourself as closer to the Republican or Democratic Party?" Some respondents might interpret this follow-up question as asking about a general partisan tendency over time, and others might think of their partisan leaning in the current election. Results gleaned from the former interpretation would come closer to the meaning of an enduring identity; results gleaned from the latter would be similar to current voting preference.

We cannot penetrate the thinking of the people who responded to this question, but we can illustrate the variability of leaning independents by examining how different partisan groups change their responses over time. In 2004 the ANES interviewed people they had previously surveyed in the 2000 election. In both years the individuals were asked the standard party identification question.

To examine the stability of party identity, we tracked whether each of the seven partisan groups in 2000 had changed their partisanship by 2004 (Figure 2.4).[26] As the party identification theory would predict, strong partisans of both camps have very stable loyalties. Less than 5 percent of strong Democrats or strong Republicans changed party loyalty across these two elections, and only a small percentage changed to become pure independents.[27] Weak partisans are also very stable in their party loyalties, with less than 10 percent switching parties.

The big difference involves leaning partisans. About 20 percent of leaners in 2000 switched to an allegiance with the opposing party between these two elections, and an additional 10 percent said they were pure independents in 2004. With nearly one-third of this group shifting their partisan leanings over four years—markedly higher than the shifts among weak and strong partisans—this indicates that they were not simply partisans hiding under the cloak of independence. Pure independents cannot change party loyalties between elections since they lacked a party preference in 2000. The figure shows, however, that only 39 percent of pure partisans in 2000 retained their purity in 2004. Most shifted to being an independent with leanings toward one party or the other.[28] This is additional evidence that the partisan leanings of independents follow their short-term party preferences.

FIGURE 2.4   How Partisanship Changes

▶ *The shift in party identities between 2000 and 2004 shows more volatility among independents.*

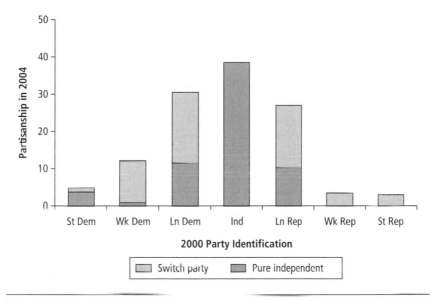

Source: 2000–2004 ANES panel.

Note: The figure shows whether partisans in 2000 switched party identifications by 2004 or were pure independents in 2004.

These comparisons suggest that leaning independents aren't simply partisans in disguise—a conclusion that Warren Miller also reached when he stated, "They are demonstrably the independents they claim to be."[29] Leaning independents are individuals who primarily think of themselves as independent of a political party while also expressing their support for the party they currently favor. If they want to vote, they have to choose between parties. When the next election comes, they may lean in the same direction, toward another party, or toward pure independence. Similarly, even the plurality of pure independents in one election is likely to express a partisan leaning in the next election as election preferences change. This lack of enduring party loyalties makes independents fluid voters. This fluidity also explains why their current voting patterns appear more congruent with their leanings, because their leanings often reflect current party support (see chapter 7 for more detail).

REGISTERING THEIR INDEPENDENCE

If the skeptics of dealignment remain doubtful because people can too easily express their independence with a simple response in a public opinion survey, a more rigorous test of partisanship comes from voter registration records. In most states, people identify themselves as a Democrat, a Republican, a member of another party, or an independent (or decline to state a party preference) when they register to vote. Registering as a partisan is important because it typically is required to vote in the party primaries to select candidates for the general election. Thus, there is a strong incentive to express support for a party lest one be excluded from primary candidate selection.

The *Almanac of American Politics* published state statistics on the percentage of people who registered as independents or declined to state a party preference for twenty-four states in 1972. These statistics are updated for the 2004 and 2008 elections in Table 2.1.[30] The vast majority of states showed a significant increase in the percentage of independent/no party affiliation (NPA) registrants from 1972 until 2004, essentially doubling the percentage of nonpartisans over time. A slight further uptick continued in 2008 despite the highly politicized and partisan nature of that year's campaign. It is also quite apparent that states vary widely in the percentage who registers as unaffiliated. This may be partially due to state rules on the ability to register as an independent and the electoral consequences of this registration. For instance, in closed-primary states nonpartisans are excluded from voting in primary elections, but this might apply to one party and not the other. In open-primary states nonpartisans can choose a partisan ballot on Election Day or change their affiliation at the polling place. But virtually everywhere, more people are registering as nonpartisans.

To further illustrate registration trends, I collected additional information for six states: California, Connecticut, Florida, Iowa, Oregon, and Pennsylvania.[31] I selected these states as they are regionally and economically diverse; span traditionally Democratic, Republican, and swing states; and have both open and closed primaries. These states display

TABLE 2.1	None of the Above

▶ *The percentage of persons registering as nonpartisan has grown in most states.*

State	1972	2004	2008	Change 1972–2008
Alaska	54	59	52	−2
Arizona	5	24	34	+29
California	7	21	20	+13
Colorado	38	33	34	−4
Connecticut	35	43	41	+6
Delaware	24	24	24	0
Florida	4	23	20	+16
Kentucky	2	7	7	+5
Louisiana	1	19	24	+23
Maine	25	42	34	+9
Maryland	4	14	16	+12
Massachusetts	38	51	52	+14
Nebraska	4	15	19	+15
Nevada	7	18	16	+9
New Hampshire	0	38	46	+46
New Mexico	6	15	16	+10
New York	15	26	19	+4
North Carolina	4	18	25	+21
Oklahoma	1	10	11	+10
Oregon	4	25	20	+16
Pennsylvania	3	11	13	+10
South Dakota	10	13	17	+7
West Virginia	2	10	17	+15
Wyoming	15	10	17	+2
Average	13	24	25	+12

Sources: 1972 figures from *The Almanac of American Politics,* 1974; 2004 figures from Martin Wattenberg, personal communication; 2008 figures from Michael McDonald, "Partisan Registration Totals," *Huffington Post,* October 12, 2010.

different patterns in the timing and rate of increase in nonpartisans, but all follow the same upward trend (Figure 2.5). The longitudinal comparisons are based on midterm elections to avoid the registration surges that might accompany presidential elections and possible confusion regarding the term "independent," since the American Independent Party has run a candidate in each presidential election since 1968.

Four of these states—California, Florida, Oregon, and Pennsylvania—began with relatively few nonparty registrants but showed a marked increase in them over time. In the late 1950s and early 1960s, only about 3 percent of Californians registered as nonpartisans. By 1990, 9 percent were independents, and by 2010 this had increased to 20 percent of the public.[32] In 1974 only 4 percent of Floridians were registered as unaffiliated, but this figure increased to 19 percent by 2010. Oregon had few people registering as independent in 1966, but this number grew steadily to about 20 percent of the electorate in 2010. In Pennsylvania the percentage of NPA (or minor party) registrants began at about 3 percent in the early 1970s but rose to 12 percent in 2010.

The two other states—Connecticut and Iowa—seem to traditionally accentuate independence, with roughly one-third of registrants lacking party ties at the start of the series. However, in both states the percentage of independents has grown slightly over the last two decades. When the figures are averaged across all six states, the percentage of nonpartisan registrations increased by about 10 percent from the early 1990s until the

| FIGURE 2.5 | Registering Their Independence |

▶ *The percentage registering as not affiliated to any party has grown over time.*

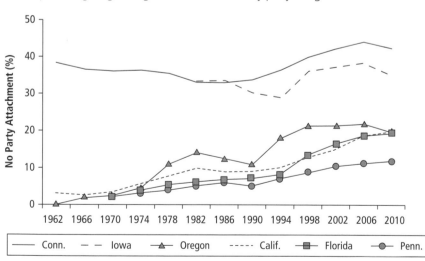

Sources: Secretary of state or election board in each state; Almanac of American Politics for Pennsylvania 1970–1994.

2010 election—even though a registered partisanship is often a prerequisite to vote in party primaries and elections continue to be about the choice of parties.

Eric McGhee and Daniel Krimm uncovered similar patterns in county-level registration records for twenty-one states.[33] Tracking the change in registration patterns from 1968 until 2008, they found a fairly steady 2 percent increase in the percentage of nonpartisan registrations over each four-year electoral cycle. Consequently, the total percentage of nonpartisan registrations more than doubled between 1968 and 2008. In other words, the percentage of Americans registering as nonpartisans has continued to increase even after the survey-based party identification plateau of 1976–1992, possibly because new voters are expressing their independence as they register for the first time.

In summary, state voter registration statistics display a significant growth in independent (or decline to state) registration over the past several decades. Moreover, these registration statistics probably underestimate the dealignment trend. First, independents are less likely to register to vote. Second, once registered, many people probably continue with their original registration rather than re-registering if their party orientation changes. This is especially apparent in areas of the South, where Democratic Party registrations remain common even though voting patterns in the area have shifted distinctly toward the Republican Party. Thus, party registration is probably a lagging indicator of current party identities.[34] People aren't just telling pollsters they are independents, they are saying this to the registrar of voters as well—even at the potential cost of disenfranchising themselves from primary elections.

WE ARE NOT ALONE

This dealignment trend is well known to scholars of American politics, even if they debate its measurement and meaning. However, the existence of parallel dealignment trends in other advanced industrial democracies isn't as well recognized.

Although the evidence of dealignment was first apparent in the United States, similar signs have appeared in other established democracies beginning in the 1970s and continuing to the present.[35] In Britain, for example, 93 percent claimed a standing partisan preference in the 1964 election study, but this figure dropped to 75 percent by the 2010 election.[36] Similarly, Sweden has experienced a slow and relatively steady erosion of partisanship over the last several decades.[37] In 1968 about two-thirds of Swedes expressed a party attachment, but this number dropped to 28 percent in 2010. Evidence of weakening party attachments has begun to appear in election studies in countries ranging from Australia to Austria.

As election-study surveys have become available for additional nations and for additional years, the evidence of dealignment has become more apparent. In other research, I compiled trends from nineteen advanced industrial democracies.[38] Among these nineteen nations, the percentage expressing partisan attachments had decreased in seventeen cases. If we focus on the strength of partisanship, it had decreased in all nineteen nations. In nations as diverse as Austria, Canada, Japan, New Zealand, and Sweden, the pattern was the same: the partisan attachments of the public weakened during the latter half of the twentieth century. Similarly, Harold Clarke and Marianne Stewart examined the decline in more depth in three nations—Britain, Canada, and the United States—and found combinations of decreasing percentages of strong party identifiers, increasing numbers of independents and nonidentifiers, and increasing individual-level instability in party identifications.[39] In fact, the decline in partisanship among Americans over the past several decades falls about in the middle of the results for other established democracies.[40]

Chapter 9 describes the cross-national patterns of dealignment in more depth. However, to illustrate the dealignment trend outside the United States, Figure 2.6 plots the distribution of party attachments among Europeans from 1976 until 2009. The figure is based on nine member states of the European Union (EU) for which continuous data are available from the Eurobarometer surveys.[41] The EU surveys use a "softer" measure of partisanship that asks whether people feel close to any party instead of a harder measure of long-term psychological identities. Nevertheless, the overall downward trend in party attachment is unmistakable. The percentage of nonpartisans in the pooled European analyses increases from 30 percent in 1976 to around 45 percent in the recent surveys. In Europe as in the United States, the percentage of

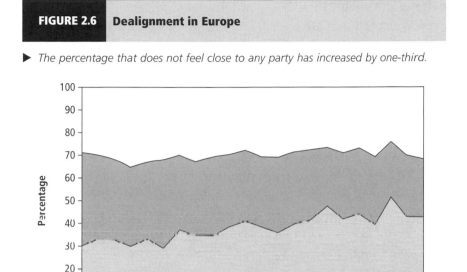

FIGURE 2.6   Dealignment in Europe

▶ *The percentage that does not feel close to any party has increased by one-third.*

Source: Eurobarometer Surveys, 1976–1994; European Election Studies 1999, 2004, and 2009. Results are based on the nine early EU member states and weighted by national population size.

nonpartisans generally exceeds adherents to any single political party. In short, Americans aren't alone in experiencing partisan dealignment.

A CHANGING PUBLIC

Many partisans are still alive and well in America today—and voting in elections. The majority of Americans still express a party identity and partisanship remains one of the most potent influences on individual political behavior.

Still, this chapter demonstrates that the number of people expressing a partisan loyalty is declining as fewer Americans possess a party identity. The percentage of independents has grown by about one-third since the early 1960s and now outnumbers either Democrats or Republicans as a share of the public. In addition, an increasing percentage of Americans express no party affiliation when they register to vote. The trends in independence being seen on survey measures of partisanship and in voters registering as independent (or with no party affiliation) are both continuing. In both attitudinal and behavioral terms, fewer people now express a partisan attachment.

It may be that these expressions of independence are ephemeral statements reflecting a changing sprit of the times that emphasizes personal individualism and a critical view of politics. The ultimate test of the meaningfulness of these trends will be in the behavioral differences between partisans and independents that we study in subsequent chapters. However, the fact that a plurality of Americans now describe themselves as independent provides a justification for probing more deeply into the sources of these changing orientations and their consequences.

Even more striking, perhaps, are the parallel dealignment trends occurring in most other advanced industrial democracies. When partisanship is weakening in one nation, it might easily be due to the specific problems that parties face in that nation or the unique effects of national history. Indeed, the research literature in many of these nations discusses how the unique events that occurred in them caused their dealignment trend. In one nation it was due to a weak economy; in another it was tensions over regional issues or another policy controversy. Scandal or debates over national identity are linked to the declines in other nations. However, the cross-national breadth of the dealignment trends speaks to a broader systematic process affecting advanced industrial democracies more widely. This should encourage us to look for such processes of change when we discuss the correlates of partisanship in chapter 3.

In addition, the cross-national breadth of the dealignment trends suggests that reformers' efforts to renew party attachments in the United States based on a narrow reading of the nation's party experience are doomed to failure, because the process isn't unique to the United States (or any single nation). Instead, the evidence presented in subsequent chapters suggests that a less partisan public is the new reality of contemporary politics, which is affecting how citizens make political choices and how politics functions.

CHAPTER

3

CAN PARTISANS GO TO HEAVEN?

Partisan bonds are weakening among the American public and in many other established democracies. What does this mean? The implications of dealignment depend on the political attitudes and behaviors of these new independents. Not surprisingly, political scientists disagree on these points, and dealignment has renewed the debate on the consequences of partisanship for the electoral process.

On the one side, a long-standing philosophical tradition has presented partisanship in a negative light and offered an idealist view of nonpartisans. For example, in the *Federalist Papers* James Madison warned about the mischief of faction, and one of his worries was the emergence of partisan factions. In his farewell address in 1796, George Washington warned about the baneful effects of the spirit of party. Thomas Jefferson stated his views even more starkly, saying, "If I could not go to heaven but with a party, I would not go there at all."[1] (The title to this chapter paraphrases Jefferson.) Nancy Rosenblum's recent work *On the Side of Angels* gives an extensive and thoughtful discussion of this antipartisan sentiment in American history and political thought, as well as the counterarguments.[2]

Indeed, the current partisan bickering in Washington and many state capitals is a modern reminder of why previous scholarship commented on the problems of excessive partisanship. When senators Chris Dodd and Evan Bayh finished their tenures in the U.S. Senate in late 2010, both gave passionate speeches about how excessive partisanship was weakening the institution and the Republic. Partisanship can be synonymous with narrow-mindedness, an unwillingness to compromise, and a tendency to put the interests of the party ahead of those of the voters or the nation. Therefore, some political scientists suggest that the ideal citizen is one who objectively makes political choices without the emotional bond to a preferred party.[3] This perspective would therefore see positive potential if affective party bonds are weakening in America.

On the other side of the debate, *The American Voter* and other research has shown that the empirical reality of independents can fall short of the theoretical ideal. Many studies have found that independents live at the boundaries of politics, not following politics in the news, not understanding political discourse, and making unfocused voting choices if they participate in elections.[4] Or, as noted political historian Michael Kazin recently wrote about independents: "What if [these voters] are really just a confused and clueless horde?"[5] This research tradition calls for an appreciation of the beneficial effects of party identity on individual political behavior and the functioning of the democratic process. From this perspective, an increase in independents would have negative effects on electoral politics and democracy.

This debate runs through many of the chapters of this book. The answer to the question of the significance of dealignment depends on whether independents conform more to the positive or negative stereotypes offered by political scientists. As a first step in providing this answer, this chapter describes some of the social and political characteristics of independents today. I argue that societal change is affecting partisans and independents in ways that challenge the early empirical descriptions of both groups. By mapping these changes we can improve our understanding of contemporary electoral politics.

WHO ARE THE INDEPENDENTS?

Who are the independents in the American electorate today? Do they differ from our traditional imagery of independents?

While this seems like a simple question, answering it isn't so easy. There are many academic theories for why the number of independents has increased. In September 2010 the Pew Center explored these ideas by asking self-defined independents why they were independent.[6] The most common answer was that they felt parties cared more about special interests than they did the average American (64 percent). A sizeable number of independents (58 percent) said that they agreed with the Democrats on some issues and the Republicans on others. In contrast, a significant minority thought there wasn't much difference between the parties (34 percent). The least frequent response was that politics was not important to the individual (19 percent).

Only the last response evokes the type of disengagement traditionally attributed to independents, and this is applicable to only one-fifth of independents. Other answers reflect contrasting but meaningful reactions to partisan politics—that it is too polarized or not polarized enough. These are examples of political awareness, not disengagement. This also applies to those who see issues in common with both parties and perhaps decide not to identify with either party as a result. There is no single explanation of dealignment, and all these factors likely make some significant contribution.

I also believe that something broader is affecting contemporary publics. Deference and loyalty to many social and political institutions have waned in recent years.[7] Experts find that brand loyalty has decreased in many consumer purchasing sectors, marriages don't last a lifetime, people are more fickle in other aspects of their lives, and even the stability of religious identities is decreasing.[8] Moreover, there are similar patterns of party dealignment in many other nations, as was demonstrated in the previous chapter. Consequently, explanations based on the unique history or circumstances of American politics are insufficient answers.

This section describes the social and political characteristics of independents over time. This should give us indirect evidence on the sources of dealignment and at least preliminary evidence on whether traditional descriptions of independents still apply.

Growing Up Independent

One way to understand who the independents are is to ask the question in reverse: How do people become partisans? This question reminds me of an interview that actor Kirk Douglas, Michael Douglas' father, gave on a TV talk show about his autobiography. In the interview, he said that his family lived down the street from Ronald Reagan's family in the

Pacific Palisades neighborhood of Southern California. The Douglas and Reagan children sometimes got into political arguments when they were playing together because the Douglases were Democrats and the Reagans were Republicans. Both sets of children knew there were good and bad politicians, but the opinion of who was good or bad differed between families. Imagine a very young Michael Douglas saying something critical about President Eisenhower or Vice President Nixon in the 1950s, while the Reagan kids thought both were good politicians. Eventually, Kirk Douglas said that the parents agreed to minimize the intermixing of their children to lessen these arguments.

The first explanation of party identification is that most people, like the Douglases and the Reagans, learn to be partisans from their parents. Socialization studies show that many children develop party IDs long before they understand the basis of these identities.[9] This is similar to a child learning that he or she is Catholic or Jewish from his or her parents, even before he or she knows the religious beliefs that accompany these labels. Initial partisan loyalties then strengthen with the passage of time, or more precisely with the repeated experience of supporting one's party in elections.[10] So if we are looking for the sources of partisanship (or nonpartisanship), we should begin with these socialization patterns.

The ideal evidence would compare the opinions of parents and their offspring from separate interviews, but such evidence is rare.[11] So we turn to recall questions from the ANES that asked people to remember the party their mother or father generally supported. There are undoubtedly errors made in recalling a parent's party ties, and naming a single party is difficult if one's parents shifted allegiance between elections. Such factors should be fairly consistent across time, however, allowing us to use these recall questions to see if socialization patterns have changed.

Figure 3.1 shows the percentage of self-defined independents according to their perceptions of their mother's partisanship across four electoral periods (patterns for the father's partisanship are very similar).[12] In the 1950s and early 1960s, most people reported their parents were either Democrats or Republicans, and less than one-fifth of those with partisan parents were themselves independents. In the late 1960s, something changed. Democratic and Republican parents became less successful in inculcating their partisanship in their offspring. This might have been a result of 1960s youthful rebellion or indecisiveness of the parents that lessened party cues. Even more dramatic, independent parents became substantially more successful in raising children who remained independent. In other words, the impact of parental socialization in creating new partisans weakened, and this weaker socialization effect persisted in subsequent years (unfortunately, the ANES has not repeated this question since 1992). One-third of partisan parents raised independent children, and two-thirds of independent parents raised children who shared their independence. Moreover, dealignment produces a growing percentage of

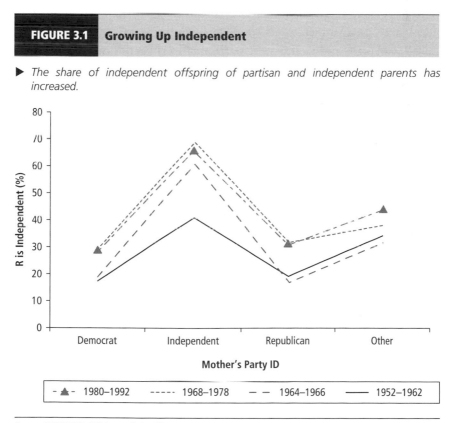

FIGURE 3.1   Growing Up Independent

▶ *The share of independent offspring of partisan and independent parents has increased.*

Source: ANES 1952–2008 cumulative file.

independent mothers and fathers, so this nonpartisan socialization effect is growing over time.[13]

The Jennings political socialization studies present a similar picture of the changes in the generational transmission of partisanship.[14] This is an intriguing project that traces a high school class of 1965—think of the students on the old television program *Happy Days*—and their parents over time. In 1965 only about one-fifth of Democratic or Republican parents had children who were independents. About two-fifths of independent parents had independent children. However, when the researchers reinterviewed these same high school students in 1997 as parents with their own children, the patterns of partisanship within the family had changed. The percentage of nonpartisan children among Democratic or Republican parents had almost doubled compared to the 1965 families. Similarly, independent parents were more likely to raise children who also lacked party attachments when compared to 1965. In short, hereditary Republican and Democratic partisanship is becoming less common among Americans.

These socialization patterns are important in several ways. They mean that even if people develop party attachments as they vote as adults, they start with a lower baseline of partisanship. Moreover, an innovative study of German public opinion found that partisan ties were more likely to strengthen with age among those who initially held a party attachment.[15] Independents who lacked this seed of partisanship were less likely to grow attachments with the passage of time.

This generational change is evident in comparing the share of independents among the young (aged 21–29) over time. Until the mid-1960s, only about one-third of youths lacked a party identification as they entered the electorate. The proportion of independents grew dramatically to almost half of this age group in the late 1960s. The lack of party IDs continued for the young across the next three decades. In 2008, 51 percent of those aged 21–29 said they were independents. Partisan ties strengthened with increased electoral experience for each of these cohorts, but they never caught up to the levels of partisanship among the prior generations.

The shift in partisanship can be clearly seen in Figure 3.2. The figure displays the percentage of party identifiers by age for two time periods:

FIGURE 3.2 **Partisanship and Age**

▶ *Party attachments normally develop with age, but today people are less partisan at every age level.*

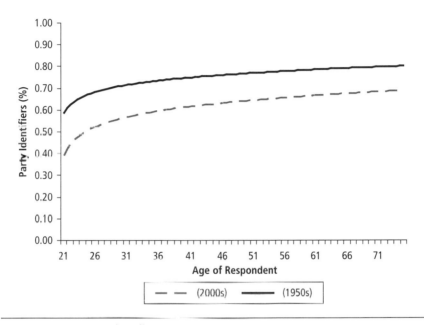

Source: ANES 1952–2008 cumulative file.

Note: The figure shows the percentage of partisans by age for the 1952–1960 surveys and the 2004–2008 surveys. The curves summarize the relationship by age.

---

elections in the 1950s and elections in the 2000s. In both periods the percentage of identifiers is greater among older respondents, which is a normal life cycle pattern. Developing a career, raising a family, and establishing a home tend to increase interest and involvement in elections.[16] Repeated experience voting in elections generally increases party ties.

Party attachments show this same age curve in the 2000s, but the starting point is initially a lower level of identification. So even if party ties strengthen with age, they remain lower than party ID in the 1950s.

These figures illustrate what previous research has shown—many younger Americans are growing up as independents. This is one locus for the rise in independents. And, all else being equal, partisanship may even weaken in the future as older generations leave the electorate and are replaced by voters who are more likely to be independents.

Cognitive Mobilization and Independents

Think of what the typical voter was like in 1952–1956 when the authors of *The American Voter* conducted their surveys. Two-thirds of the public had less than a high school education. Many women and minorities remained outside of the electoral process. Overall interest in politics was modest, and even if a person *was* interested, access to information was limited. Newspapers and magazines were a major news source, but remember the limited education of most voters. And according to the 1950 census, only 9 percent of homes had a television, so people could not even passively get their information from that source; many relied on the radio instead.

Society and the political world have changed dramatically since the 1950s.[17] Education levels have transformed the skills of the contemporary public. For instance, in the 1952 election only about 14 percent of the public had at least some college education; in 2008 this had increased to well over 60 percent. While there is not a one-to-one relationship between education and political sophistication, this tremendous increase in educational levels completed should increase the political skills and resources of the average citizen. Numerous studies illustrate how education improves the breadth and/or depth of the public's cognitive skills and understanding.[18]

Additionally, access to political information has expanded in ways that could not even be imagined in 1952. Television provides access to an incredible wealth of knowledge through news programs and soft news programs and even in the content of entertainment shows. One can see the world rather than read about it in newspapers and magazines. Today, cable news channels compete with the Internet to give people information on a twenty-four hour basis, often tailored to their own political leanings. Markus Prior, for example, used diverse evidence to show that the expansion of media choice has increased the total consumption of political information.[19] In addition, general interest in politics has increased over time, partially as a consequence of growing skills and resources and partially due to the government's expanding role in society. A larger percentage of women and minorities are also now integrated into the political process.

These tremendous socio-economic changes have increased the *cognitive mobilization* of the public.[20] Cognitive mobilization means that more people now possess the political resources and skills that better prepare them to deal with the complexities of politics and reach their own political decisions with less reliance on affective, habitual party loyalties or other external cues.

It is important that these civic skills—represented by education—are combined with a motivation to apply these skills to politics—represented by political interest. If citizens focus their skills on other life domains, then the impact of increasing cognitive mobilization on politics will be limited. *But if these two traits are combined*, this can produce groups of citizens that vary in substantial ways from our traditional images of independents and habitual partisans. In short, cognitive mobilization may yield a new type of nonpartisan: unaligned but also politically engaged.

Cognitive mobilization may also change the characteristics of some of those who decide to identify with a political party. Researchers such as Joseph Bafumi and Robert Shapiro argue that a new type of partisan has developed.[21] These new partisans do not function solely on the basis of affective party loyalties but give greater weight to ideological and issue-based decision making.

Debate exists on whether cognitive mobilization actually decreases the functional need for partisanship and thus contributes to the decline in party identities.[22] Growing skepticism of political institutions and a rise of self-expressive values also may lessen the likelihood that cognitively mobilized individuals will develop strong affective bonds to a political party, as has typically happened in the past. However, this book is more concerned with the consequences of a dealigned and cognitively sophisticated public, regardless of the causal relationship between the variables. Even if the growth of cognitive mobilization does or does not directly increase the percentage of nonpartisans, it means that a new type of nonpartisan may be developing in contemporary democracies. The new independents lack identification with a political party, but they possess greater political abilities because of the expansion of cognitive mobilization.

This book treats each mobilization process as a distinct characteristic of the electorate to create a *Cognitive-Partisan Index* (Cog-Partisan Index).[23] People are categorized by whether they have a partisan identity or not and by their level of cognitive mobilization (Table 3.1). This typology yields four groups that represent distinct mobilization patterns used in the following chapters.

"Apolitical independents" conform to the image of independents as originally described by Campbell and his colleagues in *The American Voter*. They are neither attached to a political party nor cognitively sophisticated. Members of this group should be less sophisticated politically, less concerned about the political issues and candidates of the day, and less likely to vote.

"Ritual partisans" are people who are guided by their partisan identity in the absence of cognitive resources. Ritual partisans should support their preferred party and participate in party-related activities such as voting or campaigns. However, their party support in elections can almost be a habitual activity, and they may possess very limited knowledge of the political issues. Political involvement or understanding is less likely to extend to areas where party cues are lacking.

"Cognitive partisans" score highly on both mobilization dimensions. Their party ID should stimulate involvement in party-related activities. At the same time, this group also possesses the cognitive resources to understand politics beyond affective partisan loyalties, like the new

TABLE 3.1	The Cognitive-Partisan Index	

	Party mobilization	
Cognitive mobilization	No party ID	Weak/strong party ID
High	*Apartisans*	*Cognitive partisans*
Low	*Apolitical independents*	*Ritual partisans*

Source: Constructed by the author.

partisans described by Bafumi and Shapiro.[24] The behavior of cognitive partisans may parallel that of ritual partisans in many areas—such as higher voting turnout and higher voting loyalty—but these behaviors are based on informed judgments rather than inherited partisanship.

"Apartisans" are the focus of this book. They are political independents, but they are independents of a much different sort. Apartisans generally have the skills and resources necessary to orient themselves to politics without depending on party labels. They may participate in elections and other party-related activities—although they are less supportive of party-based politics—and their political involvement may extend beyond the partisan sphere.

The important feature of this typology is that it separates different types of people who are normally combined when either dimension is considered alone. For example, *The American Voter* offered a very negative description of independents. The cognitive mobilization thesis suggests that sophisticated apartisans may comprise an increased share of the independents, which would change the nature of nonpartisans. Similarly, ritual partisans and cognitive partisans are routinely combined in studies of electoral behavior, although this book proposes that each group approaches politics in a substantially different manner. Therefore, separating these four groups should clarify our understanding of the contemporary public.

To study the groups in this typology, I used measures of party attachments and cognitive mobilization in the ANES and the standard ANES party identification question to identify partisans and nonpartisans. Cognitive mobilization implies that people possess the skills and resources necessary to become politically engaged with less dependence on external cues. In addition, cognitive mobilization implies a psychological involvement in politics so that latent abilities are applied to politics. Following a series of prior studies, I constructed a cognitive mobilization index by combining education (to represent the skills component) with interest in public affairs (to represent the political involvement component).[25] Chapter 4 explores some of the attitudinal correlates of cognitive mobilization in more detail.

It isn't clear how the expansion of cognitive mobilization has affected the distribution of these four cog-partisan groups over time. Because party mobilization and cognitive mobilization were positively correlated during the "stable state" period of *The American Voter* study, the growth of cognitive mobilization over time should have strengthened partisan ties if the initial relationship was constant. But partisanship has obviously weakened, and thus the question is whether these new independents are located primarily among the apartisans or the traditional independents.

Figure 3.3 summarizes the distribution of mobilization types since 1965, when the necessary survey questions first became available. From 1964 to 1966, the distribution of groups broadly reflected the patterns described in early electoral research.[26] Ritual partisans—those with party identifications and low cognitive mobilization—were nearly a majority (47 percent). These are the people who necessarily depend on party cues to manage the complex world of politics. If one could push the series back to the 1952 and 1956 elections, this group would be even larger.[27] In contrast, cognitive partisans were a modest proportion of the public (27 percent) in the mid-1960s.

Among nonpartisans, most (16 percent) were initially the apolitical independents who lacked party cues and cognitive skills and thus remained at the margins of electoral activity. The proportion of sophisticated apartisans was much smaller (10 percent)—the smallest of the four groups in the early 1960s. In these terms, *The American Voter's* description of independents was generally accurate at the beginning of this series (and even more so back in the 1950s).

Over the next four decades, however, the erosion of party ties and the growth of cognitive mobilization transformed the public. By the 2002–2008 elections, the percentage of ritual partisans had decreased by nearly half, to 24 percent. Far fewer citizens today rely primarily on habitual party cues as a guide to their behavior, which was the logic of the functional model of partisanship. The number of cognitive partisans has grown to become the largest group (39 percent).

Of equal importance, the decline in identifiers and the rise in cognitive mobilization have altered the character of nonpartisans. Nonpartisans were once predominately composed of the less sophisticated, apolitical independents, but now apartisans are slightly more numerous and account for one-fifth of the American public.

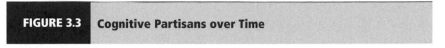

FIGURE 3.3   Cognitive Partisans over Time

▶ *The number of cognitively mobilized partisans and apartisans has grown over the past five decades.*

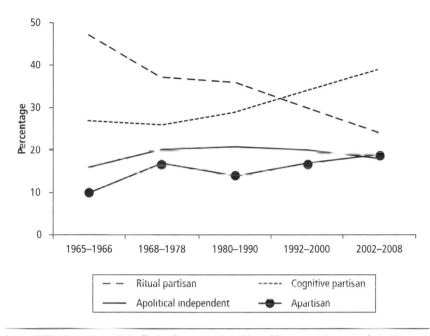

Source: ANES 1952–2008 cumulative file. For the construction of the mobilization typology, see endnote 25.

The literature on partisanship often maintains that independents who lean toward a party are hidden partisans because their behavioral profile is often closer to that of partisans than pure independents. This is a theme discussed several times in this book. I believe this argument has things backward. From 1964 to the present, two-thirds of "pure independents" (those without party leanings) are what I label apolitical independents, and these less engaged citizens should fit the standard critical descriptions of independents. In contrast, a majority of leaning independents are apartisans. Because of this concentration of apartisans, leaning independents should be more politically aware, be more active in politics, and use different bases of voting choice. In short, differences in cognitive mobilization produce the intransitivity patterns that appear to make leaning independents look like partisans in some ways; it is not that leaners are hidden partisans.[28]

Thus, the American electorate today is significantly different than the one studied in *The American Voter* and early electoral research. It is less partisan, but also more likely to possess the cognitive skills and resources to manage the complexities of politics. The growth of nonpartisans isn't primarily a function of demobilization, as some have suggested. In contrast, growing sophistication has expanded the pool of apartisans, as well as that of cognitive partisans. At the same time, the proportion of people who approach each election based on ritual dependence on party cues has decreased dramatically.

If we combine our discussion of generational change with the evidence of cognitive mobilization, we can more clearly see the full process of change. Let's use the example of the 1964–1966 generation, which came of age during the tumultuous events of that decade.[29] This generation experienced the conflict over the civil rights reforms and the massive protests and urban riots of the period. This was followed by the rising tide of the peace movement opposing the Vietnam War, the assassinations of Martin Luther King Jr. and Robert Kennedy in 1968, and the Watergate break-in and resulting scandal after the 1972 election. This generation lived through the rapid dealignment that occurred in the late 1960s—just as its members were entering the electorate. We can track how the orientations of this generation changed across the next forty years of the ANES surveys as the generation members matured, entered middle age, and began to contemplate retirement.

In 1964–1966, slightly more than one-third of this generation said they were nonpartisans, with a three-to-two ratio between apolitical independents and apartisans (Figure 3.4). As members of this generation aged, their cognitive mobilization increased—some finished additional schooling or became more interested in politics. Slowly but steadily, the percentage of apolitical independents decreased until they comprised only 13 percent of this generation by 2002–2008. The percentage of apartisans grew from 12 percent to 19 percent. Cognitive mobilization also depletes the number of ritual partisans over time and increases the percentage of cognitive partisans. Consequently, by

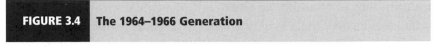

FIGURE 3.4   **The 1964–1966 Generation**

▶ *As this generation ages, increasing cognitive mobilization shifts the characteristics of partisans and independents.*

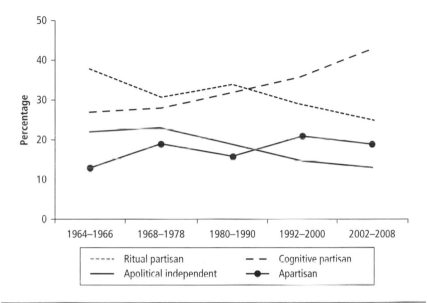

Source: ANES 1952–2008 cumulative file. The figure is based on respondents who were aged 21–29 in either the 1964 or 1966 elections.

2002–2008, when members of this generation were entering their sixties, most nonpartisans were apartisans and most party identifiers were cognitive partisans. Only a minority of this cohort still fit the modal patterns of traditional independents and ritual partisans as described in *The American Voter*. The fact that the percentage of apartisans increased modestly over time further suggests that apartisans are relatively immune from developing enduring party attachments even as they vote, which normally nurtures party ties.

Attitudes and Nonpartisanship

The abrupt drop in partisan attachments in the late 1960s leads to a natural assumption that the tumultuous events of the period changed the nature of partisanship in America. To an extent this is true. Americans have become more cynical about parties and political institutions, and this trend also dates to the late 1960s. Disillusion with Lyndon Johnson's administration led to Richard Nixon's victory in 1968, and then voters experienced the Watergate scandal in 1972. The downward trends in political trust have generally continued to the present.[30] This spreading distrust might have changed the spirit of the age, making expressions of independence from partisan politics more politically acceptable.

To explore this idea, I correlated overall trust in government with our Cog-Partisan Index (Figure 3.5). The feeling that one can trust the government to do right is a broad measure of political support.[31] Although these relationships are only modest, they point in the expected direction. That is, the percentages of ritual partisans and cognitive partisans increase as we compare those who never trust the government versus those who trust the government all of the time. There is roughly a 10 percent increase in the percentage of both partisan groups with higher levels of trust in government.

Those who distrust government are modestly less likely to have a party attachment, as shown in the figure, but there are some significant variations in this relationship. As the percentage of distrustful Americans grew after 1966, this skepticism led many people to become traditional independents. That is, after being jilted by both the Democrats and the Republicans, many people seemed to move away from partisanship. The relationship between distrust and apolitical independence was thus strongest in the 1968–1978 period, although it persists to the present. The substantial growth in distrust since the early 1960s has had a weaker impact on increasing the percentage of apartisans. Apartisans are less trustful of government, but this effect is substantially weaker for them than for apolitical independents.[32] A closer examination of the relationship over time (not shown) suggests that spreading distrust does not seem to be the major driving force behind the growth of apartisans.

A different explanation, and one somewhat related to the cognitive mobilization thesis, is that the norms of citizenship are changing. Rather than showing deference toward elites and political institutions, Americans have become more autonomous in their political orientations.

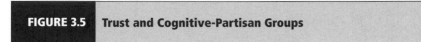

FIGURE 3.5 Trust and Cognitive-Partisan Groups

▶ *Those who trust government are more likely to be mobilized or ritual partisans.*

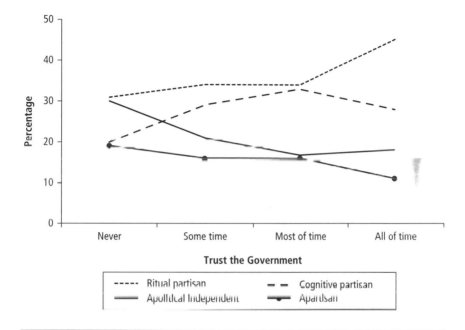

Source: ANES 1952–2008 cumulative file. The figure is based on all surveys from 1964 to 2008 that included the trust in government question.

Ronald Inglehart describes this as the growth of postmaterial, or self-expressive, values.[33] Individuals holding postmaterial values are more likely to be interested in politics, but they value individualism, which may spur a desire to remain independent of political parties. In addition, postmaterialists are only weakly integrated into most party politics because their policy goals do not fit either party closely. Thus, in an earlier work based on five advanced industrial democracies, I showed that postmaterialists are significantly more likely to be apartisans.[34]

Figure 3.6 displays the relationship between postmaterial values and the groups defined by the cognitive-partisan typology. Postmaterialists are more likely to be better educated and politically involved, and thus

▶ *The percentage of apartisans and cognitive partisans increases among postmaterialists.*

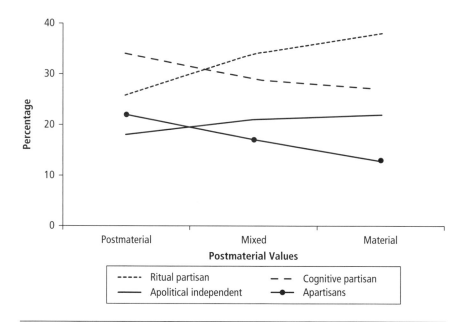

Source: ANES 1952–2008 cumulative file. The figure is based on all surveys from 1972 to 1992 that included the postmaterial values question.

they are more likely to be either apartisans (if they lack a partisan identity) or cognitive partisans. Materialists, in contrast, are more likely to be ritual partisans and apolitical independents. In other words, postmaterial value change runs across the partisan/independent line, encouraging the more mobilized subgroup on both sides. This means that the simple relationship between postmaterial values and independence is weak across the ANES surveys because of this cross-cutting effect.[35]

CONCLUSION

Virginia (a pseudonym) was interviewed in the 2008 ANES. She followed the campaign closely and claimed to discuss politics every day of the week before she was interviewed. The interviewer reported that she was better informed than most other survey respondents. Virginia seems like a typical Republican voter in many ways: she lives in the South, attends church every week, has a bachelor's degree, and works as a health care professional. She even voted early to cast her ballot for John McCain.

But Virginia is an apartisan. She is thirty years old and says she is an independent who leans toward the Republican Party. When asked what she disliked about the Democratic Party, she naturally had a number of complaints: "Their agenda, I feel, is contrary to what the Bible teaches. And at this point I think that they are very socialist and they are opposite to everything that is important to me. There is corruption in the Democrats." But at the same time, she also had harsh words about the Republican Party: "There is corruption in any politics. And I don't agree 100% with what the Republicans do. Some tend to be pro big business, like Wall Street." In fact, although she supported McCain in the 2008 presidential election, she did not vote for the Republican congressional candidate in her district.

Virginia—like Lyse in chapter 1—illustrates the new type of apartisan. In contrast to the apolitical independents, who are less interested in politics and less skilled in dealing with the complexities of politics, apartisans have the cognitive skills to understand politics and are interested in them. Thus, in contrast to the *The American Voter*'s initial description of independents, apartisans seem closer to the nonpartisan ideal that Angus Campbell and his colleagues found lacking in America. Moreover, the number of apartisans has grown significantly over the past four decades—enough that they outnumbered traditional independents in the 2008 and 2010 elections.

Of equal significance, the composition of partisans is changing in parallel ways. When Jefferson criticized partisans in his quote at the beginning of this chapter, he was probably referring to ritual partisans. Ritual partisans have limited cognitive skills and limited political interests, but they have strong party attachments and are loyal supporters of their party. Jefferson probably disliked the blind loyalty of some partisans. Cognitive partisans, in contrast, are more informed about political matters and their partisanship blends with knowledge about politics. In sports terms, the former partisans are the loyal, but unsophisticated, fans of the team; the latter are the fans who regularly follow the team on the sports page and know the statistics of the team and its players. Over the past four decades, there has been a marked decrease in the percentage of ritual partisans and a substantial increase in the number of cognitive partisans.

The statistically savvy might ask whether these correlates of partisanship endure when we consider the potential overlap between the variables. The appendix to this chapter presents a multivariate analysis describing apolitical independents and apartisans. For example, postmaterialists are more likely to be apartisans and materialists are more likely to be apoliticals, even when controlling for other factors. In short, even with multivariate controls, the patterns described here endure.

In summary, the Cog-Partisan Index argues for distinguishing between different groups of people that are normally combined in analyses of party identification. Partisans include two distinct types— ritual partisans and cognitive partisans—that bring different abilities and orientations to their electoral behavior. Similarly, nonpartisans include two distinct types—apolitical independents and apartisans—that also differ substantially in their political orientations. These contrasts are lost in analyses that simply compare partisans and nonpartisans. The goal in the remainder of this book is to show how this detailed typology is important to understanding contemporary electoral politics and the changes American politics has experienced over the past half century.

APPENDIX: MULTIVARIATE ANALYSIS

This chapter has described patterns of partisanship and independence across several different social and political characteristics, such as age, trust in government, and postmaterial values. However, some of these relationships may overlap. For example, postmaterialists also tend to distrust the government. So how do we separate out these discrete effects to tell which are due to one specific variable and which are due to overlapping effects with another variable? The answer is to conduct a multivariate analysis that includes all these variables in a single model and use statistical methods to estimate the effect of each variable while holding constant the effects of the other variables in the model.[36] This yields a more precise description of the social and political characteristics of partisan groups.

Since we are primarily interested in the growth of independents, I conducted two regression analyses. The first predicted who was an apolitical independent; the second predicted who was an apartisan. To explain each, I used the set of variables presented in this chapter: age, trust in government, and postmaterial values. In addition, these analyses include several demographic variables that might describe these two groups: income as a measure of affluence, gender, and a north/south regional division.[37] For each of these variables the statistical procedure estimates the impact of the variable controlling for all the others (standardized regression coefficient).

Figure 3.7 summarizes the results of these two regression analyses. Although there is some overlap in the factors that explain apolitical independents and apartisans, the differences are more striking. For instance, even while controlling for all the other variables, postmaterialists are still more likely to be apartisans (a positive effect of postmaterial values) and materialists are more likely to be apoliticals (a negative effect). Similarly, higher-income respondents are more likely to be apartisans, while lower-income respondents are more likely to be apolitical independents. Men are slightly more likely to be apolitical independents, while women lean more clearly toward being apartisans.

Some variables also have disproportionate effects for these two groups. For example, the percentage of apoliticals decreases substantially with age, but the age effect for apartisans is a quarter as large. Distrust of government similarly has a much stronger effect in predicting apolitical independents than apartisans.

In summary, these multivariate results follow the same pattern described in the body of this chapter. This should inspire confidence that this book's descriptions of apolitical independents and apartisans—and the contrasts between these two groups—in terms of social and political characteristics are accurate. Independents are not a single group of disengaged citizens, but reflect two very different groups of people.

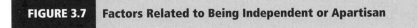

FIGURE 3.7   **Factors Related to Being Independent or Apartisan**

▶ *Apartisans are more likely to be postmaterialists, high-wage earners, and female. Apolitical independents are more likely to be low-wage earners, materialists, and distrustful of government.*

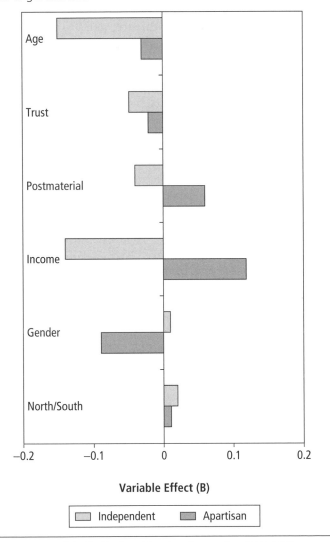

Source: ANES 1952–2008 cumulative file. The figure is based on all surveys from 1964 to 2008.

Note: The figure presents the standardized regression coefficients measuring the impact of each variable while controlling for the others, using pairwise deletion of missing data.

4

COG-PARTISANS AND DEMOCRATIC CITIZENSHIP

Are You Smarter than a 5th Grader? is an interesting television show to a social scientist. It provides a small insight into the minds of average Americans and an occasional celebrity. Adults compete with fifth-grade students on their knowledge of what might be considered basic facts. Often—and this is the appeal of the program—the fifth-graders appear smarter than the adults.

One of my favorite episodes, since I also teach European politics, featured a popular singer who was asked a third-grade geography question: "Budapest is the capital of what European country?"[1] She first said she thought Europe was a country and that she had never heard of Budapest before. She knew they spoke French in Europe, so she thought it might be France, if France was a country. In the end, she thankfully relied on fifth-grader Nathan, who correctly knew the answer was Hungary. Nathan won $25,000 for the celebrity's charity.

There are a number of possible explanations for results such as this. The students have recently had classes in the subjects of the questions, such as third-grade world geography or fourth-grade history. But many of the questions are what might be considered common knowledge. It might be that older people are a bit addled, something I consider at every meeting of the political science department faculty (just kidding). Or, the producers might select dumb people as contestants to make the show more interesting. But many of the contestants are successful in their careers and have advanced education. The singer described above is very accomplished, and I am a fan of her singing. Another explanation is that everyone cannot know everything, and we tend to compartmentalize learning to certain topics.

Being informed and thoughtful are valuable traits—in life as well as on this TV program. This book focuses on cognitive mobilization because I believe the expanding skills and resources of contemporary publics are reshaping the characteristics of democratic citizenship in positive ways. Previous political psychology research suggests that cognitive mobilization changes citizens' orientations toward politics, decision making, information seeking methods, and citizenship norms.[2] Cognitive mobilization is what makes us smarter than a fifth grader when it comes to politics.

This chapter compares the influence of partisan mobilization and cognitive mobilization on some of the citizen attitudes that underlie the democratic process. These analyses help us understand the foundations of citizenship in American politics today.

ENCOURAGING DEMOCRATIC CITIZENSHIP

Politics is not easy to understand. The issues are often very complex, even for the elected representatives who vote on legislation. Politicians and political analysts offer seemingly unending, and typically conflicting, advice on political news programs. Americans are asked to decide on a wide array of offices at election time—more than in virtually any other democracy in the world—and then make a whole new set of choices in the next election, which is at most two years away and often sooner. Being a well-informed citizen and making reasonable choices is difficult.

This is one reason why the authors of *The American Voter* placed such emphasis on party identification.[3] As discussed in the previous chapters, partisanship provides a cue for evaluating political information, integrating information into one's belief system, and making reasonable choices. Partisanship should stimulate people to participate in politics to support their party (see chapter 5). People place greater reliance on political cues from trusted sources,[4] and partisanship is a way to identify sources that one would trust: fellow partisans. Party cues are useful in local, state, and national politics. These cues apply to most issues, since the parties typically take diverging positions on the issues of the day. In a very real sense, partisanship is a superheuristic in orienting people to politics.

In addition, partisan ties and the behaviors they produce may encourage the norms of democratic citizenship. By participating in elections and campaigns, partisans may improve their knowledge of politics and their feelings of political efficacy. Electoral activity may spill over to participation in other political activities. Partisans may also improve their general skills in thinking and talking about politics through these activities. These accumulated benefits are what make partisanship so important for many people.

At the same time, the reliance on cues such as partisanship is a shortcut to actually making decisions. To a large extent, heuristics mean relying on others to give advice on what policies might benefit people like oneself or what candidate best represents one's interests—and then following this advice. Often the advice is correct, but this process abdicates political choice to others. There is an active debate about whether the use of cues is a satisfactory basis for democratic citizenship.[5]

Cognitive mobilization offers a different choice mechanism. Cognitive mobilization signals an individual's greater involvement in politics. People still might use political cues; in fact, this is a reasonable strategy for almost everyone. However, these cues are more critically evaluated because cognitive mobilization reflects a greater ability to make informed political choices on one's own.

Cognitive mobilization is an imprecise term, so I have emphasized two elements in measuring it (also see chapter 3). The first is education.[6] Education ideally signifies the cognitive development of the individual, partly because smarter people generally go further in their schooling and partly because they become more cognitively advanced by the additional years of study. Education is also related to life chances and success, so better educated people have more resources to devote to politics, more time available for discretionary activities like politics, and often more extensive social networks that mobilize them to become politically engaged.

The significance of education to democratic citizenship has long been recognized. Philip Converse summarized this position in stating:

> *There is probably no single variable in the survey repertoire that generates as substantial correlations in such a variety of directions in political behavior material as level of formal education. . . . Whether one is dealing with cognitive matters such as level of factual information about politics or conceptual sophistication in its assessment; or such motivational matters as degree of attention paid to politics and emotional involvement in political affairs; or questions of actual behavior such as engagement in any of a variety of political activities from party work to vote turnout itself: education is everywhere the universal solvent, and the relationship is always in the same direction.*[7]

Subsequent research on citizen norms and political participation has reinforced Converse's point.

I agree that education is very important in identifying the skills and resources that can benefit democratic citizenship, but a second factor is equally important: motivation. An educated person might be turned off by politics to the degree that he or she doesn't follow political affairs and doesn't even register to vote. Cognitive mobilization requires that people apply the skills and resources that they possess to politics, and so interest in politics is the second factor in our cognitive mobilization index. *The combination of both education and interest produces citizens who are significantly better at following politics and reaching their own political decisions.*[8]

In summary, both partisan mobilization and cognitive mobilization can benefit democratic citizenship. And, not surprisingly, these two traits are empirically related within the public. Partisans tend to be slightly higher in their cognitive mobilization than nonpartisans. Our goal in the rest of this chapter is to compare the independent and joint effects of both variables on a range of traits that contribute to good citizenship.

THE EFFECTS OF MOBILIZATION PATTERNS

Norman Nie and his colleagues examined the relationship between education and democratic citizenship and claimed that education enhanced "democratic enlightenment."[9] We will follow their study and examine the impact of mobilization patterns on three aspects of democratic enlightenment: political information seeking, political knowledge, and support for democratic values. In each of these areas, they found strong education effects, which should also be the case for cognitive mobilization. In addition, party identification should have similar effects in many of these areas by mobilizing partisans to be politically aware.

Political Information Seeking

One of the first steps in being an informed citizen is to acquire the information that is needed to understand politics and make political choices. Part of this information comes from personal networks, which are very important in providing context for political facts. An equally important source of information is the media, which are the main information conduits between the public and what occurs in politics.

The first expectation is that both party identification and cognitive mobilization stimulate people to follow politics in the media. I tested this expectation with a standard battery of questions on media usage for information on the presidential campaign from the 2008 ANES.[10] The survey asked how much attention people paid to politics in various media sources.

Figure 4.1 shows that both mobilization factors stimulate information seeking. The highest level of media usage is among cognitive partisans whose political interest is stimulated by their party identities and their cognitive mobilization. Conversely, the lowest level of information seeking is attributed to apolitical independents. For instance, about 45 percent of cognitive partisans say they devoted a "great deal of attention" to television news on the campaign, compared to only about 15 percent of apoliticals. I suspect the specific media outlets utilized also vary across cog-partisan groups, with partisans more likely to use television and radio programs that generally support their political orientations (e.g., MSNBC for Democrats and Fox for Republicans) and nonpartisans less likely to follow partisan media outlets.

The low level of information seeking among apoliticals reaffirms the critical evaluations of this group in previous research. However, apartisans follow a different pattern. Their level of information seeking rivals that of partisans (sitting slightly above ritual partisans and below cognitive partisans). This is a first bit of evidence that cognitive mobilization can generate democratic involvement even in the absence of party identification.

FIGURE 4.1   **Seeking Information**

▶ *Apartisans pay attention to the news in various media almost as much as partisans and substantially more than apolitical independents.*

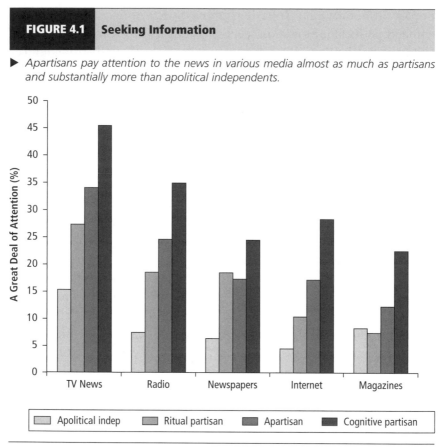

Source: 2008 ANES, postelection survey.

Note: The figure shows the percentage that pays "a great deal of attention" to the news in each of these media outlets.

Political Knowledge

Information seeking is the means to an end: acquiring the information that citizens need to make informed choices. People should understand the issues they are deciding on in order for elections to be meaningful. Even following Jon Stewart's banter on *The Daily Show* requires knowledge of current events. Measuring political information is complicated because different people know different things. Civics-type factual knowledge is routinely more common among people with longer experience as active citizens, and specific policy areas appeal to different demographic groups.[11] Knowledge of office holders may be biased toward partisans who follow "their team" more closely.

Political knowledge requires access to information and a belief system that enables the individual to understand and retain information. Consequently, cognitive mobilization—and partisan mobilization—may be important in describing the distribution of knowledge within the public.

The 2008 ANES had several ways to measure political knowledge, and multiple measures lessen the potential biases from any single item. The first question from the survey asked whether one party was more conservative than the other and asked the respondent to name the more conservative party. This seems like an easy question for *Are You Smarter than a 5th Grader?* and about two-thirds of Americans correctly answered "the Republican Party." Figure 4.2 shows the distribution of right answers by cog-partisan groups. A full 80 percent of apartisans and 78 percent of cognitive partisans gave the correct answer, but less than half of ritual partisans or apolitical independents did. Since one would be correct 50 percent of the time just by guessing randomly, this suggests that people low on cognitive mobilization might need a fifth-grader to answer this question.

Another measure of political knowledge asked people to identify the office holder for four political positions: Speaker of the U.S. House of Representatives, vice president of the United States, prime minister of England, and chief justice of the United States. These aren't topics of everyday conversation in most households, but an informed citizen should get at least half of these right.[12] The figure shows that this political knowledge was again more common among apartisans and cognitive partisans, with two-thirds knowing the names of at least two of these officials. This number dropped to half for ritual partisans and only one-third for independents.

Yet another political knowledge measure comes from the interviewers in the ANES survey. After an hour or two discussing politics with each survey respondent, the interviewers gave their overall assessment of that respondent's level of information about politics and public affairs.[13] Cognitive mobilization is strongly related to these evaluations. Interviewers were most likely to identify apartisans as having "very high" information levels (39 percent), closely followed by cognitive partisans (37 percent). In contrast, only a small minority of ritual partisans (11 percent) or independents (7 percent) received this same evaluation.

Enlightened Citizenship

The enlightened democratic citizenship of Nie and his fellow researchers includes the norms that underlie the workings of the democratic process.[14]

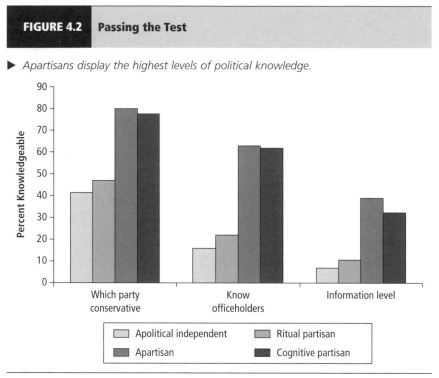

FIGURE 4.2 **Passing the Test**

▶ *Apartisans display the highest levels of political knowledge.*

Source: 2008 ANES.

Note: The figure shows the percentage scoring as "knowledgeable" or "informed" on each question.

For instance, if people feel they can have an effect on politics, then they are more likely to actually participate. Democratic politics also requires a distinct set of political norms, such as a commitment to political tolerance and support for minority rights. These feelings encourage people to be engaged as a positive force in the democratic political process.

Just as Nie's group showed that education was strongly related to these political values, we should expect that cognitively mobilized citizens will more closely fit this model of enlightened citizenship. The cognitively mobilized should feel more efficacious, be more politically tolerant, and be more supportive of democratic values. Partisanship, in contrast, yields more ambiguous predictions. Partisans should have a greater sense of political efficacy because of their ties to the political parties and their participation in electoral politics. However, it is unclear whether partisans are more tolerant and have a more enlightened definition of citizenship. This might be a function of the cues they get from party leaders, and right now political tolerance and collective interests seem to be suffering in Washington.

Figure 4.3 presents an array of items that fit the general idea of enlightened citizenship. The first two items are standard measures of whether people feel they can effectively participate in politics. Both items show a clear divide between the two groups high in cognitive mobilization and the two groups low in cognitive mobilization.

Political tolerance is a core element of a democratic political culture, and previous research demonstrates a strong relationship between such tolerance and educational levels.[15] The Citizenship, Involvement, Democracy (CID) survey measured political tolerance by asking respondents about their least-favored group from a long list and then assessing tolerance for that group.[16] The next item in Figure 4.3 measures support for democratic values from the CID survey.[17] The democratic values index is based on beliefs such as "free speech is just not worth it if it means that we have to put up with the danger to society of extremist political views" and "the government should have some ability to bend the law in order to solve pressing social and political problems."

Both political tolerance and democratic values clearly vary as a function of cognitive mobilization, and apartisans are especially high in democratic values. There is little indication that partisanship stimulates these democratic values once levels of cognitive mobilization are considered. In fact, apolitical independents score slightly higher than ritual partisans on both indices.

The final item in Figure 4.3 is a measure of engaged citizenship that I constructed in another study.[18] Engaged citizenship involves several elements: the idea that a good citizen is politically and socially active, the belief that one must be attentive to others' interests, and concern for the well-being of others. An engaged citizen is also somewhat skeptical of government. As with other traits, there are clear differences between the more and less cognitively mobilized groups in the figure.

In summary, these are all very encouraging results. The growth of cognitive mobilization appears to be deepening the democratic foundations of American political culture.

IS IT JUST POLITICS?

It might not seem surprising that cognitive mobilization stimulates what we have called "democratic enlightenment." After all, one component of

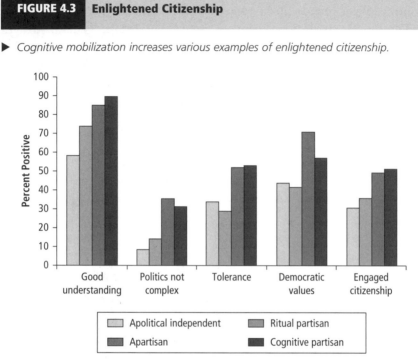

FIGURE 4.3   **Enlightened Citizenship**

▶ *Cognitive mobilization increases various examples of enlightened citizenship.*

Legend:
- Apolitical independent
- Apartisan
- Ritual partisan
- Cognitive partisan

Source: The first two items are from the 2008 ANES; the last three are from the 2005 CID survey.

cognitive mobilization is interest in politics. One might easily theo-rize that political interest drives many of the patterns described in this chapter. In addition, education contributes to feelings of demo-cratic enlightenment within the American public. However, the basic point is that cognitive mobilization is important in producing enlightened citizenship, even when people lack a party identity. Party identification has only limited influence in stimulating information seeking or political knowledge once cognitive mobilization is taken into account. The big gap in most figures is between the two groups high in cognitive mobilization and the two groups with low cognitive mobilization.

However, cognitive mobilization can be more than just a marker for the distribution of politically relevant skills and resources among Americans. There is some evidence from political psychology that we are tapping differences in individuals' cognitive style with our measure of cognitive mobilization. For instance, better-educated individuals are more likely to vote on the basis of their issue positions and place less weight on social cues.[19] They may relish the opportunity to make choices, while others try to avoid too many choices. While the average person might shun complexity, the cognitively mobilized individual might accept complexity and look at daily choices in a different way.

To explore the thought processes possibly related to cognitive mobilization, this chapter closes with some nonpolitical evidence from the 2008 ANES.[20] The ANES asked a battery of questions about the cognitive orientations of people. These questions were not framed in terms of political examples, but rather in terms of general life experiences.

Figure 4.4 shows that the cognitively mobilized—apartisans and cognitive partisans—were more like to say they held opinions on most issues, while opinion holding was much less common among the two groups lower in cognitive mobilization.[21] A second question was even more direct in assessing cognitive style; it asked whether the person liked being responsible for situations that required a lot of thinking.[22] Again, while two-thirds of the cognitively mobilized said they liked such situations, these situations were much less appealing to the ritual partisans and traditional independents. Finally, another question asked if people liked to solve simple or complex problems.[23] It is a bit surprising to me that anyone prefers complex problems. Are these the people who like doing the *New York Times* crossword puzzles, solving hard Sudoku puzzles, and answering difficult questions on midterms? Indeed, a majority of respondents preferred simple problems, and this was especially the case among ritual partisans and apolitical independents. However, two-thirds of the cognitively mobilized preferred complex problems.

CONCLUSION

Democracy demands a lot of its citizens, and it is easy to point to the examples of flawed choices in politics and in life. Yet democracy endures, and I would argue it has improved over time. I think this is at least partially because we have become better citizens.

The process of cognitive mobilization has contributed to this trend. Cognitively mobilized citizens apparently approach politics differently than the less mobilized, which is reflected in a more active search for

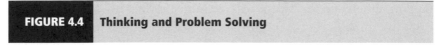

FIGURE 4.4 **Thinking and Problem Solving**

▶ *High cognitive mobilization may reflect different patterns of thinking and problem solving.*

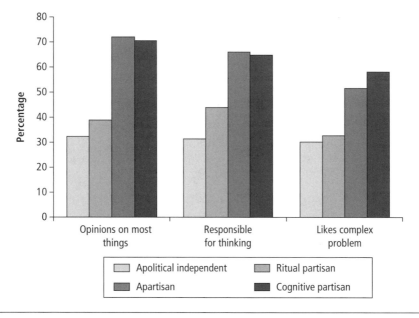

Source: 2008 ANES.

Note: The figure shows the percentage scoring as "knowledgeable" or "informed" on each question.

political information, a higher level of political knowledge, and a more enlightened set of political values. Such stratification has always been present in the public. However, the balance of these traits has shifted substantially over the past several decades because of the dramatic increase in cognitive mobilization. Moreover, the patterns in political orientations across cog-partisan groups observed in later chapters may reflect a deeper difference in how cognitively mobilized citizens approach decision making.[24] In comparison, partisan mobilization seems to yield weaker differences in the survey questions examined in this chapter, but it may be more important for behaviors more directly related to vote choice. The overall lesson is that simple assertions of the basic contrast between partisans and independents seem suspect because cognitive factors are equally or more important.

5

BECOMING ACTIVE IN POLITICS

I have a friend who bleeds Dodger blue. When he was young, his father took him to see Los Angeles Dodgers games. He has special memories of the early games that were played in the L.A. Coliseum before the new stadium was completed in Chavez Ravine. At "Roy Campanella Night" in 1959, over ninety thousand people attended the ballgame between the Dodgers and the New York Yankees in the coliseum. While my friend was in school, he followed the team through the good years and the bad, reading the box scores in the newspaper, listening to games on the radio, and going to a game when he could.

After my friend established his career and his income grew, this loyalty to the Dodgers prompted him to buy season tickets. This is a real sign of Dodger loyalty because season tickets are not cheap. He attended more games than I could imagine. He even travelled to Vero Beach for spring practice at those legendary facilities, and there is a collection of baseballs signed by Dodger greats in his den. At the start of every year he thinks that his team will win the World Series and eagerly offers his reasons for its expected success; he's been waiting since 1988. In short, his life-long identification with the Dodgers leads him to follow the team in the news and support it emotionally, and it mobilizes him to be an active fan and attend games regularly.

For partisans, their identification with a party can have similar effects. The party ID model holds that partisanship stimulates people to participate in the electoral process—to care about their party winning, to follow the campaign in the news, to maybe attend a campaign event or show support for their party, and eventually to vote on Election Day. This happens year in and year out, as the "team" has good years and bad years.

The level of participation in politics is inevitably a sign of the vitality of democracy. Moreover, this is an instance where both partisan mobilization and cognitive mobilization may stimulate participation. However, the countertrends in both factors—partisanship weakening and cognitive mobilization strengthening—offer different predictions about participation trends over time. Therefore, it's no surprise that political scientists are intensely debating the participation patterns of contemporary publics, with some scholars arguing that participation is broadly eroding and others speaking of an expansion of political engagement.

Another important question is whether these mobilization effects carry over to political activity beyond elections. Does the party identifier also engage in more expressive activities, direct contacting, or protest? Are cognitively mobilized citizens oriented to one form of political participation over others? Most experts agree that something is happening, but there isn't a consensus on exactly what.

This chapter looks at the relationship between the Cog-Partisan Index and various forms of political participation. It can be expected that the identities of strong partisans will mobilize them to be active in electoral politics, and this may carry over to other forms of activity. Similarly, cognitive mobilization provides the skills and resources that are often deemed essential to political action. Our question is the relative weight of these two mobilization forces in shaping contemporary participation patterns. This provides a first test of the behavioral importance of the Cog-Partisan Index.

MOBILIZATION IN ELECTIONS

The mobilizing effect of partisanship has been apparent since the advent of electoral research. This is one of the factors that led to the negative imagery of nonpartisans, because their lack of a psychological identification with a party diminished their involvement in the sport of electoral politics. According to *The American Voter*:

Independents tend as a group to be somewhat less involved in politics. They have somewhat poorer knowledge of the issues, their image of the candidates is fainter, their interest in the campaign is less, and their concern over the outcome is relatively slight.[1]

The American Voter and subsequent studies showed that independents were less likely to participate in a campaign and less likely to vote.[2] In 1952 only 49 percent of pure independents said they voted, compared to 82 percent of strong partisans. Martin Wattenberg observed that "people with stronger party identification are bound to think they have more at stake on election day."[3] If this pattern persists, the declining percentage of partisans should signal declining involvement in electoral politics and perhaps politics in general.

A countertrend is the growing cognitive mobilization of contemporary publics. General interest in politics and levels of education have increased, and participation research consistently shows that these factors strongly encourage political activity.[4] Political interest is the equivalent of a sports fan's interest in the sport, and education provides the resources to follow the game of politics and manage the complexities of political activity.

Electoral politics is the natural setting to begin our examination of how cognitive-partisan mobilization affects political behavior. I first consider how groups differ in their psychological engagement in elections. Cognitive partisans should have the greatest interest in elections and the most concern about election outcomes because they are mobilized by their partisanship and their high cognitive mobilization. Apolitical independents should be the least involved. The major question is where apartisans position themselves between these two extremes—closer to cognitive partisans because of cognitive mobilization or closer to apoliticals?

Figure 5.1 compares the four cog-partisan groups on their attitudes toward elections. As Campbell and his colleagues stated in *The American Voter*, apolitical independents are relatively distant from electoral politics. They are least likely to care about the election, least likely to believe that elections make the government pay attention to the people, and least

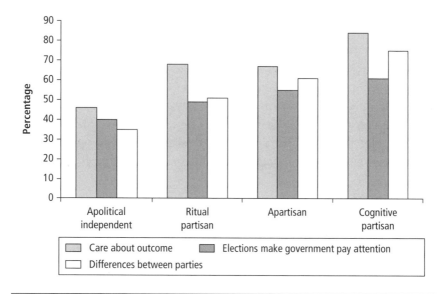

▶ *Apartisans give slightly more importance to elections than do ritual partisans.*

Source: Results for 1964 to 2008 are from the ANES 1952–2008 cumulative file.

likely to see significant differences between the parties. Even in highly contested and polarized elections, such as in 2004, independents remained aloof. In contrast, cognitive partisans score highest on each of these measures, as expected. To them, elections really matter.

The most striking pattern, however, involves apartisans. Their cognitive mobilization stimulates their concern about elections despite their lack of party ties. They scored higher than ritual partisans on two of these three attitudes, approaching the levels of the cognitive partisans. For instance, 55 percent of apartisans said elections make government pay attention, compared to 49 percent of ritual partisans. These patterns are significant because they mean that apartisans are very different from apolitical independents and thus are more likely to actually follow the campaigns and turn out on Election Day. Apartisans' independence does not reflect a disinterest or disillusion with electoral politics.

Voting

Americans' turnout in elections has gradually declined from the high points observed in the early 1960s.[5] This is problematic for democracy because elections are a primary basis of political legitimacy and one of the key aspects of representative democracy. Elections not only select government officials, they are also an ongoing civics lesson that informs the public about the issues facing the nation and the choices available to address these issues. What role do partisan and cognitive mobilizations play in encouraging turnout?

Figure 5.2 tracks the self-reported turnout of Americans categorized by the Cog-Partisan Index. Admittedly, some people overreport their turnout in an opinion survey, but these effects are probably constant over time.[6] As we would expect, cognitive partisans claim the highest level of

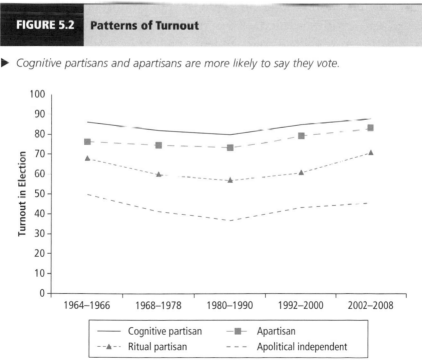

FIGURE 5.2   **Patterns of Turnout**

▶ *Cognitive partisans and apartisans are more likely to say they vote.*

Source: Results for 1964 to 2008 are from the ANES 1952–2008 cumulative file.

turnout, averaging about 85 percent over these five decades. Like the Dodgers fan at the beginning of this chapter, these are the superfans who turn out regularly to support their party because they identify with it and have the skills and resources to be engaged.

A close second in voting turnout are apartisans, averaging over 75 percent across these elections. These are not Angus Campbell's independents. Rather, apartisans are aware of the importance of elections but lack a habitual loyalty to a party. In a sense, apartisans are campaign managers' worst nightmare (or their best hope): Apartisans will normally vote in an election, but since they do not have a standing party commitment, their voting choices should be less predictable. Chapters 8 and 9 will show that this group produces a disproportionate share of electoral volatility because of these traits.

Those least likely to vote are the two groups ranking low on cognitive mobilization: ritual partisans and apolitical independents. Less than half of apolitical independents claim to vote in most elections, which is consistent with the standard description of independents. The contrast between apolitical independents and apartisans is even more striking if we look at voter registration. A full 41 percent of apoliticals say they are not registered to vote, which implies persisting electoral disengagement. In comparison, only 12 percent of apartisans say they are not registered, which is only slightly more than cognitive partisans (7 percent).

Ritual partisans are similar to apolitical independents in their cognitive resources, but their party loyalties bump up their stated turnout by about 20 percent in most elections. Yet even among ritual partisans, 21 percent say they are not registered and thus can't even vote for their party come Election Day. If we are concerned about decreasing turnout, which was most evident in the 1990s, it is worth noting that the greatest drop-off was among the two groups that lacked cognitive resources. Electoral politics was not losing its engaged citizens, it was losing those with limited political resources, even if they had a party attachment.[7]

These trends imply substantial change in the characteristics of the electorate over the past half century. If we project these patterns back to 1952,[8] the electorate in the Eisenhower-Stevenson contest was disproportionately composed of ritual partisans (almost two-thirds). Apartisans and cognitive partisans combined accounted for only about one-third of those who voted in 1952. The remainder were apolitical independents. This matches *The American Voter's* description of the 1950s electorate. The imbalance is even more pronounced in off-year congressional elections. However, the changing size of the cognitive-partisan groups is magnified by their differential turnout rates. Consequently, by 2008 ritual partisans had shrunk to comprise barely a quarter of the voters. Apartisans represented roughly one-fifth of all voters, and cognitive partisans comprised another two-fifths—their combined size had nearly doubled. The contemporary electorate is thus far different from that described in early electoral research.

Campaign Activity

One may argue that voting is the most important single form of political participation, but it is only one example of a repertoire of activities available to citizens. American elections depend on an army of volunteers. These volunteers assemble information packets for precinct walks, staff the campaign offices, show up at campaign events, spend hours making calls on phone banks, and work on Election Day to turn out their voters. Even informal conversations about the campaign are an important part of elections. These campaign activities require a greater commitment to politics than just voting, and thus they should provide an even clearer example of how partisan and cognitive mobilization can shape electoral participation.

The American National Election Studies have monitored campaign activity since 1952, asking respondents about a range of different activities. Even though the nature of campaigning has changed with technological and social modernization, this still provides a good measure of how much activity occurs during campaigns. The comparisons focus on campaign activity for the elections from 2000 until 2008 to describe current patterns of participation. In addition, I also examined the 2005 Citizens, Involvement, and Democracy survey (CID) conducted by the Center for Civil Society and Democracy at Georgetown University.[9] For both studies I used a statistical technique that produces a summary index of campaign activity.[10]

Figure 5.3 shows the patterns of campaign activity across the four cog-partisan groups. I normalized campaign activity scores so that values of 0.0 are the average for the entire public; negative values denote lower than average and positive values higher than average. The results highlight the importance of cognitive mobilization in explaining campaign activity: Apartisans and cognitive partisans both score above the national mean in both surveys, and apolitical independents and ritual partisans both score below the mean. Apartisans participate in campaigns even though they lack a long-term party loyalty; they are interested in the "game of politics" rather than in one team. In the CID survey, there isn't a significant difference in electoral activity between apartisans and cognitive partisans. In general, partisan mobilization has a secondary effect, encouraging people to be a bit more involved after taking into consideration their level of cognitive mobilization.

FIGURE 5.3   **Patterns of Electoral Activity**

▶ *Cognitive partisans and apartisans are more engaged in a variety of electoral activities.*

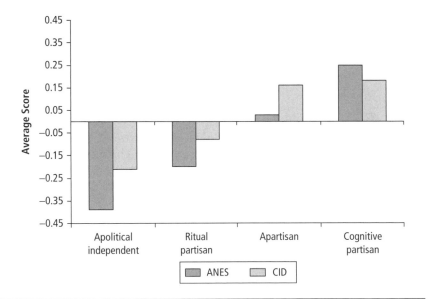

Source: 2000–2008 ANES; 2005 Citizens, Involvement, and Democracy Survey.

To some extent, these patterns of electoral participation are consistent with earlier participation studies that stressed the importance of skills and resources in predicting political activity, with partisanship playing a secondary role. However, two factors make these results more noteworthy. First, apartisans are engaged in campaigns and voting, which is in contrast to the traditional image of independents. Second, the apartisan share of independents has grown substantially over the past fifty years, so we have to reconsider our traditional image of independent citizens. Their participation makes apartisans an electoral force to be reckoned with since they will show up to vote on Election Day—in even greater numbers than ritual partisans.

PARTICIPATION BEYOND ELECTIONS

In *The Social Contract*, Jean-Jacques Rousseau made the implicit argument that democracy requires a politically active citizenry between elections, because otherwise people are only free on the day they cast their votes.[11] The American public increasingly shares Rousseau's views, even though few know of him or can correctly spell his name. Over the past several decades, participation in political activities beyond elections has increased.[12] More Americans are contacting politicians and the media and sharing their opinions in letters, e-mails, and blogs. More Americans are working with others in their community to solve local problems. And the repertoire of participation has expanded to include contentious forms of action and new types of Internet-based activism.

This section examines how partisan and cognitive mobilization affect political participation beyond elections. This provides a basis for judging the full participatory consequences of the changing characteristics of the American public.

Direct Action

Alix lives in Northern California. She switched shampoos due to animal testing and won't buy clothes produced by child labor. She yells at people who don't recycle. During her last year in high school, she helped organize a protest over the genocide in the Sudan, raising $13,000 for Darfur relief. All this was before she was even eligible to vote.

Perhaps you know Alix or are involved in some of these activities yourself. They illustrate an important form of direct action in which citizens try to influence government and society directly through their actions. These activities present an interesting test case for partisan and cognitive mobilization. While there is a natural motivation for partisans to support their party in elections, the ability of partisanship to mobilize nonpartisan activity is less clear. At the same time, the skills and resources defined by cognitive mobilization should carry over to direct action and other types of political participation.[13]

I used the 2005 CID survey to construct an index of direct action. The index includes activities such as signing a petition, buying or boycotting a product for political or ethical reasons, wearing a political button, giving money to a nonpartisan group, or contacting a politician.[14] As in the previous figure, scores are normalized so that values of 0.0 are the average for the entire public, with negative values denoting lower than average activity and positive values higher than average.

Figure 5.4 presents one of the clearest examples of how cognitive mobilization shapes political participation. Apartisans are most likely to participate in the various forms of direct political action, followed by cognitive partisans. Among the cognitively mobilized, having party loyalties does not stimulate additional direct action. Conversely, among those who rank lower in cognitive mobilization, party attachments can provide an alternative way to engage these individuals in direct activity. Ritual partisans rank below average in their level of direct action, but they are more active than apolitical independents, who again display their limited political involvement. The Cog-Partisan Index is more strongly related to direct action than to any of the other four participation examples presented in this chapter.

Protest Activity

The nature of protest in advanced industrial democracies has broadened from an activity mainly engaged in by the disadvantaged to one involving a wider spectrum of society.[15] Gray Panthers protest for senior citizen rights, consumers actively monitor industry, and environmentalists call attention to ecological problems. Public interest groups of all types are proliferating. A sampling of the large protests organized in Washington,

FIGURE 5.4   **Patterns of Direct Action**

▶ *Apartisans are most likely to use direct forms of political action.*

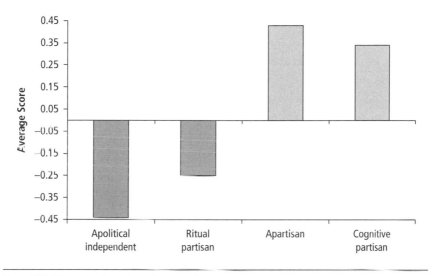

Source: 2005 Citizens, Involvement, and Democracy Survey.

DC, during 2009–2010 illustrates this diversity: the Tea Party's Taxpayer March on Washington; the LGBT Equality March; the antiwar march on the seventh anniversary of the Iraq invasion; the March for America that called for immigration reform; the Restoring Honor Rally organized by Glenn Beck; the March for Jobs, Peace, and Justice; the Rally to Restore Sanity and/or Fear organized by Jon Stewart and Stephen Colbert; and a Veterans for Peace Rally.

Historically, protests often challenged the basic legitimacy of political institutions. Contemporary protests are seldom directed at overthrowing the established political order—because the affluent and well-educated participants are some of the primary beneficiaries of this order. Reformism has therefore replaced revolutionary fervor. A modern protest is typically a planned and organized activity in which a political group consciously orchestrates its actions to occur when the timing will most benefit its cause. For many individuals and groups, protest has become simply another political tool for mobilizing public opinion and influencing policymakers.

Who protests today? Figure 5.5 presents the patterns of protest activity in 2005 compared across the categories of the Cog-Partisan Index.[16] In this instance, both cognitive mobilization and partisanship stimulate protest activity, but with only weak effects. Indeed, this is the weakest relationship across the five examples of participation compared in this chapter. Both cognitively mobilized groups are slightly above average, and both less mobilized groups are below average. This reaffirms previous studies that show protest is more common among the better-educated and more sophisticated citizens than among disadvantaged population groups. Partisans are also slightly more active than equivalent nonpartisans, but again these differences are modest. These patterns indicate that cog-partisan traits are only minimally relevant for protest activity, and other factors are needed to describe protest among Americans.

FIGURE 5.5   Patterns of Protest Activity

▶ *Both apartisans and cognitive partisans are more likely to participate in protests.*

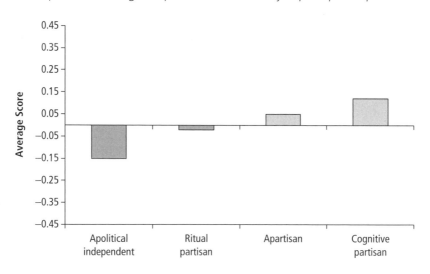

Source: 2005 Citizens, Involvement, and Democracy Survey.

Internet Activism

The newest forms of political action take advantage of the Internet age. Many Internet activities now replicate in online form earlier customs of political activity. For instance, wearing a candidate's campaign button now competes with posting an affinity button on your Facebook page. One can attend a rally through an online video stream or watch the video later on YouTube. Instead of letters mailed to an elected official through the U.S. Post Office, the vast majority of constituent mail now comes through e-mails. Campaigns are increasingly turning to the Internet as a fundraising tool in place of traditional receptions and meet-and-greets. The Internet makes it possible to do old things in new ways.

The Internet also makes it possible to pursue new forms of action. For instance, in 2008 the Obama campaign used the Internet to provide a social networking opportunity, MyBo, for dispersed supporters who otherwise would not connect. The campaign networking site also allowed local activists and supporters to interact and coordinate efforts without the guidance or intervention of the campaign. Daily e-mails from campaign headquarters reminded supporters of the issues and goals of the campaign. YouTube also played a prominent role in getting out the message of the campaign, and supporters and opponents could post their own videos, such as Will.i.Am's ode to Obama and Obamagirl's various postings. (President Obama currently has over 10.1 million followers on Twitter.) The 2008 election was the first full-fledged Internet campaign, which will influence the way future campaigns are run.

A host of studies show that Internet-based activism also has a strong generational component. A Pew Internet and American Life Project survey in 2008 asked people about their online and offline political activism.[17] The survey found that young people (18–24 years) were more active in online activities such as sending a political e-mail, signing an online petition, or contributing to a campaign online. Conversely, seniors (65 and older) were more likely to participate in comparable offline political activities. Similarly, 29 percent of the young made political use of a social networking site, compared to only 1 percent of seniors. Another survey in late 2010 found that the Internet was the most common news source for the young—for the first time outstripping even television.[18] For seniors, the Internet comes in third as a news source, matching the radio. Other recent studies show similar generational contrasts in Internet usage.[19]

The Internet has generated debate on how it will affect traditional patterns of political mobilization, including the impact of social status and party-based mobilization. Some experts have claimed that the Internet will lower the barriers to participation, while others worry that it will increase the gap between the technologically sophisticated and the less sophisticated (which would overlap with our cognitive mobilization measure). Other experts are asking whether online activism might circumvent traditional party-based forms of political mobilization and thus lessen the relevance of partisanship as a predictor for participation. With online social networks, one does not need a party organization to organize action. Indeed, it seems that many of these new online methods are embraced by individuals and groups that want to criticize both political parties and the standard processes of government action.

Figure 5.6 explores the patterns of Internet activism across cog-partisan groups.[20] The figure clearly shows that cognitive mobilization is the major factor stimulating online activism. Both apartisans and cognitive partisans are more likely to engage in these activities, while apolitical independents and ritual partisans rank significantly below average in these forms of participation. Equally evident, party ties do not stimulate participation in online activities, since partisans are no more active than nonpartisans at the same level of cognitive mobilization.

THE PATHS TO POLITICAL PARTICIPATION

This chapter has repeatedly asserted that an active citizenry is an essential aspect of democracy. While discussions of political participation often focus on turnout in elections, the range of political activities is much broader. As Rousseau would advise, people need to vote and then remain active between elections contacting politicians, expressing their views, engaging in public discourse, and influencing government policy making.

This chapter focused on how participation is shaped by the two mobilization factors comprising the Cog-Partisan Index: party mobilization through identification with a political party and cognitive mobilization.

FIGURE 5.6 **Patterns of Internet Activity**

▶ *Apartisans and cognitive partisans are more likely to participate in Internet activities.*

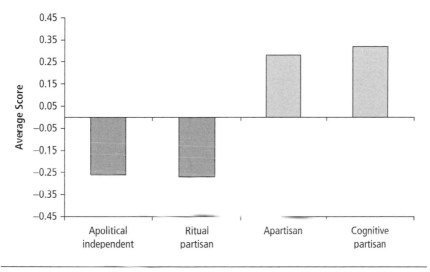

Source: 2005 Citizens, Involvement, and Democracy Survey.

What is the relative importance of both factors, and how does their impact vary across different types of politics participation? Certainly other things influence whether people participate, but these two factors are central to our inquiry about the changing nature of the American electorate. Cognitive mobilization consistently correlates with participation in virtually all forms of political action. Partisan mobilization has significant effects on campaign activity, voting, and other activities where parties are the focus of participation, but even in these instances its impact is limited.

The total impact of both mobilization factors is seen in Figure 5.7, which presents an index of overall political activity combining the separate activities examined earlier in this chapter.[21] Two patterns are most apparent in comparing cog-partisan groups. First, cognitive mobilization is most important in predicting activity because it provides the skills and resources that facilitate political action. Thus, both apartisans

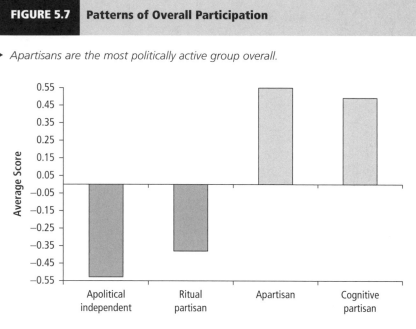

FIGURE 5.7   Patterns of Overall Participation

▶ Apartisans are the most politically active group overall.

Source: 2005 Citizens, Involvement, and Democracy Survey.

and cognitive partisans score significantly above average in their overall participation. Second, the overall mobilizing effect of party identification appears limited. Cognitive partisans are actually slightly less active in overall terms than apartisans. Partisanship seems most effective in mobilizing those with limited political skills and resources who might not otherwise participate. Party loyalties provide a way to get marginally skilled citizens to still participate. Yet even this is primarily effective for party-focused activity.

Political participation is thus the first behavioral evidence of the importance of the cog-partisan framework. Apolitical independents do display limited participation in politics, justifying *The American Voter*'s initial negative description of independents in the 1950s. But even in the 1950s there was a small group of cognitively mobilized independents, and their numbers have grown substantially in the subsequent decades. Apartisans are virtually the opposite of traditional independents in their political involvement. While apolitical independents are the least involved across all areas, apartisans are the most politically active overall and even display high levels of electoral activity. Apartisans have doubled in size since the 1950s, making it essential to distinguish between the two groups and move beyond the negative image of independents held in the past.

Of equal importance, the characteristics of partisans have changed because they have also experienced cognitive mobilization. Early electoral researchers were correct to emphasize the ability of party identification to mobilize a less sophisticated public to participate in electoral politics. This pattern is evident even in the 2000s surveys. But the percentage of these ritual partisans has decreased by more than half in the past several decades. Instead, more Americans have become cognitive partisans who have clear party attachments and the cognitive skills to be more active beyond electoral politics.

One might discount these findings because the cognitive mobilization index includes a measure of political interest, which should be a strong predictor of participation. However, the very point of the Cog-Partisan Index is to show that some independents have substantial political skills and resources, and some partisans lack these traits. In fact, if one disaggregates the cognitive mobilization index, both the education and interest items have a significant independent impact on participation that generally exceeds the mobilizing potential of party attachments.[22] In short, despite the emphasis on party identification as a stimulant to political participation in electoral research, it matters less whether one has a partisan identification or not. *More important are the skills and resources of partisans or independents.*

These developments have several implications for contemporary politics. First, this should affect the nature of election campaigns. In the past, partisans predictably showed up and normally supported "their" party, with only minor deviations from election to election. Independents were electorally disengaged, and so they had limited impact on election outcomes. We expect both ritual and cognitive partisans to remain loyal to their party—each election should begin with their predispositions set. But a growing number of apartisans means that these citizens will participate in elections (and beyond), and their voting choices should be based more on the issues and personalities of each campaign since they lack a fixed party loyalty. This should introduce new fluidity and volatility into elections—an idea examined in the next three chapters.

These changes in citizen orientations have potentially even further-reaching effects. Cognitive mobilization has likely contributed to the increase in nonelectoral forms of political action in instances where party cues are weak or lacking. This broadening of the repertoire of political activity should strengthen the voice of the American public and thus strengthen the democratic process.

CHAPTER 6

IMAGES OF PARTIES AND THE PARTY SYSTEM

Alexis de Tocqueville expressed mixed feelings about political parties in his chronicle *Democracy in America*. He called them an evil inherent in free governments. This doesn't sound like a ringing endorsement of parties.

The American public seems to share Tocqueville's views. When the Comparative Study of Electoral Systems asked people whether political parties are necessary to make our political system work, nearly three-fifths said yes.[1] But when asked if parties care what ordinary people think, about three-fifths said no. This imbalance is even greater in other democracies. For instance, 80 percent of Germans agree that parties are necessary, but only 18 percent feel that parties care what people think. These mixed sentiments about political parties are widely evident in public opinion, which leads to conflicting claims about Americans' true images of the political parties. Some experts talk about growing negativity toward parties, while others discuss the resurgence of parties in public opinion.

This chapter begins a section on partisanship and voting by describing how broad images of the Democrats and Republicans have changed in the modern era and discussing the link between party identification and these images. Scholars debate whether Americans are becoming more critical of partisan politics or perhaps indifferent about political parties in general. Another question focuses on the relationship between images of the Democratic Party and the Republican Party; perhaps instead of feeling critical or apathetic, people are becoming more polarized in their partisanship. That is, the growing partisan polarization among members of Congress in Washington may be making people's feelings toward the two parties more polarized as well.

As a side point, it's important to note that some electoral researchers consider citizen perceptions of the parties as a measure of party alignment or dealignment. *Our use of the term dealignment explicitly focuses on the level of party identification among the public.* If Americans have more or less polarized images of the political parties, this can reflect the parties' policy positions or the actions of party leaders in Washington and the state capitals. This is an important factor in how people may act politically or think about partisan politics, but such perceptions are distinct from whether people identify with one party or the other.

This chapter examines the changes in party images over time. Then the analysis is expanded to examine the variations of party images across the four cog-partisan groups. Elections end with a party choice; they begin with citizens' images of their choices.

THE SALIENCE OF POLITICAL PARTIES

One explanation for dealignment claims that political parties have become less relevant to the political process or at least have become less visible actors in it. Some experts suggest that other actors perform some of the functions of political parties, thus diminishing their relevance.[2] For instance, the mass media are now the prime source of campaign information and general political information, supplanting a pattern in which the parties spread information through in-person contacting, political rallies, and other activities. Interest groups have assumed some of the articulation functions that parties once performed. Parties were once the dominant actors on the political stage, but now they share that platform with a variety of other groups and organizations.

Other research claims that the parties have responded to dealignment by decreasing their emphasis on partisanship, which reinforces the dealignment trend. Arthur Miller and Martin Wattenberg, for example, attributed the initial decline of partisan ties to the reduced visibility of parties.[3] In a similar vein, Wattenberg charted the media's increasing attention to the presidential candidates over the political parties and claimed it has drawn attention away from the party organizations.[4] If political parties are more hesitant to stress party loyalties in the campaign in order to attract independent voters, this could further weaken party ties.

There is an element of truth to these claims about the diminished role of political parties, but the parties are still central institutions of the democratic process. The parties' roles in the selection of candidates, the structuring of political debate, the organization of elections, and the administration of government still remain dominant.[5] It's difficult to think how democratic politics could function without political parties despite the skepticism about parties described in previous chapters.

The American National Election Studies make it relatively straightforward to track the salience of the political parties over time. Since 1952 each ANES survey has asked respondents what they like and dislike about the Democratic Party and the Republican Party.[6] This open-ended question allows people to express their opinions in their own words rather than responding to choices given by the interviewer. The responses could be very philosophical, such as comments about the liberalism of the Democrats, or very basic, such as "I just don't like them." This chapter describes the broad patterns of the responses, and chapter 7 examines the content of these analyses in more depth.

The first question is whether people are now less aware of political parties or less cognizant of their actions; if so, the total number of likes and dislikes should decline over time. Figure 6.1 displays the total number of responses for the Democratic Party and the Republican Party for each presidential election. This only counts the salience of parties rather than the content of these responses. The elections of 1952 and 1956 generated a relatively high level of awareness, especially in comments about the Democrats.[7] With the exception of the highly politicized election of 1968 in the midst of the Vietnam War, the salience of the parties then slipped off in subsequent elections until hitting its nadir in the 1980 election. Even the highly charged Johnson-Goldwater election of 1964 or the Carter-Reagan election of 1980 did not stimulate much comment about the parties. Since 1980, however, the salience of the parties has increased to roughly the same levels as in the 1950s.

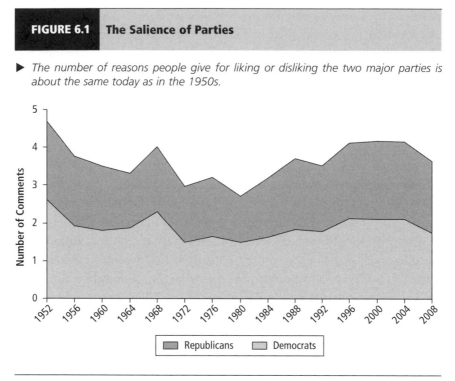

FIGURE 6.1   **The Salience of Parties**

▶ *The number of reasons people give for liking or disliking the two major parties is about the same today as in the 1950s.*

Source: ANES 1952–2008 cumulative file; 2008 coded by author.

Note: Figure entries are the number of likes or dislikes for the two parties, cumulated together.

In summary, the salience of the parties did not follow a single trend over these six decades. Simply correlating the year of the survey with the total number of comments for both parties yields a statistically insignificant relationship. The decreasing salience of political parties during the first half of this period did overlap with the decline in party identifiers. But even though the salience of parties has grown since 1980, the percentage of partisans hasn't increased. Without describing the specific content of people's images of the parties (see chapter 7), people today are as likely to have some opinions about the two parties as they were a half century ago. Fewer Americans now identify with a party, however, so the level of party salience isn't correlated with levels of party alignment or dealignment.

COGNITIVE-PARTISAN GROUPS AND PARTY SALIENCE

Studying the salience of parties is one way to see how the cognitive-partisan groups view partisan politics in general—a separate issue from their specific images of the Democrats and the Republicans. The classic view of party ID holds that independents should have less awareness of the parties because independents are less politically engaged. *The American Voter* was quite harsh in describing independents as "having somewhat poorer knowledge of the issues, their image of the candidates is fainter, their interest in the campaign is less, and their concern over the outcome is relatively slight."[8] Martin Wattenberg reinforced this point by showing that independents are more likely to be neutral toward both parties.[9] Conversely, election experts see partisans as more knowledgeable about political parties—at least their own party—and thus more vocal in expressing their likes and dislikes. Partisans have a team to root for and presumably follow the performance of their team (and the opposing team) on the field of politics.

Our expectations become more complex, however, when cognitive mobilization is added to these comparisons. Ritual partisans have strong party loyalties, but their modest cognitive skills may limit their knowledge about the political parties or at least their ability to articulate these points. Cognitive partisans are most likely to express multiple party likes and dislikes because they have party loyalties and are cognitively skilled. The uncertainty lies with the apartisans. If they are disengaged from partisan politics, they may display the same limited partisan awareness as apolitical independents. And, even if they *are* politically engaged, apartisans lack the partisan loyalties that typically shape and reinforce party images. At issue is the relative importance of their cognitive resources in the absence of party loyalties.

Figure 6.2 shows the total number of responses that individuals give to the party likes and dislikes questions, categorized by cognitive-partisan groups for 1962–2004. The two most different groups fit our expectations. Cognitive partisans offer nearly three times as many comments about the parties as compared to apolitical independents—and this is a persisting pattern over time. Despite their partisan loyalties, ritual partisans offer relatively few likes and dislikes about the two major parties. This limited vocabulary is somewhat surprising because up to ten

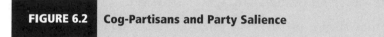

FIGURE 6.2   Cog-Partisans and Party Salience

▶ *Cognitive partisans and apartisans are more likely to give reasons for liking or disliking the parties.*

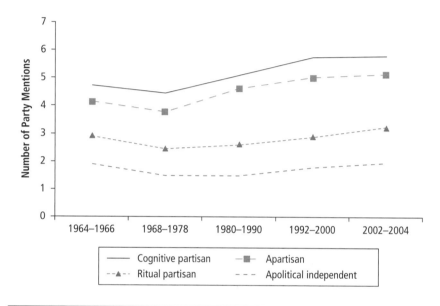

Source: Results from 1964 to 2004 from ANES 1952–2008 cumulative file.

Note: Figure entries are the total number of likes or dislikes for the two parties for each group.

likes and dislikes could be coded for the respondent's own party and another ten for the opposition, but ritual partisans average less than three responses in total.

Apartisans, despite their lack of party ties, have a considerable amount to say about the parties. The number of likes/dislikes they offer is only slightly less than that of cognitive partisans and considerably more than ritual partisans. In addition, the gap between the two cognitively mobilized groups and the other two groups has increased over time.[10] As has been argued in previous chapters, this demonstrates the need to separate apartisans from the traditional image of independents. Apartisans' lack of party ties doesn't denote a void of political interest and awareness.

PARTY LIKES AND DISLIKES

What do people say about political parties when asked about their likes and dislikes of them? It seems the spirit of age is to be *critical of political parties* (as well as of other institutions of government). Indeed, the previous chapters cite evidence of this zeitgeist. A growing share of the public lacks party identities, fewer people are voting in elections, and fewer people actively participate in many party-focused political activities. Americans' images of political parties are only slightly better than their images of real estate agents and used car salesmen. Stories of politicians' expense scandals, corruption and graft, and sexual infidelities fill the mass media almost on a daily basis.

I have written about a growing public negativity toward political parties and the current system of party government.[11] Popular trust in political parties is quite low, often hovering near the lowest evaluations across a variety of political and social institutions. Anti-incumbent sentiments in recent elections are further evidence of general dissatisfaction with both the Republicans and the Democrats, and perhaps with the current system of party-based representative democracy. One option is that Americans may be becoming more negative about both major parties and the general system of party government over the past several decades, paralleling the decline of party identifications.

Another perspective suggests that people are becoming *neutral or apathetic* toward the parties.[12] We have all heard the claims that the parties are like Tweedledum and Tweedledee—with not a dime's worth of difference between them. Martin Wattenberg showed that the percentage of the public that was neutral toward both parties grew from about one-seventh in the 1950s to one-third in the 1980s—a change potentially related to the decrease in party attachments during this same period.[13] This pattern may also reflect the less ideological nature of party politics in the 1980s. The Carter-Ford campaign in 1976 was markedly different from the Johnson-Goldwater contest in 1964. It appears that the percentage of the public expressing neutral sentiments toward both parties has decreased in recent years. Still, this remains an important category to compare across different categories of party identification.

A very different perspective argues that policy differences between the parties have actually increased in both Washington and the state capitals—and presumably stimulated *greater partisan polarization among the citizenry* as a whole. The evidence of a widening party gap in Congress is the clearest indication of this heightened polarization,[14] vividly portrayed in the often hostile partisan exchanges seen on television talk shows. If there is an "R" or a "D" after the name of the elected official being interviewed, their answers can be easily predicted—with the reverse prediction if the letter is changed. Electoral politics is an adversarial process.

Some experts say that growing elite polarization has stimulated perceptions of greater party differences among the public. Most famously, we are divided into blue states and red states, blue voters and red voters, with nary a shade of purple moderation to be seen.[15] People supposedly see the parties as highly polarized, and they divide themselves by their party identities. Often these contrasts are sharply drawn.[16] Blue Democratic partisans are described by their opponents as godless, unpatriotic, pierce-nosed, Volvo-driving, France-loving, left-wing communist, latte-sucking, tofu-chomping, holistic wacko, neurotic vegan, weenie perverts. And from the opposite perspective, red Republican partisans are seen as ignorant, fascist, knuckle-dragging, NASCAR-obsessed, cousin-marrying, roadkill-eating, tobacco-juice-dribbling, gun-fondling, religious fanatic rednecks.

Less incendiary research by academics provides some support for citizen polarization. Marc Hetherington made the widely cited claim of a resurgence of parties in the electorate because feelings of party affect polarized in the elections of the 1990s.[17] Karen Kaufmann and her colleagues used feeling thermometer questions to show that affect toward the two parties became more polarized between 1980 and 2000.[18] Especially in the 2004 and 2008 elections, it appeared that Republicans and Democrats were more sharply divided in their sentiments toward the parties and their presidential candidates. From this perspective, a growing polarization in party sentiments—strongly liking one party and strongly disliking the other—might suggest that partisanship is alive and active in contemporary politics, even if people don't label themselves as such on the party identification question.

These alternatives reflect quite different claims about how the public's images of the parties have changed over time. Some of the differences between authors occur because of how the authors measure public opinion. There are also differences in the time span studied in various articles, which can produce divergent findings. Therefore, this book goes beyond past studies by being more precise in measuring all the logical possibilities and tracking opinions from 1952 until the present.

The same set of open-ended questions is used as in the previous section. (A substantial amount of the previous research on party images uses these questions.)[19] Based on the balance of likes and dislikes, respondents' images of each party are categorized as positive, neutral, or negative. Then the opinions of both parties are compared in terms of their relative affect (see Table 6.1). At this point we aren't examining whether people prefer the Democrats or Republicans, which is considered in the next chapter, but whether opinions fit the patterns of negativity, neutrality, or polarization that are suggested by various election experts. I also separate those who gave no response to either the likes or dislikes question for both parties. This allowed the construction of an *Index of Party Affect* with six categories:

- **Positive:** Both parties receive generally positive comments.
- **Polarized**: Clearly divergent opinions of both parties. Positive toward one party and negative toward the other.
- **Preferred**: There is a modest preference for one party over the other. This might be positive toward one party and neutral toward the other, or neutral toward one party and negative toward the other.
- **Neutral:** Total comments about both parties are neutral. This results from either an equal mix of positive and negative comments or neutral comments for one party and no content for the other party.
- **Negative:** Both parties receive negative comments overall.
- **No content:** No mention of any like or dislike for either party.

These categories describe the broad patterns in how Americans view the party system and whether these options have systematically changed over time.

Figure 6.3 shows the pattern of these party images from 1952 until 2008. These images don't follow any of the three general patterns described in the political science literature. First, a very small percentage of the public is negative toward both parties. Negativity reaches 10 percent

TABLE 6.1	Comparing Party Affect		

▶ *Measuring various patterns of party affect.*

	Democratic Party		
Republican Party	Negative	Neutral	Positive
Negative	Negative	Prefer Dems	Polarized
Neutral	Prefer Dems	Neutral	Prefer Reps
Positive	Polarized	Prefer Reps	Positive

only in 1968 in the midst of the Vietnam War and the conflict over civil rights, but otherwise it is in single digits throughout this time span. Similarly, few people are positive toward both parties. Second, the share of the public that is truly neutral toward both parties is very small—consistently less than 5 percent from 1952 until 2008. In retrospect this isn't surprising. It's hard to be neutral in an election, since the point is to choose between the two parties. Third, the percentage that sees a stark polarization of the two parties—positive about one party and negative about the other—actually decreases over time. The elections of the 1950s display higher levels of party polarization than those of the 2000s.

What changed? The "no content" group doubled in size over these six decades despite advances in education levels, access to the media, and the general rise in political interest. These respondents gave *no responses* to any of the four party likes or dislikes questions. They numbered 10 to 12 percent of the public in the 1950s and have accounted for a quarter of it in recent elections. This is a striking finding because it implies an almost complete lack of political information or of an ability to discuss the two major parties. Imagine the social pressure of the University of Michigan interviewer coming to your door and asking you what you like and dislike about the Democratic Party and then what you like and dislike about the Republican Party—and repeatedly saying to these questions and the follow-ups that you don't have any opinion, or being unable to even fake an answer.

The extent of this "no content" group is a negative sign for the vitality of American electoral politics. This category doesn't imply a complete

FIGURE 6.3   Party Images

▶ *Americans' images of the parties are less polarized than they were in the 1950s, but an increasing percentage has no opinions about either major party.*

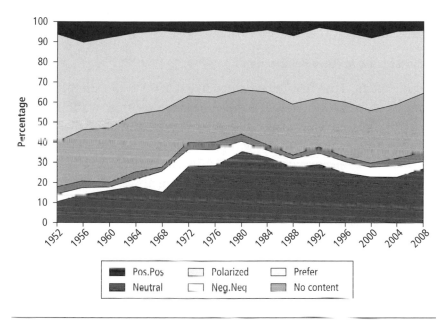

Source: ANES 1952–2008 cumulative file; 2008 coded by the author.

lack of political awareness, since many of these "no content" respondents express some interest in politics, and over three-quarters typically express some like or dislike about the presidential candidate in the same election. But parties are essential to the system of representative government, and the lack of positive or negative images toward either party suggests that many people feel distant and uninvolved from party politics. If people are neither attracted to nor repulsed by either party, it's no wonder they don't vote in elections or participate in campaigns. This may be another sign of decreasing partisanship or the consequence of the increasing political gap between the cognitively mobilized and the less mobilized.

These results thus paint an image of how partisan politics has changed that is different from most previous studies. The most striking contrast with past research may involve the claim that partisan images have polarized in reaction to elite policy polarization. This has been a common argument among those who criticize the evidence of partisan dealignment. Therefore, it's worthwhile to take a second look at the evidence of polarization.

A Closer Look at Party Polarization

A critic might claim that the typology in Table 6.1 is too simple because it measures polarization as a positive/negative contrast without giving weight to the degree of polarization. Even voters who differ markedly in their positive (or negative) images of both parties may not be counted in the polarized category if they don't cross the positive/negative divide. Also, small positive/negative differences count the same as maximally different opinions. So we should consider other ways to assess the polarization of party images.

One way of thinking about polarization involves examining the simple difference in affect between the two parties. A starting point is to subtract the number of dislikes for a party from the number of likes; this produces separate indices of affect for the Democratic Party and the Republican Party.[20] One polarization measure simply computes the absolute difference in these two affect scores. If the gap in party images between red and blue voters is increasing, then the difference in affect between the parties should increase over time. A second method correlates the affect scores for each party. The polarization thesis would predict that affect for the two parties is negatively correlated and that this relationship is strengthening.

Figure 6.4 shows that levels of polarization have not systematically grown over time. The solid line (and scale on the left) represents the average gap in party affect between the Republicans and Democrats. There is nearly a three-point gap in the 1952 election; that is, there are three more likes for the preferred party (or three fewer dislikes) compared to its opponent. It's unlikely that this primarily reflects the presidential contest, since the ideological gap between Dwight Eisenhower and Adalai Stevenson in 1952 was more moderate than in previous elections. More likely this pattern reflects the deeper ideological differences between the parties that flowed from the New Deal policies of the Democrats. This gap slowly narrows over time, reaching a nadir in 1980. Polarization then grows slightly to the present. There are numerous reasons one might describe the Bush-Kerry election of 2004 as highly polarized, many of which stem from the different policy orientations of the candidates, the political interest stimulated by the jihadist terror attacks on September 11, 2001, and the opposition to the Iraq War. The 2008 election occurred in the midst of economic recession, a falling housing market, and the potential collapse of the banking system. Nevertheless, polarization in 2004 and 2008 ranks below the public's polarization in party evaluations in the 1950s and 1960s.

The dashed line in the figure shows the correlation between affect toward the Democrats and the Republicans (the sign is reversed for

FIGURE 6.4   Party Polarization

▶ *Public images of the Democrats and Republicans are not more polarized today than in the 1950s and 1960s.*

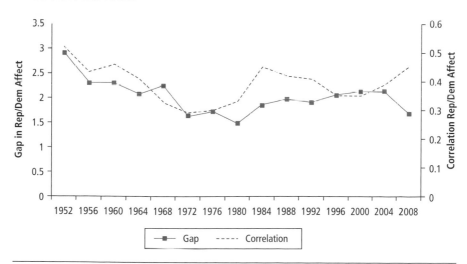

Source: ANES 1952–2008 cumulative file; 2008 coded by the author.

Note: Figure entries for the left axis are the absolute difference between Democratic and Republican Party affect; entries for the right axis are Kendall's tau-b correlations between affect toward the Democratic Party and the Republican Party using the party likes/dislikes; the signs of the correlations are reversed for readability.

readability, and the scale is on the right). Party images are most strongly polarized in 1952 and then polarization diminishes until the 1970s. There is a bump up in polarization during the Ronald Reagan and George H. W. Bush administrations, but then it declines after 1992. The public's affect toward the Democratic and Republican Parties is not more polarized today than it was in 1952.

A Second Look at Polarization

While sentiments toward the parties haven't become more polarized with the passage of time, much of the literature on mass polarization compares the issue differences between the parties.[21] This research suggests that the gap between party camps is increasing on issues that are at the core of contemporary political debate. Indeed, the polarization of party elites seems to show there are deep ideological divisions between the parties on issues such as the role of government, cultural issues, and even foreign policy. To many observers, the intense ideological polarization between the parties during George W. Bush's administration seemed the culmination of a long-term trend. This hyperpolarization appears to have continued into the Obama administration—at least in Washington.

One concern when studying polarization is what issues to compare, and, since there is an inevitable change in the salient issues between elections, it can be difficult to discern long-term trends. To provide the broadest and most robust measure possible, I used the public's perceived liberal/conservative positions of the parties as a measure of their broad ideological positions.[22] The liberal/conservative scale is generally used as a summary for political positions on the major issues of the day, even if the list of issues changes over time. In short, has the broad ideological gap between the parties systematically increased over time?

Figure 6.5 presents the gap between the public's placements of the two parties on the liberal/conservative scale. The series begins with the 1972 election, when the two measures of party affect showed more modest levels of party polarization than in the previous figure. In 1972 Americans saw the Democrats as almost two scale points to the left of Republicans—a modest level of ideological polarization.

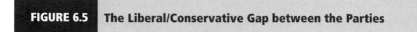

FIGURE 6.5 **The Liberal/Conservative Gap between the Parties**

▶ *Ideological polarization varies across elections, but does not have a general trend over time.*

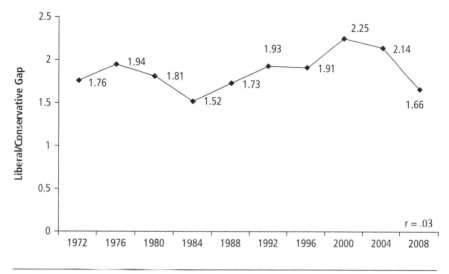

Source: ANES 1952–2008 cumulative file.

Note: The figure plots the average difference between respondents' placement of the Republican Party minus the Democratic Party on the liberal/conservative scale.

The next three decades show an ebb and flow in ideological polarization across specific elections, which reached a low point in 1984. Although Clinton tried to highlight the new centrism of the Democrats, the liberal/conservative gap increased in 1992 and 1996. Al Gore followed a more ideological course in 2000, and the public perceived this widening distance between the parties. From this zenith in 2000, the public's perceptions of party ideological differences moderated in the last two elections. In 2008 the perceived liberal/conservative distance between the Democratic and Republican Parties was actually the second lowest in this series!

Political scientists are often skeptics, and there *are* reasons to be skeptical of these patterns in liberal/conservative polarization. One might argue that these are only public perceptions of the parties, and perceptions may differ from the reality of politics in Washington. However, these perceptions are the reality when it comes to explaining people's own behavior, since they shape the electoral choices of those people. One might also argue that liberal/conservative is too broad a measure, and polarization has grown on certain subsets of issues. It's easy to understand that parties are divided on current issue controversies—the very sort of issues that are likely to be included in an election study survey. Other issues have passed from the political agenda, in part because they have become consensual (and thus are no longer included in surveys). Racial desegregation, equal voting rights, and the introduction of Medicare were highly divisive issues in the 1960s but now receive broad support from the electorate. Overall liberal/conservative differences thus provide a way to tap widespread ideological differences by summarizing party positions on the issues of the day.

The lesson taken from these three measures is that polarization has been a dynamic feature of the American party system.[23] Polarization increases and decreases in reaction to the issues and candidates of an election, and studies of a single election or a single decade present an incomplete picture of the American electorate. However, none of these three measures show the stark affective or ideological polarization that might produce a resurgence of party identities, as some experts have suggested.

VARIATIONS IN PARTY AFFECT

Partisanship is similar to a sports loyalty. It provides a cue about whom you root for and who your opponents are. Partisanship's cue-giving influence should be very apparent in feelings of party affect, even without knowing the content of these feelings. Strong partisans should have very positive feelings about their preferred party and critical feelings toward their partisan rivals. Similarly, if one is an L.A. Dodgers fan, then there is usually some degree of negativity toward the San Francisco Giants (and vice versa).

The traditional notion of independents, in contrast, claims that they are less aware of the parties and somewhat ambivalent about both the Democrats and the Republicans. They are like people who don't follow sports and wonder why others get excited by a ballgame. Thus, the direction and strength of party identification should be a strong predictor of party affect.

Figure 6.6 displays the patterns of party affect across the seven categories of party identification summarized across the six decades of the ANES. As one should expect, strong partisans overwhelmingly have more positive things to say about their own party than the other party. For instance, 80 percent of strong Democrats prefer the Democratic Party, and only 3 percent are more positive toward the Republican Party. Strong Republicans display nearly the mirror image (77 are more positive toward the Republican Party and only 4 percent toward the Democrats). Although I don't show the data, the same general pattern appears if partisans evaluate the good and

FIGURE 6.6   **Party Identification and Party Preferences**

▶ *Party identification is strongly related to party preferences.*

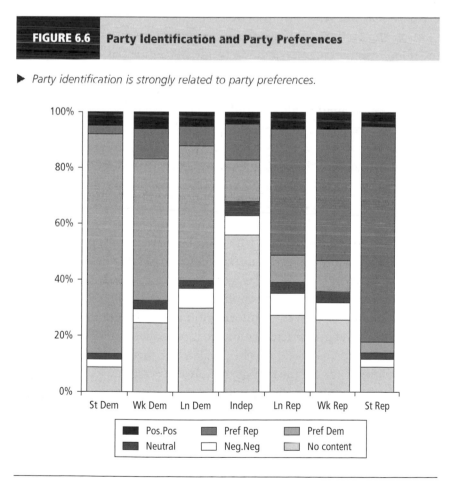

Source: ANES 1952–2008 cumulative file; 2008 not included.

bad points of the parties' presidential candidates.[24] This pattern is persuasive evidence that long-term party attachments strongly influence identifiers' images of the parties (and also the candidates) of the day.

The responses of independents also follow a pattern that is familiar to electoral researchers. The percentage of those lacking any comment about the two parties is substantially higher among independents—especially pure independents where a majority (56 percent) doesn't have anything to say about either party. However, the opinions of leaning independents are more mixed; a plurality favor the party to which they lean and a minority express no content about either party.

Of course, the relationship between party ID and party affect in an opinion survey may raise questions of what causes what. Theory and previous research suggest that party identification has the dominant effect, although there is some modest tendency for changing party images to shift party identities. But since party identifications are formed early in life and tend to endure and strengthen, they generally influence the opinions of parties in a specific election.[25]

While party affect varies by party identification in a way that matches previous research, I think that levels of cognitive mobilization affect party images in ways that aren't apparent with the standard party ID question. For example, ritual partisans should be less likely to articulate clear differences between the parties when compared to cognitive partisans. The former is a sports fan who roots based on loyalty; the latter is a sports fan who knows the statistics of the team and its players. Similarly, apolitical independents with limited cognitive resources should vary markedly from apartisans. The apolitical exists at the boundary of politics with limited interest in or information about the political parties—consistent with the characterization of independents in *The American Voter*. Apartisans may lack a party loyalty, but they are knowledgeable about politics. They are the fans of the sport of politics without having a strong loyalty to any specific team. One would expect them to recognize party differences nearly as much as party identifiers.

Cognitive-partisan types display significant differences in their patterns of party affect (Figure 6.7). One striking pattern is the contrast between apartisans and apolitical independents. Apoliticals fit the pattern of having little to say about the parties (55 percent give "no content"

FIGURE 6.7   **Cog-Partisans and Party System Images**

▶ *Political independent Ritual partisan Apartisan Cognitive partisan*

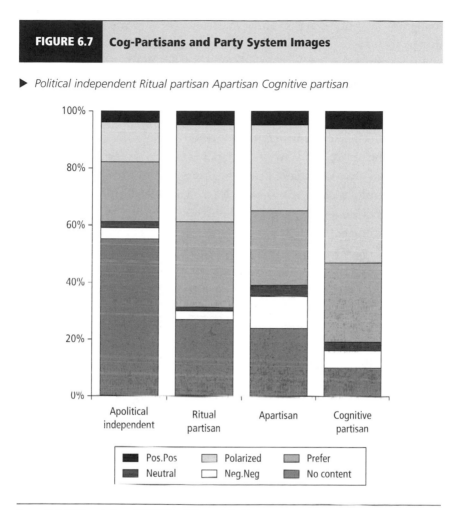

| Pos.Pos | Polarized | Prefer |
| Neutral | Neg.Neg | No content |

Source: 1964–2004 results from ANES 1952–2008 cumulative file.

responses), and only a fifth feel more positive toward one party than the other. In other words, apoliticals are largely indifferent toward the two parties, seeing them as equally appealing or unappealing, or they have nothing to say about either party. Apartisans are very different. The plurality prefer one party or the other, and barely a quarter fall into the "no content" category. A significant number of apartisans have negative feelings toward both parties or are neutral toward both. In their immediate images of the two parties, apartisans are more similar to partisans than to apolitical independents. However, these two contrasting groups of independents are blended together in the typical party identification analysis. Figure 6.7 shows that these are two very different groups, which is even more politically significant since their relative sizes have changed over the past several decades.

There are also modest differences between ritual partisans and cognitive partisans in their sentiments toward the parties. The cognitive partisans are the most likely to see party politics in polarized terms (47 percent, and an additional 28 percent prefer one of the parties over the other). Cognitive partisans are also least likely to fall into the "no content" category (only 10 percent). As we should expect, this group's feelings toward the parties reflect its loyalties. In contrast, a quarter of ritual partisans don't express any reasons for their partisan preference, and we have previously seen that the breadth of their comments is limited. Many of these ritual partisans apparently base their identity on party loyalty without a deep understanding of the parties.

If anything, the contrasts between cognitive-partisan groups have become more distinct over time. Longitudinal analyses, not shown, found that the gap in affect between the parties has actually decreased over time for apoliticals; they have become more ambivalent about seeing differences between the Republicans and Democrats.[26] Meanwhile, the gap in party affect has grown among apartisans, and since the 1980s this gap has been greater than the polarization gap for ritual partisans. Rather than being ambivalent toward the political parties, most apartisans express support for the party they currently favor, even though a significant minority are negative toward both parties.

Furthermore, if we examine the perceptions of the liberal/conservative differences between the parties, the contrasts across cognitive-partisan groups are even clearer.[27] Apolitical independents and ritual partisans see only modest ideological differences between the parties. Barely a single scale point separates the Democratic and Republican Parties in their views. But apartisans and cognitive partisans see liberal/conservative differences that are nearly twice as large.

IMAGES OF THE PARTY SYSTEM

The study of elections is a study of change. With each new campaign, experts begin to speculate on what party will gain or lose and how this election will be different from the previous election—or how it won't be. This tendency, coupled with limited empirical evidence, means that analysts often focus on short-term changes rather than the longer-term electoral patterns. More often we are interested in how this election differs from the last poll rather than how this election differs from the one fifty years ago. However, to understand the changing nature of American politics and how this influences current elections, we need a long-term perspective.

This chapter has focused on these long-term patterns, testing previous ideas about public images of the parties and the party system. With sixty years of electoral surveys at our disposal, this provides a broad context to study electoral trends.

One frequent claim is that parties have become less central to the public's political consciousness as other actors now crowd the political stage. While the latter is true, the former is not. There hasn't been a long-term decline in the salience of political parties as measured in responses to the party likes/dislikes question since 1952. Instead, there is shift in salience from election to election that without a longer-term perspective might look like a trend in decreasing or increasing attention to parties. However, the gap in party salience between the cognitively mobilized and the less mobilized has generally increased over the past six decades. The politically engaged are becoming more aware of party politics—even if they are apartisans and lack a party attachment—and the cognitively disengaged are becoming more disengaged.

The other area of debate on current party images involves the levels of affect toward the Democrats and the Republicans. By various accounts, Americans are becoming more negative, or more neutral, or more polarized in their images of the parties. We can find periods over the past sixty years that fit each of these patterns. Miller and Wattenberg, for instance, showed that party images became more neutral from 1952 until about 1980; Kaufman and her colleagues found that they became more polarized from 1980 until the present.[28] When we broaden our perspective to cover the entire period since 1952, however, none of these generalizations are accurate. The percentages of the public that are negative toward both parties, neutral toward both parties, or even polarized in their images of both parties have not increased systematically over time. Even in terms of broad liberal-conservative orientations, the perceptions of the Democratic

Party and Republic Party have not become more polarized. The only clear long-term trend since 1952 is an increased percentage of Americans who have nothing to say about either party. These are the political disengaged, and they are concentrated in the less cognitively mobilized share of the public.

Beyond these specific conclusions, our findings hold two broad implications for American electoral politics. First, party images validate the importance of the Cog-Partisan Index. Apolitical independents conform to the classic description of this group as having lower levels of party awareness. However, apartisans are substantially different from apoliticals and even ritual partisans. Simply combining both types of independents into a single category defies political reality. Apartisans are in a distinct position: they have relatively clear preferences about which party they like or dislike in an election and clear perceptions of the parties' ideological positions, but they aren't habitually committed to either party. This implies that they are more likely to evaluate candidates and parties based on current policies and performance and by definition rely less on long-term party loyalties. If elections emphasize the study of political change, then our attention should be on apartisans as the focus of potential change.

Second, the growing gap in party awareness between more and less cognitively mobilized citizens is a potential concern if it signals that a significant share of the public is turning away from parties and electoral politics. This mirrors the finding that turnout is also decreasing the most among those with less cognitive mobilization. It's also, true, however, that the number of less mobilized citizens is steadily declining over time. Thus, this gap may occur because those with lower levels of cognitive mobilization are more clearly at the margins of society and politics. As education levels have increased, those without college education have become a more distinctive group than in prior generations. Still, political inequality—regardless of the reason—remains a concern for democratic politics.

MAKING CANDIDATE CHOICES

S everal years ago, a European political scientist was visiting Irvine during the elections in California. The unique nature of American elections could be seen through the eyes of this visitor. She was amazed by the experience. Instead of the short campaigns of her home country, the campaigns began early in the year (or the year before) as candidates geared up for the primaries. Then, after the spring primaries selected the party nominees, the campaign began again in earnest after Labor Day and lasted until the vote in November. Television programming was full of advertisements—typically making conflicting claims—and the mailboxes were full of campaign mailers. In her nation the television ads were limited and organized by parties rather than individual candidates. Instead of the one or two decisions to be made on the ballot, as she experienced at home, she was surprised by the long ballots of American elections—and the substantial election guidebook that the government sent to voters. A citizen voted for governor and all the cabinet positions, members of the state assembly and senate, and local offices down to the water district board. There were also government bonds to approve or reject and a host of policy initiatives to consider. She took all of this very seriously and thought that American voters faced a challenge comparable to taking a PhD exam in political science. How does the American voter decide?

Like much of life, elections are about making choices and making good choices. Electoral behavior research stresses the importance of heuristics (cues) in guiding the citizen through the complex world of politics. This is part of the genesis of party ID; partisanship provides a cue to help people organize the political world and make decisions, and it mobilizes them to participate in politics. Many people with limited political interest or limited skills made reasonable political decisions at elections by following party cues.

However, cognitive mobilization may be changing the calculus of political decision making for at least some people. More people today possess the skills and resources that better prepare them to navigate the complex world of politics. Instead of voting primarily on the basis of habitual party loyalties, cognitively mobilized citizens may give more weight to issues and candidate evaluations as part of their calculus of voting. If people are interested in politics, more information is available on the candidates through the mass media, the advice of political groups, the Internet, and even voting-advice Web sites such as VoteSmart.

This chapter examines how cog-partisan groups vary in the factors that structure their voting choices. Most research has focused on presidential elections, and I extend this work by comparing presidential and congressional elections. The first is a high-profile election where a lot of information is available to the public; the second is a lower-profile election where media coverage and interest is less extensive (and turnout is lower). Examining these two types of elections enables us to see whether cog-partisan traits have a differential impact on high- and low-stimulus campaigns. The chapter first examines the basic relationship between party ID and voting choice. The study then expands to examine differences in the content of political evaluations as a function of mobilization patterns. Finally, the chapter explores the correlates of electoral choice. The results provide a better understanding of how voters today reach their electoral decisions.

PARTISANSHIP: THE BASELINE

If you walked into the ballot booth on Election Day and didn't know anything about the many candidates on the ballot, how would you decide who to vote for? You might pick randomly (it sometimes seems like people do this) or choose based on the listed occupations of the candidates. But a better solution is relatively straightforward: you look to see whether there is a "D" or "R" associated with a candidate's name and vote for the person who plays for "your team."

This is the underlying logic of partisanship as a heuristic for making voting choices. Philip Converse has discussed this logic in terms of the "normal vote": How would people decide if a campaign was equally balanced between the two candidates?[1] Partisan loyalties are the default value for making electoral choices for many people because the party and its candidates generally represent the people who identify with the party. Thus, in all the elections between 1952 and 2008, over 80 percent of Democratic identifiers voted for their party's candidate for president, as did over 90 percent of Republican identifiers. The statistics for House and Senate elections are very similar—more than 80 percent of partisans supported their party. Even in recent elections, party identifiers are sharply divided in their voting preferences.

Partisanship is still an extremely potent predictor of voting choice, and I don't want to diminish its importance. In fact, several election experts have pointed to this persisting effect on presidential vote choice to argue that dealignment isn't really occurring and the partisan camps are supposedly still as divided as ever. Warren Miller and Merrill Shanks noted that the relationship between party identification and presidential vote choice began to increase from a low point in the 1980s and interpreted this as a sign of dealignment reversing.[2] Larry Bartels extended this voting time series to the end of the 1990s and similarly found a persisting relationship for presidential voting. He concluded: "[Dealignment claims] would have been mere exaggerations in the 1970s; in the 1990s they are outright anachronisms."[3]

Figure 7.1 summarizes the relationship between party ID and vote choice across the elections from 1952 to the present. (The coefficient estimates the increase in the percent voting Republican for each step in the Republican direction across the seven-point party identification measure.) The first conclusion is that partisanship does have a strong and persisting overall relationship with the two-party presidential vote. In 2008, for example, 97 percent of strong Democrats voted for Barack Obama, and 95 percent of strong Republicans voted for John McCain. Partisan loyalties still strongly influence voting preferences.

Our discussion of voting choice should not end here, however. Figure 7.1 also shows that party-line voting for House and Senate elections has not followed the same pattern. Partisans were initially more divided on these elections, but partisan voting for both elections is now slightly

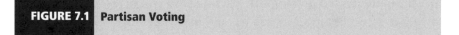

FIGURE 7.1   Partisan Voting

▶ *The relationship between party identification and presidential vote has increased slightly over time, but party-line voting for the House of Representatives and the Senate has become relatively weaker.*

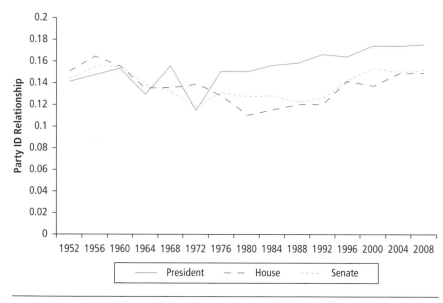

Source: ANES 1952–2008 cumulative file.

Note: The figure presents the relationship between party identification and two-party vote preference in each election (unstandardized regression coefficient).

weaker than it is for presidential vote. Moreover, other changes in the electorate can affect partisan voting over time. For instance, the mobilization of African Americans into the Democratic Party undoubtedly benefits party-line voting. The realignment of southern voters and the sorting of liberals and conservatives between the parties also increases the appearance of partisan voting.[4] If some partisans change their party identification because of their issue positions, this would also increase the apparent impact of partisanship on vote choice.[5]

Let's also think a bit more about what the relationship between party identification and vote tells us. It does show that the partisan poles are still very divided, and thus partisanship seems to shape the voting preferences of identifiers. However, the thrust of the dealignment the-sis is that fewer people now belong to these two partisan camps. So the test of dealignment is what happens among the nonpartisans, who have grown in number over time. Another caveat is that party ID is very useful in predicting continuity between elections, as it tells us who routinely supports the same party regardless of the candidates and issues of the campaign. But an equally important question is what explains change between elections: Why did Bush win a majority of the vote in 2004 and Obama in 2008? Stable party identifications cannot explain electoral change, which is an essential aspect of democratic politics. Finally, the simple correlation between partisanship and vote doesn't explain the content of voter decision making. Are people voting out of habit or because they think about the issues and the same party always best represents their views? How do nonpartisans reach their voting decision?

CANDIDATE AWARENESS

Voter choice starts with candidate awareness. Sometimes voters know a great deal about presidential candidates, such as when an incumbent runs for office or the challenger is a long-established politician. But each presidential election also presents a challenge for voters because one of the candidates has likely never run in a national election and is only well known to voters of his or her home state. In some elections the track record of the candidates is relatively short, such as with Barack Obama in 2008 or George W. Bush in 2000. The issues also change over time, and sometimes the candidates alter their own positions. The John McCain of 2008 was a different candidate than the McCain of 2000. Moreover, it is often hard to know much about House elections because there is mark-edly less media exposure of the candidates and their views. So the task of learning about candidates and judging their positions is a challenge for people who have other things to do besides study political science.

To examine citizens' images of the candidates and the factors that shape their vote choice, we turn to open-ended questions on the good and bad points about the candidate that are similar to the party likes and dislikes questions studied in chapter 6. The ANES survey asked people what they thought were the good points about one candidate, then asked about that candidate's bad points, then repeated this procedure for the other major party candidate. The project coded up to five responses for each of the four basic questions.[6] This is a tremendously valuable research resource because it provides insights into how people think about the candidates that aren't possible with fixed-choice questions. These questions also reflect the salience of the candidates, as well as the content of these perceptions. Later in this chapter these perceptions are used to study the factors affecting candidate choices.

The differential salience of presidential and congressional elections is seen in Figure 7.2, which shows the percentage of the public that expressed some opinion for the good/bad points of the candidates. In the 1998 House election, a staggering 60 percent of the public said they didn't know anything about either of the candidates or had nothing to say (good or bad) about either of them.[7] Other research shows somewhat higher levels of opinions for candidates in U.S. Senate elections.

Understandably, people tend to be much more aware of presidential candidates of both parties.[8] Across the last three elections, about four-fifths of the public expressed some opinion about the Republican and Democratic nominees. As one might expect, the one incumbent in this series (George Bush in 2004) generated reactions from about 90 percent of the public. There were similar imbalances between incumbents and challengers in both House and Senate elections.[9]

Paralleling the patterns of party awareness in chapter 6 (Figure 6.2), cognitive mobilization strongly influences candidate awareness. For instance, about 40 percent of cognitive partisans and apartisans have opinions about the congressional candidates, compared to 15 to 25 percent of ritual partisan and apolitical independents. Having a party ID does little to stimulate candidate awareness once cognitive mobilization is considered.[10] Holding an opinion about the presidential candidates follows the same pattern.

The low levels of opinion holding for House candidates should give us pause when considering electoral choice outside of presidential elections. Many political pundits and academics are critical of the quality of the public's judgments when it comes to presidential elections. However, presidential elections are the high point of public awareness of the candidates and the campaign. Figure 7.1 shows a sharp drop-off in awareness for House elections. The lack of knowledge is even lower in state and local elections where media coverage and public attention is yet more limited. How does a person vote if he or she doesn't know the choices?

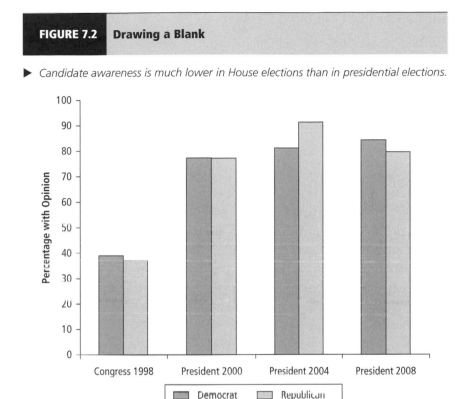

FIGURE 7.2   Drawing a Blank

▶ *Candidate awareness is much lower in House elections than in presidential elections.*

Source: 1968 ANES and ANES 1952–2008 cumulative file.

Note: Figure entries are the percentages that expressed any good or bad points about the candidates in each election.

In part, the answer is that the majority of those who said they didn't know one of the candidates or who had no opinion about a candidate didn't vote in the House election, while the majority who held an opinion did. A similar pattern probably occurs for low-profile state and local elections. This pattern lessens the number of voters with low levels of information, but it doesn't eliminate the problem. Instead, the lower candidate awareness for nonpresidential elections highlights the inevitable importance of heuristics in voting choice. When a large number of people can't say anything specific about either candidate even after the election, they must be using some shortcuts to make their choices.

THE CONTENTS OF CANDIDATE IMAGES

For candidates, election campaigns call to mind the theme song from the television show *Cheers*: First, you want everybody to know your name. If people don't know who you are, it's less likely they will vote for you. But the second step is managing the content of these images. There is an ongoing debate on how citizens evaluate the candidates.[11] Some people judge the candidates by their policy positions and their qualities as political decision makers, or they use party traits as a heuristic for policy positions. Other voters consider the personal characteristics of candidates—such as family history or even appearance—in their voting decisions. While giving credence to policy and party criteria fulfills a model of reasonable policy voters, a reliance on purely personal characteristics implies that nonpolitical judgments shape voting choice. Gary Jacobson has shown that since the late 1970s people are less likely to cite personalistic criteria and more likely to mention policy and partisan factors when describing their likes and dislikes of congressional candidates.[12]

Table 7.1 uses the specific responses to the candidate good and bad points questions to describe the content of these images. Unfortunately, at the end of 2011 the ANES had still not coded the likes/dislikes of Obama and McCain in 2008. Consequently, we compare images for the House candidates in 1998 and the presidential candidates in 2000 and 2004. To adjust for differences in visibility across offices, the table shows the results only for those who had something to say about each candidate (leaving out the "no content" and "don't know" categories). I combined responses into a set of standard categories: candidate abilities, candidate characteristics, government management, policy factors, group ties, party factors, and miscellaneous responses.[13]

Three factors are most common in how the public sees the candidates for both offices. First, since people are selecting an individual for office, characteristics of the candidates themselves are commonly cited for both types of elections.[14] People most frequently comment about the personal qualities of the candidates, such as their perceived honesty and integrity. Even for Bush, running as an incumbent in 2004, comments about his personal qualities (both good and bad) were almost as

TABLE 7.1	Content of Candidate Images

▶ *In both House and presidential elections, people cite the candidates' traits and their policy positions as the main bases of evaluation.*

	1998 Congress		2000 President		2004 President	
Criteria	Democrat	Republican	Gore	Bush	Kerry	Bush
Personal qualities	39.8	41.9	34.3	36.4	38.4	42.6
Candidate abilities	30.2	35.7	27.0	25.9	45.4	29.2
Policy	27.3	35.4	44.4	44.6	48.1	54.4
Management	7.3	6.5	7.6	5.9	6.5	18.4
Party factors	21.3	21.6	25.5	20.2	18.1	5.1
Group ties	6.8	9.6	7.8	10.1	8.2	9.8
Miscellaneous	4.2	8.1	12.5	11.0	21.2	18.3
	136.9%	158.8%	159.1%	154.1%	185.9%	177.8%

Source: 1998, 2000, and 2004 ANES; coded responses from 2008 are not available.

Note: Table entries are the percentage of each group who use each criterion at least once in discussing the good and bad points of the congressional or presidential candidates. Respondents who did not offer any responses are excluded from the table. Totals exceed 100 percent because multiple responses were possible.

common as references to the policies of his administration. Using the verbatim responses from 2008 as an example of these comments, one person described McCain in terms of his Vietnam War experiences: "I like that he was a prisoner of war, and decided to stay. The fact that he was a military man and fought for our country shows that he cares about the country. His political experience is far greater than Barack's."[15] In contrast, Obama attracted voters because of his youth, oratory skills, and his sense of energy.

Almost equally common are responses that reflect on the candidates' experience or leadership qualities, such as general references to their representation of the district, their overall voting record, or their commitment to public service. Most of these candidate-centered responses focus on criteria that are relevant for good governance, and far fewer deal with ephemeral aspects such as a candidate's looks or their simple likeability. Overall, about two-thirds of all comments about the candidates focus on some aspect of their persona.

The second most common factor involves images of the candidates' public policy positions. These cover a wide variety of issues—everything from agricultural policy to broad evaluations of economic policy or the ideological orientations of the candidates. Often the recorded comments are quite brief and telegraphic, but some voters give a range of policy examples. Again using the verbatim responses from 2008 as an example, one person described Obama by saying "I believe that he is going to help the middle class get reestablished. He is not going to continue tax breaks for the oil companies and the very rich. I think he's really going to try to make positive changes. I don't think that he will escalate any military actions that are going on right now. I believe he really will try to get everyone in the country insured with health insurance." We can't be certain that the public's perceptions of the candidate are correct, but they do contain frequent references to the policy issues facing the government.

The third most common factor in candidate evaluation is linked to the political parties. Answers in this category often express a sense of party loyalty: the candidate is a "good" Democrat or a "good" Republican, or the respondent states his or her own partisan identity as a reason for liking the candidate. When evaluating presidential candidates, people often compare them to other party leaders of the past. One person in 2008 said, "[Obama] is the first Democrat since Kennedy that raises the hopes of many layers across the social strata." Another opined, "He reminds me of Kennedy." John McCain was also the subject of such presidential comparisons, and a significant number of Republicans listed their approval of Sarah Palin as a reason to like McCain. For House candidates, people frequently referred to the candidate's likelihood of winning the constituency for the party or the candidate being a good supporter of the party in Washington. These people were thinking of the candidates as representatives of the political parties.

Each of these aspects of candidate image has a different implication for how we judge political choices. If a citizen stresses the personalistic aspects of candidates, for example, this might be interpreted as only indirectly related to specific public policies. Or, party-based evaluations might reflect the party loyalties of the respondents. Thinking of candidates in terms of their policy positions should lead to elections serving as instruments of issue voting.

In a prior study I demonstrated that the content of candidate images in the 2000 presidential election was partially derived from the public's mix of partisan and cognitive mobilization.[16] I expect that partisan references to candidates are more common among party identifiers, for example. In addition, research generally argues that policy criteria are more common among the cognitively mobilized. *The American Voter* thus argued:

> *Presumably, among people of relatively impoverished attitude who yet have a sense of partisan loyalty, party identification has a more direct influence on behavior than it has among people with a well-elaborated view of what their choice concerns. . . . The voter who knows simply that he is a Republican or Democrat responds directly to his stable allegiance without the mediating influence of perceptions he has formed of the objects he must choose between.*[17]

Thus, ritual partisans should emphasize party cues and less often cite policy criteria or ideological factors in judging the candidates. Partisanship is their shortcut for evaluating candidates: If you play for "my team," you are someone I will support.

In contrast, cognitive mobilization may produce more sophisticated individuals who have a richer basis of political evaluations. Apartisans should be a mirror image to ritual partisans: they should place less weight on partisan aspects of candidate images and give more weight to policy criteria. Cognitive partisans might have the richest images of candidates, including party criteria, because of their own partisan loyalties and the policy issues that give content to party labels. Finally, apolitical independents should have the shallowest basis of evaluation.

Table 7.2 displays the distributions of candidate perceptions for our four cog-partisan groups in the 2000 and 2004 presidential elections.[18] In both elections the table separates responses for the Democratic and Republican candidates. The first obvious pattern is the variation in the richness of political evaluations across mobilization types. Cognitive mobilization stimulated a fuller account of the good and bad points of a candidate. For instance, apartisans had more than twice as many comments about Bush in

TABLE 7.2	Cog-Partisans and Candidate Images

Criterion	Ritual partisan	Cognitive partisan	Apartisan	Indep.	Ritual partisan	Cognitive partisan	Apartisan	Indep.
	Gore 2000				Kerry 2004			
Candidate abilities	24	33	34	21	33	45	48	27
Personal qualities	30	44	43	23	28	36	40	22
Group ties	8	9	11	4	7	9	11	5
Govt. manage	6	11	9	4	3	7	7	6
Party factors	31	27	30	16	15	20	14	9
Policy factors	27	57	56	25	37	47	49	25
Miscellaneous	17	14	18	9	18	17	20	15
No content	23	11	14	38	18	11	11	31
Total	166%	206%	215%	140%	159%	192%	200%	140%
Mean responses	1.99	2.90	2.93	1.32	1.41	1.80	1.82	1.09
	Bush 2000				Bush 2004			
Candidate abilities	18	34	37	18	22	34	35	16
Personal qualities	34	44	44	26	31	45	51	31
Group ties	8	13	15	4	7	9	12	7
Govt. manage	4	8	8	4	17	21	18	13
Party factors	26	23	19	12	4	5	6	2
Policy factors	37	58	54	29	45	59	58	34
Miscellaneous	12	12	14	8	22	17	15	16
No content	28	9	13	39	12	3	3	20
Total	167%	201%	204%	140%	148%	193%	198%	139%
Mean responses	1.78	2.85	2.80	1.38	1.49	1.90	1.94	1.18

Source: 2000 and 2004 ANES; coded responses for 2008 are not available.

Note: Table entries are the percentage of each group who use each criterion at least once in discussing the good and bad points of the two presidential candidates. Totals exceed 100 percent because multiple responses were possible.

2000 when compared to apolitical independents; cognitive partisans had half again as many mentions than ritual partisans. The gap between partisans and nonpartisans is much smaller. There is also an intriguing change in the basis of Bush's evaluations between 2000 and 2004. As a challenger in 2000 he received many more comments based on his party ties, which declined in 2004. Conversely, references to his management of the government increased when he ran as an incumbent in 2004.

In summary, two important patterns emerge from these results. First, nonpartisans now include two strikingly different groups that are nearly equal in size but polar opposites in their characteristics. Apolitical independents conform to the traditional image of independents as lacking political sophistication and/or engagement, which produces fewer comments about the major-party presidential candidates. Apartisans, in contrast, have extensive views about the candidates and tend to especially evaluate them in terms of policy—much as we would expect of a rational independent voter. Second, cognitive mobilization appears more important than partisanship in shaping both the extensiveness of the information that citizens have about political actors—such as presidential candidates—and also the content of this information.

FROM CANDIDATE IMAGES TO PREFERENCES

Each aspect of candidate image can be a reasonable basis of voting choice, and the transcripts of the open ended questions illustrate this point. Most people see good and bad points about the candidates for president of the United States. However, some factors may weigh more heavily on election choices than others. People might like a candidate's oratory skills but base their judgment on the policy content of these speeches. Others might praise a candidate's vice presidential choice but give this limited weight in deciding their presidential vote.

So the next step is to link the content of candidate images to candidate preferences. The criteria that people use in making electoral choices are complicated, and empirical studies of voting behavior often yield extremely complex statistical models. Our goal is simpler than building a comprehensive model to explain the maximum variance in voting choice. Instead, we want to see if the relative weight of the three candidate factors varies across high/low visibility of elections and by mobilization patterns.

I developed a simple two-step model to capture the factors affecting candidate preferences. The appendix to this chapter explains the methodology in more detail. The first step uses the candidate good and bad points questions to create three core factors: partisan cues, candidate images, and policy preferences. In the second step, the *total impact of each*

factor is calculated. The three factors are used to predict candidate preferences as measured by the thermometers. Then the strength of the factor's
relationship with candidate preference is multiplied by how frequently
each factor is cited. For instance, one factor might be strongly related to
candidate choice but mentioned infrequently. Another factor might have
the same relationship to candidate preferences but is more commonly
cited and thus has a larger total impact. This method is similar to Donald
Stokes' calculation of the components of electoral decision making.[19] I
examined presidential elections and a House election in order to compare high and low stimulus elections.

Figure 7.3 presents the total impact of the three predictors of candidate preferences for House candidates in 1998 and the presidential
candidates in 2000 and 2004. The most obvious difference is the stronger impact for all three factors in presidential elections compared to the
1998 congressional election. This means that evaluations of presidential
candidates are more grounded in each aspect of candidate images. The
relationships between each factor and candidate preferences (unstandardized regression coefficients) are relatively similar for both presidential candidates and House candidates (see chapter appendix). The
contrast between the two types of elections occurs because of the
greater information base in presidential elections. People typically give
twice as many comments about presidential candidates compared to
House candidates for all three factors. Thus, multiplying relationships
by a factor of twice as many comments produces stronger total effects
for presidential elections.

These elections also show that candidates' characteristics (combining
their personal qualities and abilities) generally have a bit more weight
than their policy positions. Candidate characteristics had a greater impact
relative to policy or party factors in the 1998 House election. This may
be because House elections are more locally based, and the successful
member of Congress is one who can connect to the district. The other
consistent pattern is the weaker impact of partisan cues, which is surprising because of the centrality of party in all of these elections. The relationship between partisan cues and candidate preferences isn't markedly
weaker than the other two factors, but far fewer party mentions are coded
for these questions (see Table 7.1). This is surprising given the centrality

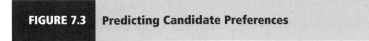

FIGURE 7.3   **Predicting Candidate Preferences**

▶ *Candidate and policy factors have a much stronger impact on candidate preferences than party comments.*

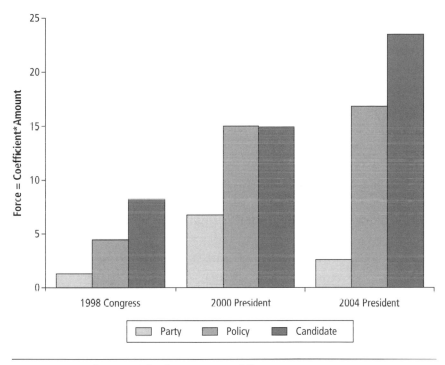

Source: 1998, 2000, and 2004 ANES; data for 2008 are not available.

Note: Figure entries are the total impact of each of the three factors on candidate preferences in each election. See chapter appendix for an explanation of how these values were determined.

of party identifications for many voters. Remember the Tallahassee voter from chapter 1 who voted for the best candidate regardless of party—but it always seemed to her that the same party nominated the best candidates. The lower impact for partisan cues may occur because partisanship is filtered through comments on a candidate's personal characteristics or policy positions. Prior research shows that candidate images are often projections of prior preferences, and not all statements on a candidate's positions or abilities are accurate.[20]

MOBILIZATION PATTERNS AND CANDIDATE CHOICE

Our discussion of the Cog-Partisan Index has alluded to how these traits may affect electoral choice. For example, partisans (both ritual and mobilized) should give relatively greater weight to party cues, as they think of elections as partisan contests. In addition, research shows that the better educated and the politically sophisticated—the cognitively mobilized—place more weight on issues as a basis of their electoral decision making; less sophisticated voters rely more on partisanship and social cues.[21] At question is whether these patterns are generalized to other elections and the possible differences between low visibility House elections and presidential elections.

Figure 7.4 presents the estimates of the causal force of three main factors—party cues, candidate image, and policy preferences—for each of the four cog-partisan groups in the three elections we are comparing. (See the chapter appendix for the calculation of these values.) The large difference in the quantity of opinions of House versus presidential candidates again appears in this figure, but we are primarily interested in the differences among cog-partisan groups. The contrasts between ritual partisans and apartisans are clear for both types of elections. Party cues exerted more than twice as much force for ritual partisans than for apartisans in all three elections. Conversely, candidate image and policy preferences have substantially greater influence among apartisans (which reflects a comparable causal weight but a much greater mass of such references among apartisans). In fact, the only case where policy factors outweigh these other two factors is for apartisans in 2000.

The pattern for cognitive partisans straddles the two previous groups: the force of party cues for cognitive partisans is roughly comparable to that of ritual partisans, and the force of the policy factor is slightly greater for cognitive partisans than for apartisans. This suggests that cognitive partisans may come closest to a model of partisanship as a rational summation of political positions, in which highly salient issue preferences and strong candidate images may alter partisan identities if they conflict with initial party ID.[22] However, the following chapter will show that their partisan loyalties are relatively impervious to change.

FIGURE 7.4

Cog-Partisans and Candidate Preferences

▲ *Apartisans and cognitive partisans have the richest basis of candidate preferences. Ritual partisans typically give the greatest weight to party cues.*

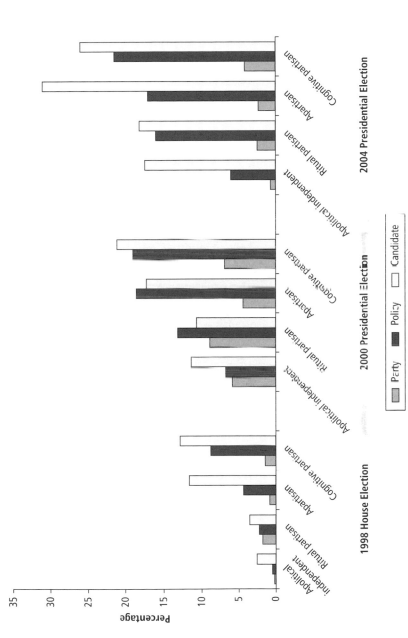

Source: 1998, 2000, and 2004 ANES.

Perhaps it is more precise to say that these are the well-informed sports fans who have a strong team loyalty and know the statistics to back up their preferences.

Finally, the relative information deficit of apolitical independents is quite apparent in all three elections. Even if one of these factors has a strong relationship with candidate preferences, there is little mass to exert much force among apoliticals. In the case of House elections, candidate preferences are almost devoid of content. Consequently, the candidate preferences of apoliticals are harder to predict when compared to the other three cog-partisan groups.

Certainly there are limitations to any one method, and data for 2008 are unavailable. So, to validate these findings, I explored another model of candidate preferences for the 2008 election. The key question is the relative weight of party cues versus issue positions across cog-partisan groups. So I created a measure of overall party preferences using the thermometer questions (the simple difference between Democratic and Republican feeling thermometer scores). To capture overall issue preferences I used each respondent's self-placement on the left-right scale to summarize diverse issue interests and positions in a single measure.

The analysis of presidential candidate preferences in 2008 yields results parallel to Figure 7.4.[23] Apartisans placed the greatest weight on left/right attitudes in defining their preference for Obama or McCain—nearly double the issue effect for either group of partisans. Conversely, affect toward the parties was the strongest for cognitive partisans and ritual partisans. Again, these factors had limited impact on the candidate preferences of apolitical independents, reflecting their marginal political involvement. In short, the patterns of cognitive-partisan mobilization shape the factors that voters consider in judging the candidates. Even apartisans give substantial attention to party factors, but they are the group that appears to come closest to our theoretical ideal of a reasonable, issue-oriented voter.

CONCLUSION

If you sit down with a friend and ask why he or she voted for a specific person for president, you probably will hear a number of reasons. Some of them might be sophisticated and ideological: "I like his new ideas and change, especially in improving [the] economy and foreign relations, where we should have been many years ago, and he will move the country forward with his new ideas. He has new ideas for energy. [He is saying many things I like about] how we do things in this country and the change for Afghanistan and our focus needs to be Afghanistan. . . . In the past I have voted Republican but he is bringing forth the ideas I think personally that we should be doing." Or they can be quite simple: "Because he is a Democrat," or "He's smart and handsome."[24] Criticisms of the candidates may be just as varied.

The point is that many different factors can enter into the calculus of voting, and seldom is there a single answer to this question. But the content of candidate and party images is a measure of the quality of the public's electoral deliberation. Ideally, we want most voters to use elections as judgments about past and future government policy rather than as a beauty contest or measure of party loyalties. All these considerations become intermixed in electoral choices.

There are many ways to disaggregate the factors affecting voter choice.[25] Our analyses use the questions on the good and bad points of the candidates to identify what factors people mention when asked their opinions about the candidates—as in the examples above—and then this research determines the weight of each factor in Americans' voting decisions.

It shouldn't be a surprise that more than two-thirds of the comments about candidates for Congress or the presidency involve the candidates' personal qualities or abilities. Most of these are relevant to their performance as elected officials and mention their experience, leadership capabilities, or personal values. Relatively few of these comments in recent elections have been trivial references to a candidate's personal appearance or a similar trait. The next most frequent responses involve what people like or dislike about a candidate's policy positions, followed by mentions of party ties or other party factors.

While the content and overall impact of these responses for the entire public are interesting pieces of information, we are primarily interested in the relative weight of these three factors across cog-partisan groups. The level of cognitive mobilization has a strong impact on the content of candidate images. Both cognitive partisans and apartisans have extensive opinions about the candidates, especially on policy issues, when compared to people low in cognitive mobilization. Consequently, the candidate preferences of the cognitively mobilized are more heavily dependent on policy and candidate images. Partisan mobilization plays a secondary role, slightly increasing the salience and causal weight of party factors in defining the candidates' images and in predicting candidate preferences. The polar opposites are thus apolitical independents, who have limited information on the candidates and base their candidate preferences largely on candidate qualities and abilities, and cognitive partisans, who have richer belief systems and place substantially greater weight on policy and partisan factors. Of equal importance to our studies, apartisans are closer to cognitive partisans in these patterns, which is further evidence of the need to separate these two types of nonpartisans.

The other important result is the contrast between low visibility and high visibility elections. Much of the research on elections focuses on presidential contests because of the importance of the office and because they engage the greatest voter interest and provide the highest turnout levels. However, our research shows that presidential elections are exceptional, and the plethora of nonpresidential elections in America involve a different type of electoral choice. Using the 1998 House election as an example—still a relatively high-visibility election compared to those for state legislatures or local offices—a strikingly large number of Americans had little or nothing to say about the candidates running for office. Even when people did have images of the congressional candidates, these were less clearly linked to their candidate preferences (see Table 7.3 in appendix). House candidate preferences are therefore ill-formed, and the relative importance of party cues is especially high among ritual partisans. Cognitively mobilized citizens have a richer belief system, but even the content of their electoral choices pales here in comparison to presidential elections.

In summary, the results of this chapter should reshape our impressions of how voters decide. Although *The American Voter* was a seminal study of voting behavior, the American public has changed in fundamental ways in the past fifty years. Chief among these changes has been the spread of cognitive mobilization. A more educated and politically engaged public decreases the overall need to base electoral choices on heuristics such as party or social group identities. Instead, the content of the campaign, the qualities and experiences of the candidates, and the issues facing government can become more important considerations in shaping candidate preferences for an increasing share of the public. But there is also great heterogeneity in the contemporary American electorate. Some people still remain aloof from politics and fit the classic image of independents as defined in *The American Voter.* Others continue to utilize habitual party loyalties as their guide to political actions. In the early 1960s, these two groups comprised about three-fifths of the entire public. Now, however, the majority of the electorate is composed of cognitively mobilized citizens who use a different calculus of electoral choice.

Finally, if these changes are real and significant, they should alter the dynamics of American electoral politics. This, perhaps, is the best test for those who doubt the significance of partisan dealignment. If dealignment and cognitive mobilization are changing the patterns of vote choice, we should be able to observe the consequences in the patterns of party support over time. The following chapter addresses this point.

APPENDIX: PREDICTING CANDIDATE PREFERENCES

I used multiple regression analysis to predict the impact of party factors, policy factors, and candidate traits on candidate preferences. I first created a measure of the relative evaluation of each candidate on these three factors based on the differences between the cited number of good and bad points of that candidate.[26] Instead of predicting voting choice, I analyzed candidate preferences as the difference between the Democrat's and Republican's ratings on the feeling thermometer scale.[27] The thermometer difference is closely related to vote choice, and it can be used for nonvoters, who are a large proportion of the apolitical independents. It also would be problematic to analyze voting in 1998 because turnout in midterm elections drops off significantly. The thermometer difference scale provides a continuous metric for our dependent variable and ranges from +100 (pro-Democrat) to −100 (pro-Republican).

The analyses had two steps. The first step used the three predictors—party factors, policy factors, and candidate traits—to explain candidate preferences in the 2004 and 2008 presidential elections and the 1998 congressional election. This yielded the relationships between each factor and candidate preferences for the entire electorate and each of our four cog-partisan groups. The multiple regression analyses predicting candidate images for the 2004 and 1998 elections appear in Table 7.3. I computed regression models for the total public and then separately for each cog-partisan group. The total public model indicates that these three predictors were fairly effective in predicting Kerry versus Bush preferences in 2004. Each of the three potential predictors—partisan cues, policy preferences, and candidate images—were significantly related to candidate preferences. I recognize this model simplifies the full complexity of candidate preferences. For instance, the simple statement of a policy being a good or bad point isn't sufficient evidence that this is an informed statement about the candidate's actual policy stance. In any case, the precise weight of the three predictors for the total electorate is less central to our research, because our goal is to compare the relative force of these three factors across cog-partisan groups.

Using the 1998 congressional results as an example, ritual partisans give party cues (b=15.7) nearly four time as great the weight as apartisans (b=3.6 and not statistically significant). Cognitive partisans give the second-greatest weight to party cues (b=5.0), although this factor doesn't dominate their decision making. Also, cognitive partisans have the richest source of political cues and thus the most structured behavior—the model explains almost three-quarters of their variance in candidate preferences, compared to less than half for ritual partisans. The three predictors explain only two-fifths of the total variance in candidate preferences for apoliticals, and only the candidate factor is statistically significant.

The second step of the analyses estimates the total impact of each of the three factors. Measuring the impact of a factor is like measuring force in physics. Force is a function of the mass of the object and the velocity it is traveling. The "mass" of each factor is represented by the amount of

TABLE 7.3	**Predicting Candidate Preferences**

Predictor	Total sample		Ritual	Cognitive		
Kerry vs. Bush in 2004	ß	b	partisan	partisan	Apartisan	Apolitical
Partisan cues	.12	12.5*	11.5*	15.1*	8.3	5.7
		(2.1)	(5.2)	(3.1)	(4.9)	(7.4)
Candidate images	.52	12.7*	11.5*	13.1*	12.7*	14.3*
		(.49)	(1.36)	(0.7)	(1.0)	(1.5)
Policy preferences	.39	10.6*	11.5*	10.8*	8.5*	6.4*
		(0.5)	(1.4)	(0.8)	(1.1)	(2.0)
Constant		−0.7	1.7	−1.6	−3.3	−0.2
		(1.0)	(2.5)	(1.8)	(1.8)	(2.3)
R square		.50	.71	.84	.78	.65
Democrat vs. Republican in 1998						
Partisan cues	.11	7.0*	15.7*	5.0*	3.6	2.7
		(1.0)	(1.9)	(1.6)	(2.3)	(3.4)
Candidate images	.46	10.5[a]	7.0[a]	11.7[a]	10.2[a]	8.2[a]
		(0.5)	(1.2)	(0.7)	(0.9)	(1.3)
Policy preferences	.31	10.1*	9.7*	12.4*	6.8*	2.7
		(.4)	(1.2)	(.6)	(.9)	(1.5)
Constant		−1.1	−2.0	−0.7	−1.2	−0.2
		(.9)	(1.4)	(1.3)	(1.8)	(0.7)
R square		.61	.43	.71	.61	.42

Source: 1998 and 2004 ANES.

Note: Table entries are the unstandardized regression coefficients using the responses from the good and bad points questions to predict differences in the Gore minus Bush thermometer scores. Standard errors are in parentheses. Statistically significant coefficients ($p<.05$) denoted by an asterisk. For the total sample I also present the standardized coefficients (ß).

information for it, which is measured by the total number of good and bad points given for both candidates in the category. That is, the "mass" of party cues is the total number of party references for the good and bad points questions on the Democratic and Republican candidates. The "velocity" of a factor is its strength as estimated by the slope in the regression models in Table 7.3. Thus, the total impact of party as a basis of decision making is the product of "mass" times "velocity"; that is, multiplying the average number of responses for each factor times the unstandardized regression coefficient in Table 7.3.[28] Again using the 1998 results as an example, the total force of partisan cues for the entire sample is 7.0 (the regression weight from Table 7.3) times 0.18 (the mean number of mentions of partisan cues for the sample). This equals 1.26, which is plotted in Figure 7.2. I repeated this procedure for cog-partisan groups in both elections (Figure 7.3).

SWITCHERS, SPLITTERS, AND LATE DECIDERS

The political scientist Samuel Barnes said that the only constant in electoral politics is that things change. Indeed, we live in such an age. After George W. Bush's victory in the 2004 election, many Republican strategists predicted a new era of Republican dominance. Karl Rove, Bush's chief electoral adviser, maintained that the Republicans were the "natural majority party." This vision ended abruptly with the Republicans' losses in 2006. Republican candidates lost thirty-one seats in the House of Representatives and six seats in the Senate, giving the Democrats majority control of both houses of Congress for the first time since 1994. The Republicans suffered a further setback in the 2008 election, as Barack Obama won the White House and the Democrats gained an additional twenty-one seats in the House and eight seats in the Senate. Many Democratic strategists then envisioned a new era of Democratic dominance. Indeed, some academic experts had previously argued that demographic change would produce a new Democratic majority.[1]

The 2010 election results were an abrupt surprise for the Democratic optimists of 2008. The Obama administration's policies stimulated the Tea Party movement and harsh criticism from the right. Many who supported the Democrats in 2008 were distressed by the slow economic recovery. There was a 9-percent vote swing toward the Republicans in the House of Representatives in 2010.[2] This gave the GOP sixty-three additional seats and a majority in the House under the new Speaker, John

Boehner, as well as six more seats in the Senate. This result stimulated calls for a new direction by the Obama administration to better prepare for the 2012 elections. And so it goes.

These recent shifts in electoral fortunes are largely due to changes in the issues of the day and the parties' and public's responses to these issues. In addition, dealignment may contribute to the volatility and fluidity of elections. The party identification model holds that most partisans will vote for "their party" and use party cues to guide them through long ballots and complex electoral choices.[3] Consequently, vote switching between elections should be fairly rare, as should be split-ticket voting, because party loyalties limit such behavior. In short, partisanship provides the stabilizing force of a party system, the "homing tendency" that guides voters back to equilibrium, and the "normal vote" that defines the structure of party competition in the United States.

However, partisan dealignment means that fewer voters enter elections with these standing party commitments. Moreover, cognitive mobilization means that a growing proportion of apartisans (and cognitive partisans) give more weight to issues and candidate images (see chapter 7). These groups should be more responsive to the issues and candidates of a campaign than apolitical independents and ritual partisans. Thus, the Cog-Partisan Index should help to identify the sources of volatility (and stability) in electoral politics.[4]

Electoral volatility is important because it signals the dynamic property of elections, with either positive or negative implications. Democracy requires that voters evaluate candidates based on their promises and performance—and sometimes vote out a government on this basis. Too little electoral change because of habitual party loyalties could yield a sclerotic system that is unresponsive to changing public preferences. The prospect that people can change their voting preferences should encourage politicians to be sensitive to the public. Too much electoral change, however, may lessen the accountability of governments if there is too much turnover in governance. It also matters why people are changing their vote, and the number of changes is important as well. In any case, the extent of electoral volatility influences the nature of democratic politics.

This chapter examines the changeability of electoral behavior and the variation across cog-partisan groups. First, we examine whether people enter a campaign with fixed party preferences or decide their vote later in response to the events of the campaign. Second, we explore how often voters change their vote between elections. This allows us to see how partisanship and voting preferences are interrelated over time. Third, we examine split-ticket voting as another possible result of dealignment.

DO CAMPAIGNS MATTER?

When do people finally make their voting decisions? The party identification model suggests that most partisans enter a campaign with standing predispositions, so they are less affected by the events and personalities of the campaign. Like sports fans, they enter the stadium knowing which team they want to win. But if party ties are weakening significantly, this implies that more voters lack these loyalties and will make their decisions during the campaign—perhaps even during its final weeks. In addition, the timing of voting decisions is an indirect sign of dealignment that is not based on reported or recalled vote choices, so it might be less susceptible to changing rhetoric about partisan loyalties.

The ANES time series generally shows a shift toward voters making their presidential vote choice later in the campaigns. For instance, in the 1952 election, 68 percent of the electorate said they had decided by the party conventions; in 2000 (a recent election without an incumbent running), the comparable proportion was 54 percent. Conversely, in 1952 only 11 percent said they decided during the last two weeks of the campaign; this increased to 23 percent in 2000. Decisions were made sooner in 2004, partly because George Bush was running again as an incumbent. As of late 2011 the ANES had still not coded the time of voting decision for the 2008 survey. However, other sources suggest that the unique nature of the Obama-McCain contest and the dramatic economic collapse that occurred during the campaign stimulated considerable volatility in electoral choices until late in the campaign. Overall, there is a clear ebb and flow in these statistics, in part depending on the individual campaign and whether an incumbent president is running for reelection. However, there is a slight time trend toward voters deciding later during the campaigns.[5]

Beyond this general trend, we expect that cognitive-partisan groups will differ in the timing of their voting decisions. Ritual partisans are often the "yellow dog Democrats" (and their Republican equivalents) who decide which party to support before the campaign even begins.

Cognitive partisans may have richer political attitudes and follow the details of the election, but their minds are also largely made up before the campaign starts. Conversely, because apolitical independents and apartisans lack party ties, they should be more likely to make their choices later in reaction to the events and issues of the campaign.

Figure 8.1 describes the percentage of each cog-partisan group that claimed to decide its presidential voting preference after the nominating conventions over the period from 1964 until 2004.[6] Clearly, many partisans enter a campaign with their preferences already decided. In 1964, for instance, only 31 percent of ritual partisans and 30 percent of cognitive partisans said they decided after the conventions. This is striking, since the Johnson-Goldwater campaign was very intense and took place in the

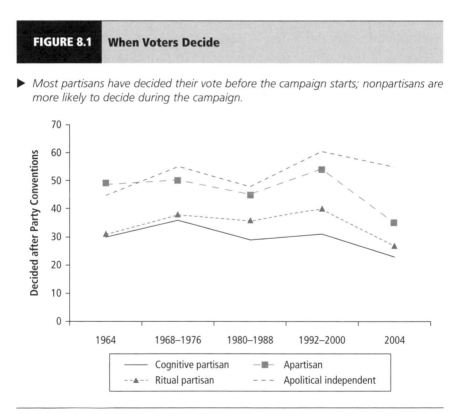

FIGURE 8.1   When Voters Decide

▶ *Most partisans have decided their vote before the campaign starts; nonpartisans are more likely to decide during the campaign.*

Source: Results from 1964 to 2004 are from the ANES 1952–2008 cumulative file.

Note: The figure shows the percentage who say they decided how to vote after the party conventions.

midst of the civil rights movement; many Americans were rethinking their issue positions and party choices during this period. Across elections for the next four decades, only a modest number of these two partisan groups said they decided their vote after the party conventions. When one is a partisan, the "right" choice is quite clear.

Conversely, almost half of the two independent groups said they decided during the 1964 campaign. This pattern persists over time. Across all elections, 30 percent of apolitical independents and 25 percent of apartisans said they decided their vote in the last two weeks of the campaign. Attention to the campaign actually seems to have been higher among apolitical independents, but this is a mirage. More than half of independents do not vote at all, and thus the proportion of all independents who do vote and decide late is the smallest among all four groups. The late decisions by apoliticals who vote may just be another sign of their indecision. In contrast, a large majority of apartisans vote and many make their decision late—presumably based on the content of the campaign.

I think these results pose an interesting question for democratic elections. How meaningful are elections if most partisans enter the campaign with their minds set even before the candidates and parties discuss the issues, the candidates hold debates, and the media have scrutinized the candidates' positions? Partisanship simplifies voting choice by having a preferred team, but is voting on the basis of such loyalty rational, democratic decision making? In contrast, apartisans are more likely to defer their electoral choices until later in the campaign when they have become familiar with the issues of the debate. The actions of apartisans seem closer to what we should expect of a good democratic citizen.

SWING VOTERS

If fewer citizens feel a deep loyalty toward a political party, then voter preferences are more likely to change between elections—or even between party candidates on the same ballot. Indeed, elections give the public a way to change the course of government if they prefer, which requires that people look beyond their party loyalty and occasionally vote for a different party that promises change. If people repetitively vote for a party based on family tradition, it raises the basic question of whether they are making informed democratic choices.

Switching party preferences between elections is the major dynamic process in electoral politics. Clinton won in 1992 because some people who voted for George H. W. Bush in 1988 didn't support him again in 1992. Obama won in 2008 because some people who voted for George W. Bush in 2004 switched their allegiance to the Democrats in 2008 (and some new voters entered the electorate). Without such change, elections would be boring (and less democratic) because people would vote the same in each election regardless of political events. Democracy requires some change to keep government accountable and politicians responsive to public preferences.

There is, however, a potential problem in measuring swing voting. One method is to ask people to recall their past vote and compare this to present voting choices. Previous research shows that such recall data are imprecise. Some people project their current preferences back to their past. Other people simply have forgotten, since the last presidential election was four years ago and much has changed in their life and politics since then. Even if we interviewed and reinterviewed the same people across two elections there would be some errors in memory and reporting.

Beyond the frailty of vote recall, defining a swing voter is complicated. Is a person who votes in one election but not the next a swing voter? How do we treat third-party candidates? Some studies delete third-party candidates to focus on two-party choices, but this seems illogical since by definition third-party voters have shifted from voting for one of the two major parties (see section below).

To address these issues I compared two measures of swing voting in presidential elections (the ANES doesn't regularly ask about vote change in congressional elections). The first measure is the simplest. It calculates whether a person reports having voted for the presidential candidate of the same party in two successive elections. Third-party voting is treated as a swing vote (except for Perot voters in 1996 who had also supported Perot in 1992). The second measure factors in nonvoting, so people who enter or exit the electorate in one election are counted as changing. As a reference standard, I also calculated the percentage of party changers in the four major ANES panel surveys, which ask for the stated voting preference of the same people across two presidential elections.

Figure 8.2 presents reported vote switching for presidential elections from 1952 to the present. The dotted line shows recalled vote switching among people who voted in at least one of the two paired elections, with nonvoting in one election counted as a switch. The solid line is based on people who said they voted in both elections. The diamonds are vote switchers based on four ANES panel surveys, which minimizes the problem of asking people to recall their vote from the previous election. The gap between the panel results and the solid line of recalled vote is fairly modest and is quite small for the two most recent panels.

There is considerable volatility in presidential elections. Based only on those who said they voted in both adjacent elections, about 25 percent switched party votes. If we include entrance or exit from voting, the switchers increase to a bit more than 40 percent of the public. Presidential election results are typically more volatile than those for the House of Representatives or the Senate.

FIGURE 8.2   Vote Switching

▶ *Vote switching between presidential elections ebbs and flows over time.*

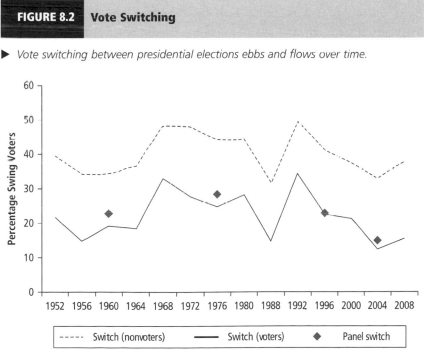

Source: ANES 1952–2008 cumulative file; 1956–1960, 1972–1976, 1992–1996, and 2000–2004 ANES panels.

Note: Figure entries are the percent switching parties between presidential election votes, including nonvoters in one election and voters in both elections. The diamond indicates the percentage of voters who switched based on the ANES panels. Third-party presidential voters are included.

Vote switching also varies considerably across different elections. When there is a significant third-party presidential candidate, this necessarily produces a spike in voting switching (such as in 1968, 1980, and 1992). Conversely, vote switching tends to drop when an incumbent is running for reelection (1956, 1984, 1996, and 2004). At the presidential level, these dynamics make it difficult to see any trend in electoral volatility over time.[7] Another ANES question explicitly asked if the respondent generally voted for a candidate from the same party for president. Those saying they switched parties increased from 29 percent in 1952 to a high of 57 percent in 1980, which was the last year the ANES asked this question.

Swing voting involves two different things. The first is the amount of change between elections, because this volatility increases the potential for majorities to change between elections. If one party has a lead in party identifiers and there is little volatility, that party can expect to win most elections. This is the idea of the "normal vote." But if volatility increases, the outcome of elections is less predictable. The second factor is which voters switch, and thus where to "hunt" if you are a candidate looking for new voters.

Of course, partisans should be more stable in their voting preferences; they can change, but that change must overcome the loyalty of their party ID. Ritual partisans may be the most stable because they are less engaged in politics and thus pay less attention to the issues and personalities of a campaign. Cognitive partisans may be more susceptible to change because they follow politics more closely and factor candidates' images and issues into their voting choices (see chapter 7).

The greatest amount of change should come from nonpartisans. Apolitical independents may shift their party votes between elections, but only half of them actually vote, and they are typically less aware of the content of campaigns. Thus, apartisans are the primary candidates for voting switching; they vote and their party preferences are more variable.

Figure 8.3 displays the percentage of each cog-partisan group that reported switching its two-party presidential vote in adjacent elections or that switched from voting to nonvoting.[8] Apartisans show the greatest amount of change, and they are nearly twice as likely to switch votes between the major parties as any of the other three groups. The least variable are the cognitive partisans because they almost always report voting

FIGURE 8.3   Patterns of Vote Switching

▶ *Apartisans vary most in major party support, while ritual partisans and apolitical independents vary in their voting regularity.*

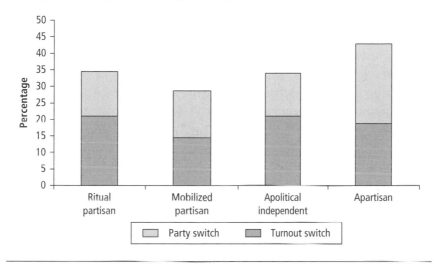

Source: Results from 1964 to 2008 are from the ANES 1952–2008 cumulative file.

Note: Figure entries are differences in the percent switching parties or switching turnout between presidential election votes, including nonvoters in either or both elections.

and are very stable in their preferences (two-thirds report voting for the same party in adjacent elections). Apoliticals and ritual partisans appear to be quite similar in the figure, but this similarity results from very different patterns of stability. Many apoliticals are stable nonvoters (45 percent in this comparison) and then swing between parties when they do vote; ritual partisans are more stable in their actual party choice (45 percent). In summary, patterns of cognitive and partisan mobilization clearly influence the stability of voting choice between elections.

ANOTHER CLOSE LOOK AT INDEPENDENTS

Embedded in discussions of dealignment is a persisting criticism that leaning independents are not truly independent. Instead, they are presumably partisans who express independence on the first party ID question to avoid the appearance of blind party loyalty. As evidence for this position, several researchers have noted that leaning independents often appear closer to partisans (and even strong partisans) in their electoral behavior.[9] For example, leaners often appear more likely to vote for the party they lean toward than do weak partisans. Although this is a somewhat separate issue from our discussions of cog-partisan groups, it has implications for how we interpret both apolitical independents and apartisans.

Chapter 2 suggested leaners are substantially more likely than weak or strong partisans to change their partisan leanings between adjacent elections, which is evidence that stable party loyalties are lacking. The previous section also showed that independents are more likely to swing their vote between parties across elections. Taking these two together, the question is whether shifts in party voting preferences produce shifts in party leanings for independents.

This is a simple question to ask, but a complicated one to answer. First, we need panel data where the same people are interviewed at two elections. I used the 2000–2004 ANES panel study. Second, we need to track both party voting preferences and party ID across both elections. For simple numerical reasons this is difficult to do, because there are only 840 people in the panel survey and many of them didn't vote in both elections. So instead of voting preferences, I used the relative preference for the two presidential candidates as measured by the feeling thermometer questions (also see chapter 7). This measures the candidate preferences of almost all respondents at both time points, even if the respondents didn't vote.

A third issue is how to compare these "voting" preferences to party attachments across both elections. One can simplify this comparison by grouping people into three categories based on their changes in presidential preferences between 2000 and 2004:[10]

- Relative opinions of one's preferred party (candidate) from 2000 became more favorable over time. For instance, those people who favored Bush over Gore in 2000 and then became even more positive about Bush compared to Kerry in 2004 (and vice versa).
- Relative opinions of the parties' candidates were essentially the same in 2000 and 2004.
- Relative opinions of the candidate from the other party improved between 2000 and 2004.

We can use these three groups to test the idea that leaning independents are "hidden partisans" by tracking whether party ID responses
follow changes in presidential candidate preferences. We would expect
people who saw no change in the relative appeal of the Democratic and
Republican presidential candidates between these two elections, or who
saw their own party's candidate as more appealing in 2004, to have
remained loyal to the same party in both elections.

The question is what happened in instances when people saw the electoral tide move away from their candidate preferences in 2000 and become
more positive toward the candidate of the other party in 2004. For
example, Democrats who favored Gore over Bush in 2000 but then
became relatively more positive toward Bush in comparison to Kerry in
2004 (or vice versa). In this case, party identification theory would predict
a high level of stability among party identifiers, who might cast a deviat-
ing vote for the other party's candidate in 2004 but still retain their initial
party loyalty. The test of the hidden partisan idea is what happens to leaning partisans in this scenario. If they are really hidden partisans, they
should retain their earlier party loyalties at the same level as weak or
strong partisans. If leaning independents are truly independents whose
party leaning reflects their current preferences, then they should be more
likely to shift their party leaning in sync with their changing candidate
preferences.

This sounds complicated, but it is easier to see by viewing Figure 8.4.
The figure plots the percentage that reported a loyalty to the same party
in 2000 and 2004 by the strength of party attachments in 2004.[11] The
lines track party stability for the three groups described in the bullet
points above: images became more favorable toward the candidate of the
party initially favored, underwent no change, or became more favorable
toward the opposing party. Strong partisans acted just as one would
expect from party identification theory. Regardless of any change in the
relative preferences for their own party's presidential candidate across
the two elections, strong partisans overwhelmingly expressed a loyalty to
the same party in both elections in all three lines in the figure. If they
were initially Democratic, they remained Democratic in all three cases. If
they were initially Republican, they remained Republican. Weak identifiers also reflect high levels of party loyalty if they see the electoral tide as

constant or moving toward their party's candidates; in these two scenarios, 90 percent or more had stable party loyalties across both elections. When weak identifiers become more favorable toward the
opposition party, over 70 percent of them still have stable party leanings.
Even the dramatic events that occurred between 2000 and 2004—
September 11th, the overthrow of the Taliban, the invasion of Iraq, and
the increase in Bush's popularity in 2004—didn't alter the loyalties of
most party identifiers.

FIGURE 8.4   Stable Partisanship from 2000 to 2004

▶ *A person's images of the parties' presidential candidates affects the stability of partisanship over time.*

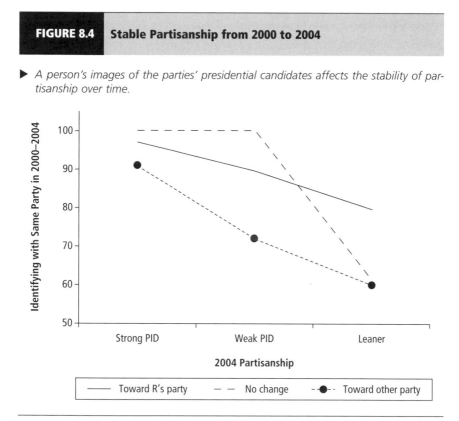

Source: ANES, 2000–2004 panel.

Note: Figure entries are the percentage of each party identification group that reported identifying with the same
party in 2000 and 2004. The lines show whether the respondent's (R's) relative preference for the two presidential
candidates became more favorable to the respondent's party's candidate in 2004, was unchanged since 2000, or
became more favorable to the other party's candidate.

The critical question is what happened to leaning identifiers across these three scenarios. When leaning independents saw their own party's presidential candidate as even more favorable in 2004, a full 80 percent had stable party leanings. However, when they became relatively more favorable toward the candidate of the other party, barely 60 percent remained committed to the same party as in 2000.[12] Keith and his colleagues also found that leaning independents were two to three times more likely to shift their partisan leanings to follow their presidential vote preferences between 1972 and 1976, but they discounted this difference as not large enough to be meaningful.[13] I disagree; a doubling or tripling of the probabilities of changing partisanship is significant. Moreover, images of the presidential candidate are only one factor in voters' electoral experience, as people vote on a large number of offices at the federal, state, and local levels. The work of Keith and his fellow researchers and our analysis only consider presidential voting preferences. Thus, a more complete measure of citizens' overall images of the political parties and their positions would likely show even clearer patterns than in this figure. In other words, it isn't surprising that leaning independents often appear like weak or strong partisans in their voting preferences in an election survey at one point in time, because leaning independents often shift their party leaning to reflect their current preferences. Some independents are undoubtedly hidden partisans, but for most their independence from a long-term affective party attachment is real.

THIRD-PARTY VOTING

Are you still skeptical that dealignment contributes to increased electoral change? Perhaps people are simply forgetting who they voted for years earlier and not actually changing votes. A pure case of vote switching exists in which questions of vote recall do not apply. This involves elections when a third-party candidate won a significant following in a presidential election. Most of these votes (except for those cast by first-time voters) represent vote switching from the last election in which nearly everyone voted for either the Democratic or Republican candidate. There have been several significant third-party candidates in modern electoral history. In 1968 George Wallace, governor of Alabama, ran as the presidential candidate of the American Independent Party. Campaigning on a strongly conservative platform of opposition to federally mandated racial integration and social liberals, Wallace garnered 13.5 percent of the popular vote, carried five southern states and their forty-six electoral votes, and nearly produced a stalemate in the Electoral College. In 1980 John Anderson, a disgruntled Republican member of Congress, decided to run as an independent because he disagreed with Ronald Reagan's positions as the Republican presidential candidate. Anderson won 6.6 percent of the popular vote, which represented almost six million voters. The next significant third-party candidate was Texas industrialist Ross Perot, who ran for president in 1992 (and then again in 1996). In 1992 Perot won 18.9 percent of the vote, almost twenty million voters, despite running what could only be described as a bizarre campaign. Ralph Nader ran a significant campaign in 2000, not just because of his advocacy of green and liberal causes, but because he siphoned off liberal votes (2.7 percent) that cost Al Gore the election. A vote for any of these third-party candidates by definition represents a swing in voter preferences between the parties when compared to the previous presidential election. In this sense it is a pure example of electoral change.

If you were the campaign manager for any of these candidates, where would you find your voters? Obviously one factor to consider is voter agreement with the issues of your campaign. We expect liberal candidates to draw votes away from otherwise Democratic voters, and conservative candidates to draw votes away from the Republicans. People who are distrustful of the political establishment also seem more likely to support a third-party movement. To an extent these hypotheses are correct.[14]

Yet another explanation follows the Willie Sutton rule. You've perhaps heard the story that when the notorious bank robber was asked why he robbed banks, he replied, "'Cause that's where the money is." Where are the potential voters for third-party candidates? If people identify themselves as Republicans or Democrats, they are less likely to reject their self-identity to vote for an independent candidate running against their party—even if they share some of the candidate's issue positions. As the campaign manager of a third-party candidate, you are likely to look for new support among nonpartisans, because that's where the voters are for your candidate.

In the past, however, this presented a problem. Independents were not politically involved and not likely to vote. Even if they supported a cause or were alienated from the established parties, apolitical independents generally would not show up on Election Day. They might not even follow politics closely enough to know that the new candidate represented their beliefs. This pattern should differ for apartisans, however. Apartisans who share an independent candidate's policy views are an exceptionally likely source of voting support because they are issue oriented and likely to vote.

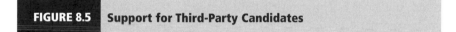

FIGURE 8.5   Support for Third-Party Candidates

▶ *Apartisans are most likely to support a significant third-party candidate regardless of the candidate's political views.*

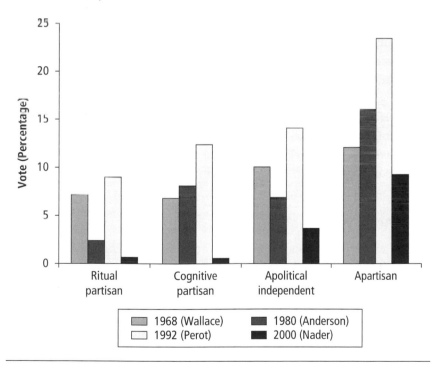

Source: Results for respective elections from the ANES 1952–2008 cumulative file.

Note: The figure shows the percentage that voted for a third-party candidate in each election; nonvoters are included in the calculation of percentages.

Figure 8.5 presents voting support for these third-party candidates across cog-partisan groups. Because we are also interested in who might be mobilized by a new third-party candidate, I included nonvoters in the calculation of percentages. Regardless of whether the candidate was pursuing a liberal or conservative program, apartisans were most likely to vote and support a third-party candidate in all four examples. Averaged across these four candidates, the third-party vote share among apartisans (15 percent) is more than double the vote share among cognitive partisans. Ritual partisans are even less likely to support a third-party candidate. Apolitical independents are more open to third-party candidates, but since only a minority of them vote, their total contribution to such candidates is modest.

Following the Willie Sutton rule, the best place for third-party candidates to find voters is among apartisans who share their policy positions. The same pattern generally has applied for other political newcomers, such as the Tea Party movement in 2010. A September 2010 survey by the Pew Center for People and the Press found that approval of the Tea Party movement was about 5 percent higher among nonpartisans and highest of all among apartisans—40 percent said they agreed with the Tea Party movement.[15] It isn't that apartisans are naturally conservative, because in other elections some apartisans have supported liberal third-party candidates. Rather, apartisans are politically aware and unaffiliated, so they are more sensitive to the winds of political competition. Thus, the changing balance of cog-partisan groups over time affects the potential for third-party candidates in America.

SPLIT-TICKET VOTING

A final example of electoral change is split-ticket voting. If you think of the choices facing the typical American voter as he or she looks at his or her ballot, the process can be daunting. The presidential election ballot normally includes votes for a member of congress, a senator, and often a host of state or local offices. Off-year elections present an extensive list of state and local elected officials and often many "nonpartisan" choices. Many states include judges, bond approvals, and initiatives or referendums on the ballot as well. These long ballots are unique to American elections, with voters in most other established democracies making only one or two choices on their ballot.[16]

Faced with a diversity of offices and candidates, it seems likely that a reasonable person might be attracted to candidates from different parties. Think of the choices you have to make. Even if you vote for the same party 90 percent of the time (which is a high estimate), with only six offices there is about an even chance that one candidate from the other party gets your vote. Split-ticket voting should be a natural behavior in the American electoral system of long ballots, especially if we look at voting across elections.

One consequence of volatility and split-ticket voting is divided partisan control of the government, which is becoming more common. Between the years 1990 to 2010, the presidency and Congress were held by the same party for twelve years. The majority in the House of Representatives shifted four times, the majority of the Senate was under different party control nine times, and the party of the president changed four times. Getting party forces in alignment to have a majority in the House and Senate and control the presidency is not a certainty

The ANES surveys ask voters what party they supported for president and Congress, which allows us to estimate split-ticket voting. Figure 8.6 displays the percentages that report split-ticket voting between their presidential vote (including third-party candidates for president) and House and Senate choices. The level of split-ticket voting varies widely depending on whether or not there is a significant third-party candidate for president, since these candidates almost invariably produce split-ticket voting. So split-ticket voting spiked up in 1968, 1980, 1992, and 1996 for both House and Senate comparisons.

A trend line would show a slight increase in split-ticket voting over time, but this is a very complex pattern to describe. One might also describe this as a curvilinear pattern, rising to a plateau in the 1980s and 1990s and then declining. One complication is that there were more third-party presidential candidates in the second half of the time series. Third-party candidates may themselves be a sign of dealignment, and excluding them from the comparisons (as many skeptics of dealignment do) significantly dampens the increase in split-ticket voting.

Another complication is the realignment in party support in the South during this time span.[17] Up until the mid-1960s, many white southerners identified with the conservative wing of the Democratic Party at the state and local levels, but they sometimes strayed from their party ID when

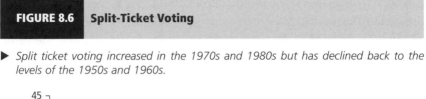

FIGURE 8.6   Split-Ticket Voting

▶ Split ticket voting increased in the 1970s and 1980s but has declined back to the levels of the 1950s and 1960s.

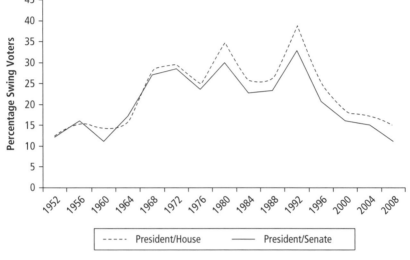

Source: ANES 1952–2008 cumulative file.

Note: Figure entries are the percentage splitting three-party vote for president/House and for president/Senate.

confronted by liberal candidates on the Democratic presidential ticket. White southerners were also more likely to split their vote when a southerner mounted a third-party challenge (such as Strom Thurmond in 1948, Wallace in 1968, and Perot in 1992). White southerners have become slightly less likely to split their ticket over time, as realignment has led them to vote for the Republicans at both the national and subnational levels. African American voters also underwent realignment over this same period, albeit in smaller numbers. In the 1950s significant numbers of blacks were apolitical or leaned toward the Republicans; today they constitute a solid block of Democratic voters.

Therefore, if one compares the level of split-ticket voting in 1956–1960 to that of 2004–2008—two pairs of elections in which one had a single-party majority and the other had divided partisan control—there was only a couple of percentage points increase in two-party, split-ticket voting for president and the House of Representatives. A simple estimate suggests that split-ticket voting has trended upward by 5 percent over the last fifty years.[18] However, for southern whites, split-ticket voting has actually decreased significantly, by roughly 10 percent. And for whites from areas other than the South, split-ticket voting has increased by approximately 10 percent. In summary, when we isolate the effects of regional realignment—such as the behavior of southern white voters—the evidence of increasing split-ticket voting becomes much more apparent.

The regional differences in party images and party positions can be partially controlled by looking at voting patterns in state and local elections. This avoids the ambiguity of a conservative southern Democrat voting for a conservative Democrat in state elections and a conservative Republican in the presidential election. The ANES probed this topic by asking people to self-report whether they generally voted for the same party or different parties at the state and local levels. In presidential elections from 1948 to 1960, less than 30 percent said they were split-ticket voters in state and local elections. By the 1980s, when this question was last asked, the split-ticket voters numbered more than half the electorate.

As with other aspects of electoral change, we expect cog-partisan groups to differ systematically in their likelihood of split-ticket voting. Ritual and cognitive partisans should follow their party loyalties, especially when voting for lower-level offices for which they may have less information. Apolitical independents may also appear relatively loyal, because half the time they don't vote, and those who do vote are typically less attentive to issues and candidates. So again we would expect apartisans to be a disproportionate source of split-ticket voting and thus the dynamic aspect of American electoral politics.

Figure 8.7 presents presidential-congressional vote splitting for cog-partisan groups in elections between 1964 and 2008.[19] Third-party voters in presidential elections are a separate category in the figure. Ritual partisans and apolitical independents both display low levels of vote splitting. However, for ritual partisans this is because they are loyal in their vote, while most apolitical independents don't vote and so the potential for vote switching is limited. Cognitive partisans typically vote and occasionally deviate in their party preferences, but more than 80 percent still voted a straight ticket for these two offices. Again, apartisans are the changeable voters. More than 20 percent of apartisans said they split their vote choice over these elections, and an additional 6 percent said they voted for a third-party presidential candidate to produce a minor/major party split.

Split-ticket voting in state and local elections presents a similar pattern.[20] About one-third of ritual partisans and apolitical independents report splitting their ballot for state and local offices. Significantly more cognitive partisans say they split their ballots (46 percent), as they presumably know more about the candidates and this sways them away from straight party-line voting. Nearly two-thirds of apartisans report splitting their votes in state and local contests. Such subjective self-statements may

| FIGURE 8.7 | Patterns of Vote Splitting |

▶ *Apartisans are most likely to vote a split ticket for president and Congress.*

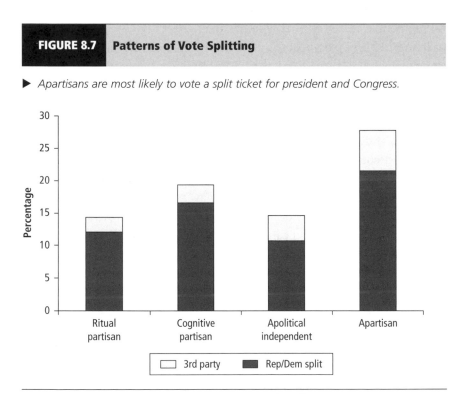

Source: Results from 1964–2008 are from the ANES 1952–2008 cumulative file.

Note: Figure entries are differences in the percentage of respondents splitting votes between parties in the presidential and congressional votes; nonvoters are included in the calculation of percentages.

overreport (or underreport) actual behavior, but the differences across cog-partisan groups likely reflect real behavioral differences.

A CHANGEABLE ELECTORATE

A colleague of mine is more knowledgeable about American public opinion and electoral behavior than almost anyone I know, myself included. He can recite the details of who won what election and the results of recent public opinion polls. Over the last decade we have developed a friendly exchange. Shortly after one election he predicts the winner's fate in the next election and is almost always wrong. Then he predicts again and is usually incorrect again. I have thought I could go to Las Vegas and bet against his predictions and do quite well.[21] It isn't that he lacks knowledge of the topic—the challenge is that elections have become more difficult to predict even for the best experts because the frozen party alignments of the past are more fluid today.

Who are these swing voters? Earlier in this chapter I recounted the story of Willie Sutton, who robbed banks because that's where the money is. If Sutton was a campaign manager—and some of them act very much like Sutton—he would know where to find new voters for his candidate. Chapter 7 showed that apartisans are aware of the candidates and are more issue-oriented in their voting choices. Consequently, they are a major potential source of support for new political figures and movements, and they are also more likely to shift their party votes between elections and to split their ballot between candidates from both major parties. This is a pattern very different from what we expect from apolitical independents, and it injects new fluidity into the contemporary party system.

In contrast, ritual partisans, cognitive partisans, and even apolitical independents contribute to the inertia of electoral politics. Ritual partisans are habitually most loyal to their party and use their party identities in lieu of a detailed knowledge of current politics. Apolitical independents are theoretically a potential source of swing voters or new voters who might be mobilized to cast a ballot, but they only vote infrequently and often don't follow politics closely enough to be attracted to a candidate who reflects their views. The situation of cognitive partisans is more complicated. They are loyal partisans, but they also are politically engaged. Their behavior is one of stability, but it is based on more than blind party loyalty.

The cumulative evidence presented across these chapters also discounts the claim that leaning independents are really partisans who hide their loyalty under the guise of independence. Most previous analyses have relied on cross-sectional surveys and inferred loyal voting based on one point in time. Panel data shows that the partisan leanings of independents are quite variable, and they track current voting preference. Hence it is no wonder that leaners look loyal in one election, because their leanings adjust to reflect their current vote choices. Independents are not hidden partisans; independents' attitudes and behaviors are significantly different from those of Americans who say they are party identifiers.

This chapter thus implies that the changing balance of cog-partisan types over time is altering the dynamics of American elections. As the number of ritual partisans decreases, this lessens some of the inertia in electoral politics caused by people who vote habitually for the same party. In their place, the growth of apartisans and cognitive partisans creates new bases of fluidity in the electoral process. People don't vote for a party because their parents socialized them to support a family tradition, but because they believe that party currently best represents their political interests. If their interests change or the party's position changes, then their voting choices may also shift. This will make current electoral politics more fluid and unpredictable, all else being equal, and it should make electoral politics more democratic.

DEALIGNMENT IN COMPARATIVE PERSPECTIVE

A re you a Republican, a Democratic, an independent, or what? The idea of a party identification comes naturally to Americans because it is part of their political DNA. Americans are familiar with the tradition of partisanship or being independent and the distinction between long-term party loyalties versus current voting preferences because these are common features of American electoral politics. In one election a person might not like a specific candidate, but most will still vote for candidates from "their" party. Americans know what partisanship means.

However, when electoral researchers outside of the United States first encountered the concept of party identification, they weren't always so understanding.[1] Some experts maintained that partisanship was unique to the United States, reflecting its long, complex ballots and the spirit of individualism in the American political culture. Another criticism claimed that fewer people held a partisan identity separate from their current vote preference in parliamentary systems because people voted for a party rather than for individual candidates. The impact of candidate image was minor in most parliamentary systems, and people did not vote directly for a president or prime minister. Even the terminology of being "an independent" was uncommon in most other democracies.

Gradually, however, researchers began to see examples of the same phenomenon of early-socialized, affective, enduring partisan loyalties in citizens in other established democracies.[2] In Germany, for example, survey researchers had to develop different question wording because there wasn't a comparable terminology for independence in the German political vocabulary.[3] The concept of partisanship, even if it was measured in different ways, became a standard question in election surveys across democratic nations. So common is the inclusion of a party identification question in election surveys and other public opinion surveys today that one might argue it is the most widespread U.S. export in the public opinion field.

Ironically, just about the same time as the concept of party ID was being accepted by scholars of voting behavior in other nations, the signs of dealignment began to appear across the established democracies. At first, it was hard to tell whether this was a long-term trend or just the inter-election volatility that is a normal part of electoral politics.[4] However, as time has passed and more evidence has been collected, the cross-national evidence of dealignment has become more convincing.

Chapter 2 summarized some of this evidence. The Eurobarometer surveys showed weakening party ties from 1976 until 2009 in a set of European nations. In an earlier cross-national study of party ID, Martin Wattenberg and I concluded that "partisan dealignment may be an indicator of systematic and enduring change in the relationship between citizens and political parties in contemporary democracies."[5] Thus, it is time to again ask whether the causes and consequences of dealignment are common across established democracies.

This chapter examines several key features of dealignment using surveys from the United States and Western Europe. There are many reasons to think that the American experience is unique because of features of our political history and political institutions. A common cross-national pattern would suggest that broader social forces are at work that transcend the specific politics of each nation. We first compare the levels of partisanship and the percentage of cog-partisan groups between the United States and Europe. Most of the chapter focuses on the correlates of the Cog-Partisan Index: predicting participation patterns, voting choice, and electoral change/stability. The commonality of the results suggests that broad social forces are changing the political orientations of Americans and Europeans in parallel ways.

THE STRENGTH OF PARTY TIES

A natural starting point is to consider the levels of partisanship in contemporary democracies. This is somewhat complicated because nations differ in their partisan traditions. In some nations, to be a partisan is considered a negative thing, indicating narrow party loyalties. To say "*Ich bin ein Sozialdemocrat*" typically means that one is a card-carrying member of the German Social Democratic Party rather than that one has a long-term, affective psychological tie to the party. Seldom does the term "independent" have the same connotation as it does in the United States. Still, in some form or another, established democracies have a group of citizens who act like the loyal, affective partisans described in the pages of *The American Voter*.

Survey researchers have struggled with this issue of measurement, and the best evidence on the extent of partisanship in a nation comes from the respective national election studies that have developed a question suited to national conditions. But this is of little help in comparing levels of partisanship cross-nationally since many nations use a differently worded question. So instead we turn to the 2002 European Social Survey (ESS), which asked a party attachment question in more than a dozen West European democracies:[6]

> *Is there a particular political party you feel closer to than all the other parties?*
>
> *Which party is that? How close do you feel to this party? Do you feel that you are very close, quite close, not close, or not at all close?*

This question exchanges the idea of a long-term partisan identity for the concept of closeness to a party. Closeness should produce a "softer" measure of partisanship, which might make it easier to express a party attachment. These attachments are also likely to be more directly tied to immediate party preferences since there is not an explicit reference to long-term, affective loyalties.[7] Still, the question taps affinity to a party and is asked separately from questions about respondents' immediate vote choice. It also includes degrees of closeness to measure the strength of party ties. Another advantage of this study is that the ESS was repeated in the United States as the Citizens, Involvement, and Democracy (CID) survey, which we used to study political participation in chapter 5.[8]

Figure 9.1 displays the levels of partisan attachments across a set of West European nations. Unfortunately, the CID survey used the ANES-type party identification question instead of the ESS closeness question. So, to compare the levels of partisanship in Europe to those in the United States, the figure includes information from the 2004 ANES survey, which had both a closeness question and the traditional ANES party identification question.

There is considerable variation in the levels of partisanship across these nations, ranging from two-thirds of those surveyed in Sweden, Portugal, and Denmark expressing a party ID to less than one-half in the five nations at the bottom of the figure. Some of this cross-national variation might come from the inevitable differences in how a standard question is translated into each language. Or, the extent of partisanship might vary with a nation's position in its electoral cycle, since partisanship tends to strengthen as an election mobilizes supporters. On the whole, more than half of Europeans (54.9 percent) say they are not close to any party. The modest levels of party closeness may be an indicator of dealignment in Europe. When half the European public says it is not close to any particular party, the potential for electoral change seems substantial.

Partisanship in the United States ranks above the European average based on either the closeness question (56.8 percent) or the standard ANES party identification question (61.8 percent). A similar party closeness question from the Comparative Study of Electoral Systems also ranks the United States relatively high in expressed partisanship.[9] Given the past emphasis on the rigid partisanship of Europeans, especially in proportional representation parliamentary systems, this is a somewhat surprising pattern. However, it may reflect the greater functional value of partisanship in the United States that exists because of the long ballots and multiple choices that voters face. A Briton who casts a handful of votes in a five-year period may feel less identification with a party than an American who casts more than a hundred votes over this same period.

Chapter 2 presented a similar closeness question showing that party attachments have generally trended downward in six European nations (see Figure 2.5). This dealignment trend is apparent across most established

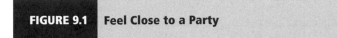

FIGURE 9.1 **Feel Close to a Party**

▶ *Barely half of Europeans say they feel close to any party. Americans are more likely than the average European to feel close to a party.*

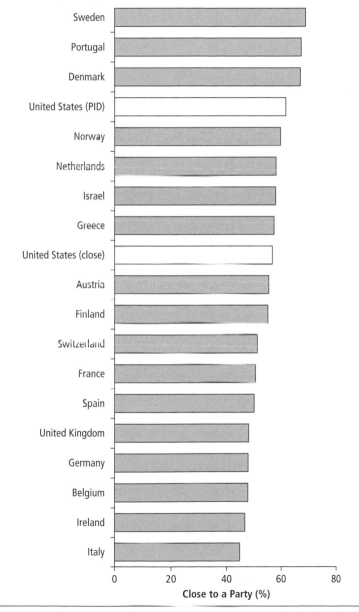

Source: European Social Survey 2002; the U.S. results are from two questions in the 2004 ANES. The "PID" result is the traditional ANES party identification question and the "close" result is for the party closeness question.

democracies.[10] The strongest evidence comes from the national election survey series that revealed long-term trends for about a dozen established democracies. The appendix to this chapter presents these results. They show that *in every nation* where long-term election surveys are available, the percentage of partisans has decreased over the past several decades.

In addition, longitudinal data from several nations points to a general decline in public support for political parties.[11] Enmid surveys show that the proportion of Germans who expressed confidence in the political parties decreased from 43 percent in 1979 to only 17 percent in 2005. Surveys in Sweden found that in 1968 a full 68 percent of the public rejected the view that parties were only interested in people's votes; this dropped to 28 percent by 2002. There is similar evidence of declining trust in political parties in most other established democracies. Indeed, very few scholars today argue that public support for political parties and the structure of party government is increasing in their nation of specialization.[12]

Given the range of nations and the varieties of institutional structures and political histories being examined, the breadth of this dealignment pattern speaks to a general process that is unlikely to be due to the unique characteristics of any national experience.[13] The complex effects of social modernization and cognitive mobilization seem to be producing common patterns of partisan dealignment that transcend national boundaries.

COGNITIVE AND PARTISAN MOBILIZATION

Many of the social and political forces that have transformed partisan attachments in the United States should also have affected other advanced industrial democracies. The skills and resources of Europeans have grown substantially in recent decades. Levels of education, for example, have increased even more rapidly than in the United States. Very few Europeans had a university education until recently. Similarly, access to information has exploded due to the same technological changes that have occurred in the United States, except the pace of change again might be greater in Europe. And Europeans' interest in politics has generally increased.

These social trends would lead us to expect that ritual partisan loyalties are decreasing among European publics. Instead, more Europeans should be cognitive partisans if they remain linked to a political party or apartisans if they lack a party loyalty. Indeed, in an earlier study Ronald

Inglehart found that the percentage of apartisans among Europeans increased significantly over a single decade (1976–1987), and we have seen that party attachments have continued to weaken since then.[14]

I used the ESS to construct the Cog-Partisan Index for European publics. The survey asked a question on political interest that I combined with education to measure cognitive mobilization. I used this item with the party-closeness question to construct the four cog-partisan groups.[15] Our analyses compare the European results to the 2004–2008 ANES surveys and the 2005 CID survey; both of these used the ANES party identification question.

Figure 9.2 shows the cog-partisan distributions for Europeans and two results for the American public. In overall terms, levels of partisanship and cognitive mobilization are lower in Europe, so there are slightly more

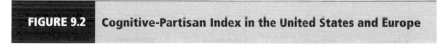

FIGURE 9.2 Cognitive-Partisan Index in the United States and Europe

▶ *The distribution of cog-partisan groups is roughly similar between the United States and Europe.*

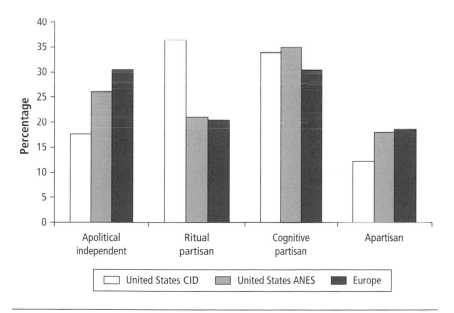

Source: 2005 CID Survey and 2004–2008 ANES for the United States; 2002 European Social Survey for Western Europe.

traditional independents than in the two U.S. surveys. The highest level of apartisans is found in affluent European democracies such as Germany and Switzerland (over 20 percent), while there are only half as many in less affluent southern European nations such as Greece, Portugal, and Italy. Conversely, these same three nations have the highest levels of ritual partisans—as we would expect because of their lower level of socio-economic development.

Because of the different wordings for the party ID questions, the United States–European statistics are not fully comparable. Still, each category exhibits only a small difference between the ESS and ANES surveys. Significantly more people said they were partisans in the CID survey, so the levels of both apolitical independents and apartisans are lower, and a correspondingly larger percentage said they were ritual partisans. But even these differences are modest. The variations in question wording limit our ability to make direct comparisons between the percentages in each category of the Cog-Partisan Index. However, we expect that if these indices are basically comparable, they should display many of the same relationships for Americans and Europeans.

DESCRIBING COG-PARTISANS

Imagine you are sitting in a pub in Manchester, England, and talking about politics with the friendly Brits around you. Depending on what part of the city you are visiting, most of your fellow pub mates would have voted for either the Labour Party or the Conservative Party at the last election. Much of the conversation would be similar to election conversations in the United States. Many British voters habitually support the same party across elections and often can trace their party loyalties back to their parents. However, if you are in a pub near the university, you will probably get a different picture of parties and elections. More British youths—especially those who are better educated—are shedding party loyalties. While their parents may be Labour or Tory partisans, young people are more likely to lack party loyalties, or they might have voted Liberal or not voted at all in 2009. The British pattern of frozen party loyalties has begun to thaw.[16]

If social modernization is the driving force behind dealignment in contemporary democracies, we would expect that the same factors that influence the distribution of cog-partisan groups in America would be evident among Europeans. Age, for example, should show the residue of social modernization, since different generations have experienced changing political contexts and cognitive mobilization has increased over time. Thus, older European generations should have more ritual partisans, while younger Europeans should be moving away from partisan ties and be more likely to have apartisan orientations.

Figure 9.3 describes the distribution of cog-partisan groups by age for the sampled European nations. The general patterns fit our expectations. The percentage of ritual partisans shrinks by half between the oldest and youngest age groups. Only one-sixth of those under age thirty are ritual partisans. Conversely, the share of apartisans doubles in size between the oldest and youngest age groups and represents 20 percent of the young.

FIGURE 9.3   Age and Cog-Partisan Groups

▶ *Younger Europeans are less likely to be ritual partisans and more likely to be apartisans.*

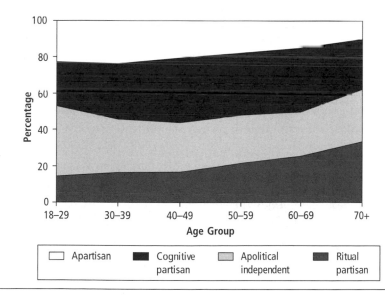

Source: 2002 European Social Survey for Western European nations.

The one anomaly in the figure is the increase in apolitical independents among those under thirty. This probably arose because many in this age group had not completed their schooling at the time the survey was conducted and were still developing an interest in politics; by their thirties they likely will score higher in cognitive mobilization and become either apartisans or cognitive partisans. Our earlier tracking of the 1964–1966 generation in the United States found such a life cycle pattern (see Figure 3.4). So, while the specific percentages in each cog-partisan group may vary between Americans and Europeans because of differences in how the index is measured, the current age differences in Europe imply an ongoing process of generational change.[17]

If the Cog-Partisan Index is tapping similar orientations among Americans and Europeans, then we should expect similar patterns in the political orientations of the cog-partisan groups. For example, by the same logic as explored in chapter 3, Europeans who are critical of the government may also be shedding their party loyalties.

Figure 9.4 shows the relationships between cog-partisan groups and trust in Congress/parliament separately for Americans and Europeans. A positive correlation (a plus bar) means the group is more likely to express an attitude, and a negative correlation (a minus bar) means they are less likely to do so. Cognitive partisans are more likely to trust the national legislature on both sides of the Atlantic. In contrast, apolitical independents tend to be distrustful, which underscores their isolation from politics. As we found with another measure of political trust in the United States (Figure 3.5), apartisans are not clearly distrustful of government—their motivation is not alienation from politics. These patterns also appear for trust in politicians and other measures of political support asked in both surveys.

Another important trait for democratic citizenship is political efficacy: Do citizens feel they can influence politics (internal efficacy) and that politicians care about their opinions (external efficacy)? The next two panels in the figure reflect these two traits. Cognitive mobilization is more important than party identities in encouraging feelings of political efficacy. For instance, both apolitical independents and ritual partisans more often feel that politics is too complicated to understand; apartisans

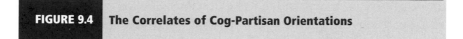

> ▶ *The largest contrast is between apolitical independents and cognitive partisans. Apartisans fall between these two groups: they are more politically efficacious and more centrist in left/right terms.*

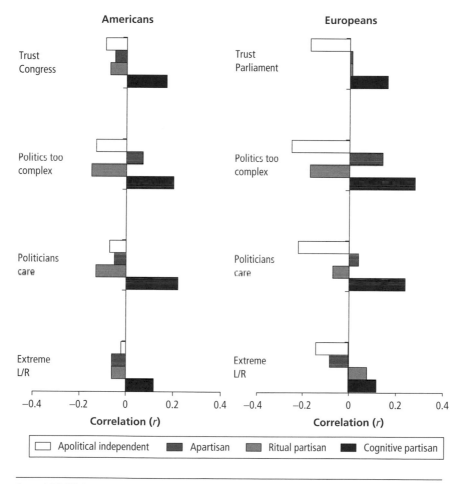

Source: 2005 CID Survey; 2002 European Social Survey.

Note: The figure presents the Pearson's *r* correlations between each cog-partisan category and each attitude.

and cognitive partisans tend to feel efficacious. Similarly, apoliticals and ritual partisans are less likely to think that politicians care what people think, while apartisans and cognitive partisans are more efficacious. These feelings of political efficacy should impact the willingness of each group to participate in politics.

Chapter 3 showed that the broad political orientations of cog-partisan groups also vary among Americans. Apartisans and apolitical independents both locate themselves as centrists, while party identifiers are more likely to take positions at the poles of political controversies—either at the extreme left or right, depending on their party. Figure 9.4 shows that these patterns are even clearer among European publics. The plurality of apartisans and apoliticals in Europe position themselves at the center of the left/right scale. Conversely, ritual and cognitive partisans are more likely than nonpartisans to position themselves at the ends of the left/ right scale. In other words, nonpartisans tend to be political centrists, although in the case of traditional independents this may signal the lack of any firm political attitudes rather than an embracement of centrist positions.[18]

In summary, Figure 9.4 nicely illustrates the varied effects of partisan mobilization and cognitive mobilization. Apoliticals and cognitive partisans generally define the extreme contrasts, but this is because they epitomize the combined effects of partisan mobilization and cognitive mobilization. In some areas, such as trust in government or left/right positions, ritual partisans and cognitive partisans tend in the same direction— which means that partisanship is important to these opinions. In other areas, such as political efficacy, cognitive mobilization prompts both apartisans and cognitive partisans to hold similar attitudes. The other general point is that the overall patterns tend to be consistent on both sides of the Atlantic, which implies that the Cog-Partisan Index is tapping similar phenomenon in America and Western Europe.

PATTERNS OF POLITICAL ACTION

The gates to the stadium are open and the fans are streaming in, wearing shirts and caps displaying their team's logo. These are the fans that fill the stands. The sport of politics is similar. Party identifiers are like sports fans. Their partisanship is a psychological mobilizer that encourages them to vote on Election Day, write their representatives, and contribute funds to their political party. In contrast, one of the repeated criticisms of nonpartisans is their limited engagement in politics because they lack a team loyalty.[19]

This same pattern regularly appears in cross-national research. In fact, party identities can be especially strong in predicting electoral participation in European parliamentary democracies where voters cast their ballots directly for a political party.[20] Even when voters choose between candidates, many are unaware of the candidates' names and are simply voting for the party's representative in their district. Other aspects of political participation, even referendums, can be organized and structured by political parties.[21] Party government is central to the European democratic experience.

Chapter 5 showed, however, that cognitive mobilization is an alternative stimulus of political action. Education is routinely related to higher levels of political activity—whether that activity is sorting through the parties' conflicting claims during elections or contacting a government official between elections. Similarly, political interest motivates one to be engaged. Apartisans can narrow the participation gap between nonpartisans and partisans because of their higher levels of cognitive mobilization. This may be especially likely for nonelectoral forms of participation in which party cues are weaker.

I first compared the participation gap between partisans and nonpartisans in voter turnout across this set of nations. Figure 9.5 describes the self-reported turnout percentages for partisans (both ritual and mobilized), apolitical independents, and apartisans. In almost every case, partisans display the highest level of turnout, as we would expect, and apoliticals consistently vote less often. On average, there is a gap of more than twenty-five percentage points between these two groups. This gap is largest in Switzerland (44 percent) and the United States (38 percent), which suggests that persistently low turnout in these nations has left nonpartisans outside the stadium.

The question is whether the cognitive mobilization of apartisans allows them to overcome this participation gap—and the answer is largely yes. Even though apartisans also lack party ties, they vote in elections at nearly the same rate as partisans. The gap between these two groups is

FIGURE 9.5 Cog-Partisans and Voting

▶ *In most nations apartisans vote about as often as partisans.*

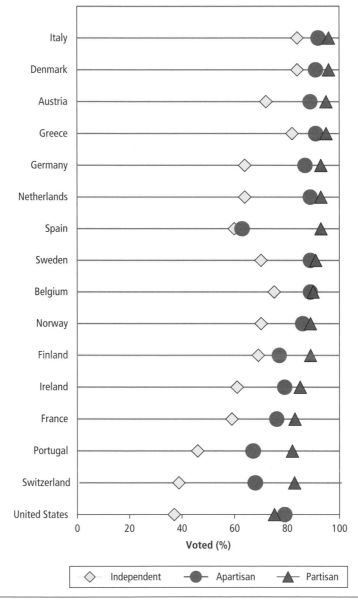

Source: 2005 CID Survey; 2002 European Social Survey.

Note: The figure presents the percentage in each group that reported voting in the previous election.

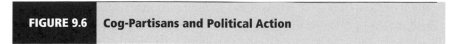

FIGURE 9.6   Cog-Partisans and Political Action

▶ *Apartisans and cognitive partisans tend to have higher levels of participation in most forms of political activity.*

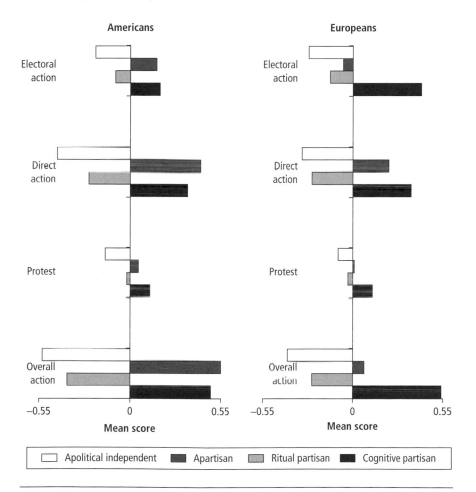

Source: 2005 CID Survey; 2002 European Social Survey.

Note: The figure presents the mean score of each activity for cog-partisan groups.

only 8 percent averaged across these sixteen nations.[22] Much as we previously witnessed when focusing on the United States in chapter 5, most apartisans will turn out to vote, and so their attitudes and preferences are an important feature in determining election outcomes in Europe.

Elections are the prime focus of party politics; they determine the parties' fates until the next election and are where most party resources are focused. When we move away from electoral politics to other forms of participation, party mobilization should weaken and cognitive mobilization may become relatively more important.

Figure 9.6 presents the cog-partisan differences in four forms of political action, paralleling the indices in chapter 5: electoral participation beyond voting, direct action, protest, and an overall participation index.[23] I constructed each index so the average value for the public is zero. For electoral participation, only cognitive partisans rank substantially above average in Europe, probably because parliamentary elections are heavily based on formal party adherents. In the United States, apartisans are also mobilized into the diversity of primaries and political campaigns.

For the other three participation examples, cognitive mobilization outweighs the importance of party mobilization. Apartisans and cognitive partisans score above average on direction action, protest, and overall participation. And in Europe, as in the United States, the greatest contrast is typically between apoliticals, who have low involvement on both mobilization factors, and cognitive partisans, who benefit from their cognitive traits and partisan ties. On the whole, these results underscore the importance of factoring cognitive mobilization into our traditional images of independents and partisans. The growing group of apartisans is broadly engaged in the political process, especially in the variety of activities that occur between elections. To push the sports analogy to the limit, these are like fans of a sport who come to a game without a habitual loyalty to either team.

ELECTORAL BEHAVIOR

Voting in U.S. national elections is relatively straightforward. There are typically only two meaningful choices—the Republican or the Democrat—and whichever gets a plurality of votes wins the seat. Elections are much more complex in most other democracies. Voters face a wide choice of parties, often ranging from two or three viable parties on the left to several viable parties on the right. They may have a choice of green parties, communist parties, religious parties, and neo-nationalist parties. Recently a new Pirate Party has emerged in several European nations. Much of electoral research argues that party choices are more structured in European party systems because the party differences are so great and because parties are more unified in their policies and actions. Thus, we want to consider whether the voting patterns presented in earlier chapters also apply to European voters with their different institutional contexts and party systems.

To examine voting choice, we turn to a different data source: a subset of national election studies.[24] I acquired the recent national election surveys for five nations: Australia, Britain, France, Germany, and the Netherlands. The choice was based on data availability and a desire to include different national experiences. Australia is an example of compulsory voting in a complex federal system that holds national parlia mentary elections every three years; compulsory voting might produce different electoral dynamics among the less cognitively mobilized because they are required to vote. Britain has a majoritarian party system based on single member districts, which is similar to the United States, except that parties are more central and unified as actors in elections. France has a rich multiparty system with considerable partisan change over time and a unique two-tour electoral system. Germany has a multiparty system with a mixed electoral system of district and party voting, and the Netherlands is a small nation with a very diverse and proportional electoral system. I expect party mobilization effects to be stronger in proportional representation systems in which citizens vote directly for political parties rather than candidates.

For each nation I constructed a measure of cognitive mobilization based on education and political interest that as closely as possible follows the methodology used throughout this book. Then I created the Cog-Partisan Index for each nation. Since the questions were phrased differently in each nation, the overall distributions of cog-partisans groups are not comparable in these five nations. But I expect that the correlates of this index will show the same general relationship if the concept of cog-partisan mobilization is meaningful. This section examines three examples of various aspects of the dealignment process: the timing of voting decisions as a sign of whether people enter elections with fixed party predispositions, the amount of inter-election change in voting preferences, and the extent of split-ticket voting in nations where this is possible.

The electoral process in most Western nations is very different from that in the United States. The election period is relatively short—a matter of a couple months rather than a couple years as in the United States. The party choices tend to be more distinct, with more parties running for office and spanning a wider range of the ideological continuum. Elections typically focus on party choices, rather than on the candidates as in the United States. So, one might expect that more European voters enter elections predisposed to a party and experience a shorter campaign period that might sway their opinions. At question is whether this increases or decreases the impact of partisan mobilization relative to candidate motivation.

Figure 9.7 displays the percentage of voters that decided late in the campaign by the four cog-partisan groups in each nation. The result should come as no surprise based on our analyses of American voters, because the figure shows that the vast majority of partisans—whether ritual or cognitive—decide who they will vote for well before the campaign has ended. Deciding early might make sense if the party clearly represents your views, but campaigns should also matter. In the 2009 German election, for instance, the last weeks of the campaign included a TV debate between Merkel (CDU) and Steinmeier (SPD) and intensifying issue debates between the parties over issues of economic reform, Afghanistan, and environmental policy.[25] Yet the majority of German partisans had decided their vote before these events occurred. In contrast, almost half of the apartisans and apolitical independents said they decided during the last week of the campaign.[26] A similar contrast between partisans and nonpartisans occurred in all five nations—in fact the gap seemed larger in Europe than in a comparable analysis in the United States (see Figure 8.1). If we expect campaigns to matter, then this figure shows that they matter mostly for nonpartisans, who do react to the ebb and flow of events and make their decision once the campaign comes to its conclusion.

An even clearer example of dealignment is the willingness of voters to shift their vote as conditions change. The potential variability of electoral outcomes is what gives elections—and democracy—meaning. The public

FIGURE 9.7   Deciding Late

▶ *Apartisans vote at high levels and decide on their vote during the campaign; partisans often decide before the campaign begins.*

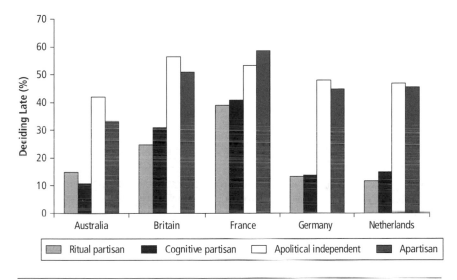

Source: 2007 Australian Election Study; 2010 British Election Study; 2002 French Election Study; 2009 German Election Study; 2006 Dutch Election Study.

Note: The definition of deciding late varies by nation: Australia "last few days of election"; Britain "during the campaign"; France "decided recently" or still undecided in preelection survey; Germany "last week of campaign"; Netherlands "last days of the campaign."

can steer the ship of state by casting their votes for a different party to set a new course. Indeed, the elections in this subset of nations highlight this dynamic aspect of representation. The 2007 Australian election produced a shift from a center-right governing coalition to a center-left one. The 2010 British election study coincided with a shift from a Labour government to a Conservative-Liberal coalition. France's 2002 parliamentary election also experienced a shift from a leftist majority after the 1997 election to a new conservative majority. The 2009 German election saw a change from a CDU/CSU-SPD coalition to a new CDU/CSU-FDP one. The Dutch 2006 election shifted the composition of the governing coalition.

The dynamism of democratic elections is illustrated by each of these nations. As an example, the Dutch 2006 election was prompted by the fragility of the incumbent government that collapsed after the withdrawal of one member of the coalition. Since the previous election, the flash movement of the List Pim Fortuyn had fragmented after the assassination of its founder. New parties—including a nationalist party and an animal-rights party—emerged to contest the election in a system that gives a party a parliamentary seat for each 0.67 percent of the national vote it wins (both of these new parties won seats in parliament). In aggregate terms, there was almost a 20-percent swing in vote outcomes for the parties that increased their vote share and a corresponding decrease of 20 percent for the losing parties. Based on the 2006 Dutch election study, almost half of those who voted in 2003 and 2006 said they had switched parties!

We would expect that apartisans are especially important in introducing a dynamic element to elections because they vote and presumably are more likely to change their party preferences with changing political conditions. Figure 9.8 displays the percentages of voters who said they switched their votes between adjacent elections for the four cog-partisan groups. The Dutch contrast is the starkest. Despite the large vote shifts between elections, only about one-sixth of partisans said they changed their party votes from 2003 to 2006. In contrast, two-thirds of apartisans and apoliticals reported voting for a different party in the two elections. The contrast between partisans and nonpartisans was similar, albeit more modest, in the other four nations. In each case, the largest percentage of inter-election switchers were the apartisans, suggesting that this cognitively mobilized group is making informed choices that change with political conditions.[27]

A final example of the variations in party-based voting is split-ticket voting. In the United States, people might vote for one party in the presidential election and a different party for Congress in the same election. Similar opportunities for split-ticket voting occur in other nations and appear to be increasing across the advanced industrial democracies.[28] Australians can support different parties in their House and Senate elections, which occur simultaneously. The French can support different parties in their presidential and parliamentary elections. In Germany,

FIGURE 9.8   **Electoral Swing**

▶ *Apartisans vote at high levels and have the most fluid voting preferences.*

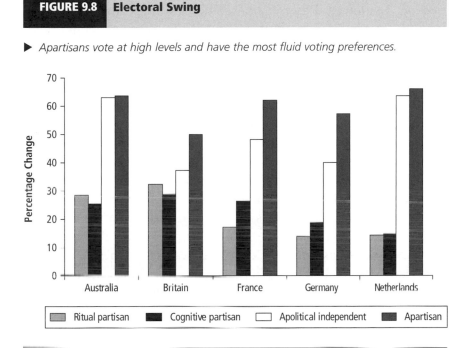

Source: 2007 Australian Election Study; 2010 British Election Study; 2002 French Election Study; 2009 German Election Study; 2006 Dutch Election Study.

Note: The figure plots the percentage that switched party support between adjacent elections among those who voted in both elections.

citizens can split their party votes between their first candidate vote (*Erststimme*) and second party vote (*Zweitstimme*).

The Australian voting patterns are especially insightful. In 2007 about 80 percent of the voters supported the same party in House and Senate elections—which is not surprising in a party-based electoral system. The consistency was highest among ritual partisans (85 percent) because these voters tend to support a party based on their party loyalties with less attention paid to the issues of the day. Cognitive partisans were also very consistent in their voting preferences (78 percent), because they have party loyalties but are also more attuned to current political debates. Apolitical independents were the next most consistent (69 percent), probably because once they make a party choice they stick with it for that election. The lowest degree of straight-ticket voting came from apartisans (55 percent), which is what we expected. In Germany about a quarter of partisans said they supported different parties with their two votes, compared to nearly half of apartisans.[29]

When John Maynard Keynes changed his position on monetary policy during the Great Depression, his explanation was simple: "When the facts change, I change my mind. What do you do, sir?" Our examination of electoral change reflects the same logic. Democratic elections provide popular input on governance, and people should change their voting decisions when the facts change. This section generally shows that apartisans are the most likely to follow Keynes' advice, since they are more fluid in their voting preferences. In contrast, partisans are much more likely to vote a straight party line across offices and across elections—and make these decisions before the campaign begins in earnest. One might legitimately ask whether the examples of electoral change among apartisans are logical and based on the facts. While we have not addressed this question in detail here, the analyses for the United States provide strong evidence that cognitively mobilized apartisans are placing heavy reliance on issues and policy positions as the basis of their voting choice. We would expect the same of apartisans in other established democracies.

CROSS-NATIONAL EVIDENCE OF DEALIGNMENT

The five national election examples in the previous section show that cog-partisan groups differ in the rigidity of their partisan preferences. If we combine this result with the shifts in the distribution of cog-partisan groups over time, this implies that the party systems of established democracies should be becoming more changeable. In other words, the frozen party cleavages of the past should be giving way to a more fluid and volatile electoral process.

At the national level, strong partisan ties can be a stabilizing influence on electoral politics. Philip Converse and Georges Dupeux were the first to argue that the potential for voters to be attracted to new parties or demagogic leaders goes down if people identify with one of the established parties.[30] More generally, widespread partisan ties dampen the impact of short-term political events on election outcomes and limit the potential electoral appeal of new political personalities. Extensive partisanship among the electorate thus works to stabilize party alignments and lessen electoral change.

Thus, one clear sign of dealignment should be a weakening of partisan consistency at both the national and individual levels. The simplest measure of electoral change is partisan volatility—the average change in party vote shares between adjacent elections. Previous research has found growing partisan volatility across established democracies.[31] Now, after a decade or more of additional electoral experience, have these trends continued over time?

Figure 9.9 presents the pattern of aggregate volatility for a set of nineteen established democracies since the mid-twentieth century.[32] In order

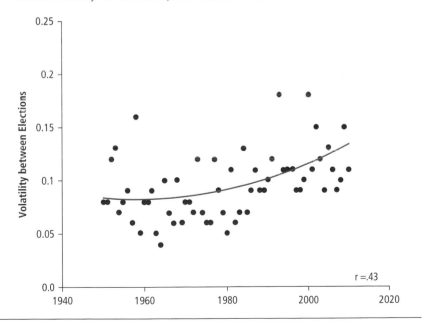

FIGURE 9.9   Electoral Volatility

▶ *Electoral volatility has trended upward since the late 1970s.*

Source: Data collected by author.

Note: The results are based on all legislative elections for nineteen established democracies from 1950 until 2010. The figure pools the national data by year.

to best illustrate the trend over time, each data point represents the average volatility score for all elections held in any of these nations in each year.

The years immediately following World War II were a period of substantial partisan volatility in many democracies, largely because of the disruptions produced by the war and the reestablishment of democratic party systems. Inter-election shifts in aggregate party support averaged 9 percent for the elections of the 1950s, although a large part of this instability was due to the reinstituted party systems of Japan and Germany. Party systems stabilized by the 1960s, and volatility decreased in many nations. Then the trend turned upward in the late 1970s. By the 1990s the average inter-election shifts in party support had increased by nearly half over those in the 1970s. A further small increase continued in the elections of the 2000s. Statistical analyses show a significant trend of increasing volatility over time.[33]

The individual nations in this set have seldom followed this simple curvilinear pattern, because a dramatic event often reshaped the party system and stimulated a spike in this trend. For example, the consolidation of the Japanese party system in the 1950s produced basic shifts in the parties and their resulting vote shares, and the French party system restructured with the formation of the Fifth Republic in 1958. In the 1970s several European party systems experienced "earthquake elections" as older parties fragmented and new parties emerged onto the political stage. In the 1990s the Italian party system restructured itself, which led to exceptionally high levels of volatility for several elections. Although the timing of such major realignments depends on unique national conditions, the general pattern is one of the unfreezing of party alignments and increased electoral volatility. More detailed country-level analyses have found that electoral volatility has trended higher since 1960 in virtually all Western party systems.[34]

Because partisanship binds voters to their preferred party, dealignment also should free more people to shift their party support to other contenders or new political parties. Established parties may fragment as the electorate becomes open to new appeals. For example, the collapse of the Italian party system in the 1990s reflected the prior weakening of party ties and further accelerated this trend, allowing new parties such as the Northern League, Forza Italia, and the Greens to emerge. At the same time, the traditionally dominant Christian Democratic Party collapsed. In the past two decades, most European party systems have experienced new political challenges from green parties on the left and nationalist or new right parties. The rise of new parties across Europe (and other established democracies) is at least partially a consequence of partisan dealignment.

Figure 9.10 presents the trends in the effective number of parties for our set of nineteen democracies.[35] Like the previous graph, this figure displays the average of all nations having an election in each year to simplify the presentation.[36] The effective number of parties—and thus

FIGURE 9.10 Parties Are Multiplying

▶ *A growing number of parties are competing in the party systems today.*

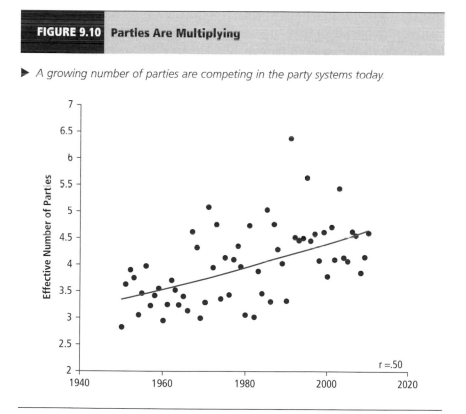

Source: Golder database and data collected by author.

Note: The results are based on all legislative elections for nineteen established democracies from 1950 until 2010. The figure pools the national data by year.

the fragmentation of these party systems—is generally increasing. The upward slope was modest until the end of the 1970s but has accelerated over the past two decades. By the mid-1990s, the average effective number of electoral parties had increased by more than half.

National patterns in the effective number of parties fill in the details of this general picture. In nearly every established democracy, the effective number of parties has increased in the postwar era (the United States is a notable exception). There are several cases, such as Belgium and Italy, in which recent turbulence and fragmentation of the party system have been obvious, but in most nations this same process of increasing partisan diversity has also been occurring, albeit less dramatically.

Often electoral analysts focus on the patterns of a single nation or the short-term trends in party fortunes. A significant shift in party fortunes, such as the collapse of the Christian Democrats in Italy or the rise of new left or new right parties in Europe, is normally explained in terms of the idiosyncratic political forces of the nation. In contrast, these results describe a pattern that generally applies to established democracies, and this pattern has grown stronger and more apparent since it was first detected. The "frozen" party systems that were once observed in Europe have become more fluid political environments in which new parties are forming and electoral change is increasing over time.

CONCLUSION

The basic lesson of this chapter is quite clear for Americans: We are not alone. The processes of dealignment and cognitive mobilization are also affecting other established democracies. As a result, many of the same correlates of the Cog-Partisan Index that we described for the American public also exist for people in other democracies.

On the one hand, this should lead us to downplay aspects of the American debate on dealignment that stress nation-specific theories and evidence. For instance, while Vietnam, Watergate, and Richard Nixon undoubtedly played a role in the erosion of party loyalties in the United States, this same weakening of partisanship is apparent in nations such as Sweden, where there was no involvement in the Vietnam War, no Watergate scandal, and no Richard Nixon. Similarly, while some discussions of dealignment in the United States pinpoint the specific institutional factors of American politics as a cause—long ballots, candidate-centered voting, and divided government—dealignment has occurred in nations (again like Sweden) with short ballots, party-based voting in a proportional representation system, and unified government. To reiterate, of the sixteen nations with long-term election study series asking a party identification question, all of them have shown some weakening of party identities over time (see chapter appendix).

This cross-national evidence also suggests the American debate on the hidden partisanship of "leaning independents" is a specious argument. Different survey questions are used to measure partisanship across nations, and few of them include the term "independent" since this is somewhat unique to the United States. Yet these other nations display the same dealignment pattern we previously described for the United States. Moreover, this chapter demonstrates that the electoral effects of cog-partisan groups are also quite similar cross-nationally. Certainly there are unique aspects of American politics and public opinion, but the broad features of partisan and cognitive mobilization work in similar ways across most democracies.

Finally, the results of this chapter underscore the importance of both partisan mobilization and cognitive mobilization. In many areas, such as voting turnout or voting choice, partisans strongly differ from both types of nonpartisans. This is the value of partisanship as a mobilizing cue. In other areas, however, cognitive mobilization plays an equal or stronger role in shaping political behavior. For instance, direct-action participation and protest activity is more common among the cognitively mobilized, whether they are apartisans or cognitive partisans. Treating all partisans as comparable is as imprecise as treating all nonpartisans as the same. A simple undifferentiated analysis based on either mobilization variable alone therefore yields an inaccurate view of political behavior on both sides of the Atlantic.

APPENDIX: NATIONAL TRENDS IN PARTY IDENTIFICATION

Perhaps the most convincing evidence of partisan dealignment comes from the respective national election studies from the established democracies. The value of these studies is that they often extend back to the 1960s or early 1970s and thus can track partisanship over a long time period. They generally use high-quality sampling designs and in-person interviews, so they are more reliable data than commercial polls. In addition, each of these projects developed a partisanship question that the researchers felt captured the political identities of the citizens; consequently, these questions differ cross-nationally. This means the level of partisanship should not be compared across different questions, but the trend over time should provide evidence of whether dealignment is occurring across the established democracies.

In earlier analyses I presented the national trends in partisanship through the late 1990s, which displayed a general weakening of party ties.[37] These trends have been updated through 2010 and now present an even clearer picture of partisan dealignment (Table 9.1).[38] The first data column shows the percentage of partisans averaged across the initial two surveys in the series. The second data column shows the trend in the percentage of the public identifying with any party as per annum change. In all of these nations, the trends are negative—a striking consistency for such a diverse array of nations.[39] For instance, 65 percent of the Swedish public expressed party ties in 1968, compared with only 28 percent in 2010.[40] The per annum change coefficient (-.85) translates into an 8.5 percent decrease in partisanship over a typical decade. The decline in partisanship in the United States, Britain, and Sweden has long been observed in the literature, and these cases are now joined by most other established democracies. However, these comparisons show that the dealignment trend in the United States has been smaller in per annum terms than in many other party systems. The parallel decline in party attachments in nearly all advanced industrial democracies offers a strong sign of the public's disengagement from political parties.

Furthermore, the striking pattern is the commonality of the decline across nations with different electoral systems, different numbers of parties, and different patterns of party cleavages. Seldom does the public opinion evidence from such a diverse group of nations follow such a consistent trend. The major variation is in the timing of the decline rather than the direction of the trend. Dealignment in the United States and Britain has been a long-term process that has moved partisanship to a lower baseline, and this lower level has remained relatively steady since the 1990s. Sweden has followed a more incremental pattern of dealignment to the present. In other instances, the changes have been more recent. For example, German partisanship, which had strengthened during

TABLE 9.1	Trends in Party Identification

▶ *In all these established democracies, party ties have weakened over the last several decades.*

Nation	% with PID	Per annum change	Period	Time points
Australia	92	−.197	1967–2010	(13)
Austria	67	−.555	1969–2009	(9)
Britain	93	−.323	1964–2010	(12)
Canada	90	−.535	1965–2006	(12)
Denmark	52	−.034	1971–2005	(11)
Finland	57	.256	1975–2007	(6)
France	73	.794	1967–2002	(6)
Germany	78	−.512	1972–2009	(11)
Italy	80	−.779	1975–2008	(9)
Japan	70	−.589	1962–2000	(12)
Netherlands	38	.192	1971–2006	(11)
New Zealand	87	−1.155	1975–2000	(12)
Norway	66	−.659	1965–2005	(11)
Sweden	64	−.854	1968–2010	(14)
Switzerland	61	−.633	1971–2007	(10)
United States	77	−.329	1952–2008	(15)

Source: The respective national election studies in each nation

Note: The percentage with a party identification in column one is the average of the percentage expressing a party identification in the first two surveys in each series.

the immediate post–World War II period, has dropped off markedly for elections held since 1990, although initial signs of dealignment existed in the late 1980s. The collapse of the Progressive Conservatives and New Democratic Party in the 1993 Canadian elections similarly accentuated a dealignment trend in Canadian politics.

In summary, since I first presented these results in 2000,[41] I have added more than three dozen elections to these series. In a few instances recent elections have increased levels of partisanship slightly, but the general pattern is a continuation of the dealignment trend. When so many nations follow a similar trend, one must discount claims that dealignment is a function of question wording, hidden partisans, or the unique political history of any one nation.

ELECTORAL POLITICS PAST AND FUTURE

The United States has experienced a series of exceptional elections in recent years. The close contest in 2000, for example, saw a few hundred votes in Florida (counted or uncounted) determine the presidential election. The September 11th attack stimulated a major shift in government policy and a strong showing for the Republicans in 2002 and 2004. Then the electoral tide shifted dramatically in 2006 as the Democrats made major gains in the House and Senate elections. The Democrats' momentum continued in 2008 with Obama's historic election victory and the party winning majorities in both the House and the Senate. The Democratic tide ebbed in 2010, when the Republicans swept to victory in the off-year elections and recaptured control of the House.

What will happen in 2012? Given the volatility in recent elections and the current economic and political situation, the outcome of the next election is difficult to predict (even though many pundits and political scientists are already on record with their predictions). However, the outcome likely depends on one group of people: independents, and especially apartisans. Nonpartisans are typically instrumental in defining the electoral tides that change results from election to election. According to CNN exit polls, less than half of independents (49 percent) voted for a Democratic candidate in the 2004 congressional elections. This number increased to 57 percent in the 2006 elections and then decreased to 51 percent in 2008. In 2010 the Democrats garnered only 37 percent of independents' votes. Party identifiers are still a large majority of the electorate, and their votes are crucial to both parties' electoral bases. However, their votes also predictably and reliably go to their party. So charting the candidate preferences of independents is a strong indicator of which way the political tides are running.

The institutional framework of elections has changed in basic ways over the past several decades. These changes include an expanded reliance on presidential primaries, a radically different media environment, new rules on funding transparency, alterations in campaign financing, and other factors. Of equal importance, we have changed as a people.[1] The contemporary electorate is now much better educated, more interested in politics, and more politically active beyond elections. This process of cognitive mobilization is altering how many people make electoral choices and practice democratic citizenship. This is the story of this book.

THE EVIDENCE OF DEALIGNMENT

Part of the debate over whether dealignment is occurring is definitional, as electoral analysts use the term in different ways or cite varied data as evidence of dealignment. So let me state my understanding of the term: "Dealignment is a period during which the party-affiliated portion of the electorate shrinks."[2] Alternatively, Ronald Inglehart and Avram Hochstein state that dealignment is "declining rates of identification with *any* party."[3] Both definitions focus on the extent of party affiliations— party identification—within the public. Thus, this study asks the central question: Do significantly fewer people today identify with a political party?

To my reading of the evidence, the answer is a convincing "yes." Chapter 2 found that identification with either of the two major American parties during the six-decade series covered by the American National Election Studies reached a historic low in the 2004–2008 elections. In the Eisenhower era, barely a quarter of the public lacked a party identification; now this group is the plurality of the public at about 40 percent. Further evidence from commercial polls in 2010 and 2011 indicates that dealignment is continuing.[4] Zoltan Hajnal and Taeku Lee reached a similar conclusion in their recent study of partisanship in

America: "We have outlined . . . the significant growth of nonpartisanship across the nation. That nonpartisanship is an important phenomenon requires no convincing for observers of recent trends in American politics."[5] A substantial dealigned segment of the public is the new reality of American electoral politics.

Still, many skeptics doubt that dealignment has occurred or argue that earlier decreases in partisanship have been reversed in recent elections. Often these claims arise because the researcher is examining something other than the trends in party identification. For instance, Americans' growing awareness of the polarization of the parties' positions is mistakenly cited as evidence of a resurgence of partisanship.[6] Or the correlates of partisanship—rather than the extent of partisanship—are used to measure dealignment.[7] For example, researchers frequently show that Democratic and Republican identifiers are still divided in their vote choice without fully acknowledging that this dichotomy includes a shrinking proportion of the American public. Dealignment is assessed by the level of partisan attachments among the public, and these attachments have weakened significantly.

Another criticism raises doubts about the interpretation of "leaning independents" and whether they are really partisans in disguise.[8] Although this is a commonly held belief in the American electoral politics literature, I think it is misguided on several grounds. Chapter 2 found that another indicator of partisanship—voter registration—has also trended downward. Since registering as independent or with no party affiliation often disenfranchises a voter from participating in the party primaries, this is an even more rigorous test of party attachments. It is not something hidden partisans would do, because it means they would lose their right to pick members of their "hidden" team. Yet, dealignment is apparent here as well. In addition, panel data indicate that the partisan preferences of leaning independents are quite variable, reflecting their preferences in the current election rather than stable party loyalties. Since these leanings shift over time, it is no surprise that leaners look like party voters at any one point in time (but will look different when their party preferences change in the next election). Indeed, two of the creators of the party identification question stated that leaners are independents who are expressing their current party preferences when asked.[9]

To me, the cross-national evidence of dealignment is equally relevant. Much of the skepticism of dealignment in the United States focuses on the specific electoral history of the nation and its unusual two-party competition. Independence does have a special cachet among Americans, and the complex electoral system makes unusual demands on the public. The growing polarization of elite politics in Washington is another prominent aspect of many writings about alignment and dealignment. But this is like focusing on the trees and missing the larger forest.

Virtually every established democracy with long-term electoral surveys shows a dealignment pattern. After updating results from the late 1990s with three dozen more elections (see chapter 9), the downward trend remains clear. The pace and pattern of change might be different in Australia than it is in Sweden, but dealignment is commonplace. Regardless of how the partisan question is asked or the nation's cultural tradition of partisanship and independence, fewer people today express an attachment. The mental gymnastics to discount dealignment in the United States because of "hidden partisanship" and Americans' affinity for an independent label seem implausible when we recognize this is a general phenomenon in established democracies.

Many people still express an affiliation with a party, and party ID remains a key concept in electoral research. On this point I strongly agree with the many studies that demonstrate the continuing importance of partisanship for the majority of the public who hold partisan ties. Given the slowing pace of social change and cognitive mobilization in established democracies, it would not be surprising if dealignment slows or partisanship even stabilizes at current levels. However, the simple truth is that fewer citizens now express long-term affective party attachments when compared to the electorates of the 1960s and 1970s.

THE IMPLICATIONS OF DEALIGNMENT

Although this book has stressed the significance of dealignment, the important point is not that the percentage of independents has increased. *More important is the fact that the characteristics of independents have changed.* If the growth of independents signals that more people are lacking citizenship norms, unable to follow the complexities of politics, ill-informed about politics, and politically disengaged—the traditional description of independents—then this will hold clear negative implications for the electoral process and democracy.

Instead, the growth of nonpartisans has disproportionately occurred among better-educated and politically interested citizens who nevertheless have not developed long-term affective party ties. This process of cognitive mobilization alters the characteristics of nonpartisans and partisans. *The American Voter* could not find the theoretical independent who is "attentive to politics, concerned with the course of government, who weighs the rival appeals of a campaign and reaches a judgment that is unswayed by partisan prejudice."[10] We found this elusive species: apartisans—cognitively mobilized independents. This group is now an important and growing share of the American electorate.[11] The changing nature of nonpartisans makes us relatively sanguine about the consequences of dealignment, but the exact consequences will depend on how the electorate, parties, and candidates respond to these trends.

Electoral Politics

The growing proportion of apartisans is already affecting electoral politics. In contrast to traditional independents, apartisans turn out to vote at levels approaching those of party identifiers. Apartisans are also less likely to enter a campaign with their votes predetermined; they tend to decide on their votes later in a campaign—increasingly in its last weeks or days. This makes campaigns more meaningful, which should be a positive development.

Not only do apartisans decide later in a campaign, the content of their decision making also differs in significant ways from that of party identifiers and apoliticals. Partisans give greater weight to their party loyalties, and these loyalties shape their images of the issues and the candidates in the election, which is to be expected of party identifiers. Apartisans, in contrast, place greater weight on candidate characteristics and issues in making their voting choice. Thus, the expansion of this segment of the electorate inevitability increases the issue content of electoral choice, especially when compared to our traditional image of nonpartisans (and even many partisan voters). Compared to other cog-partisan groups, apartisans come closest to the rational voter who has been praised in democratic theory but seldom found in early electoral surveys.

Cognitive mobilization also affects the composition of party identifiers. The percentage of ritual partisans—those who have a party identity but limited cognitive mobilization—has decreased substantially in most established democracies. In their place, most partisans today are cognitively mobilized and bring a greater understanding of the issues and candidates to their voting choices. They may ultimately vote as reliably as ritual partisans, but they are likely to be more demanding of party leaders, more sophisticated in their criticisms of the opposition, and more informed about politics in general. Because of their concern for issues, cognitive partisans may also be more likely to adjust their partisanship to reflect their political views, following a pattern of evolving partisanship that Morris Fiorina has described.[12] This would produce another source of electoral change.

Dealignment and cognitive mobilization are thus producing basic changes in electoral behavior and citizens' relationships to parties. The basis of electoral choice is shifting from long term habitual party cues that were used as a heuristic by an unsophisticated public to greater weight being given to the issues and candidates of a campaign by a more evaluative and sophisticated electorate. This contributes to the growing volatility and fluidity of electoral politics in America and other established democracies. As this book has shown, the rise in split-ticket voting, inter-election volatility, and decision making later during a campaign can at least partially be traced to the shifting sources of political mobilization within the electorate. Such trends contribute to the ongoing partisan dealignment of contemporary electoral politics.

Certainly there are reasons to be cautious about the growth of apartisans. Some apartisans are inevitably ill-informed or hold inconsistent policy views, and their egocentric voting choices may not always yield reasonable outcomes. Because they lack party attachments, apartisans may also be more susceptible to the appeals of charismatic new politicians or new parties in parliamentary systems. Apartisans in the United States have contributed disproportionately to the votes of third-party presidential candidates, both liberal and conservative. Following the Willie Sutton principle, apartisans are a lucrative place for the Tea Party movement to find new supporters. Apartisans are similarly a natural voter pool for new European parties as diverse as the Pirate Party in Sweden or

the List Pim Fortuyn in the Netherlands. This may be a positive development when it provides citizens with new representation for their political
views, and the number of political parties is increasing in most parliamentary systems. But some new parties may not have the experience to
be effective and may not be honest in their public statements.

In summary, the debate over the electoral impact of party identification
reflects two sides of the same argument. If one wants to predict how people
will vote, partisanship is still a very strong predictor of voting choice for
most citizens—as demonstrated in chapter 7—and it is likely to remain so
for the foreseeable future. Partisans vote often and they vote loyally for
their party. But, if one wants to predict which voters might swing their vote
between elections or support new candidates or political parties, then we
should shift our focus to independents and especially apartisans.

In the run-up to the 2012 presidential election, Mike Huckabee expressed
this reality. He told a meeting of the Republican Leadership Conference that
elections are not decided by partisan identifiers who routinely support their
party, but by those who shift their votes from one election to the next. He
stated, "The [2012] election will be decided by a little sliver of people, about
20 percent of the American voters, who do not see politics horizontally, as
the left or the right. . . . They ask themselves this simple question: if we elect
this guy, will things get better or will they get worse?"[13] This is the nature
of electoral politics in contemporary democracies.

Political Engagement

A second aspect of the party identification model was that these identities mobilized individuals to follow and participate in the political process. Thus, research routinely found that in comparison to independents,
partisans were more interested in politics, participated more in campaigns, and voted more often.

While this study has not directly challenged this claim regarding party
identification, I have maintained that political mobilization overall is a
more complex process. Cognitive mobilization stimulates people to seek
out political information, to become politically knowledgeable, and to
think of themselves as engaged citizens (see chapter 4). These orientations
stimulate participation in a diverse set of political activities, ranging from
voting to participation in protests. For instance, chapter 5 showed that

apartisans turn out to vote at almost the same level as partisans, and they participate more than partisans in other types of activities. This is not to deny that party identities also mobilize people to participate in electoral politics, but the impact of party identification is focused on electoral politics and has more limited effects on other types of political activity. And, overall, cognitive mobilization outweighs the effects of partisan mobilization in stimulating people to be engaged in most types of political action.

Thus, the joint forces of dealignment and cognitive mobilization are reshaping patterns of political participation. Turnout in elections has declined slightly in the United States and most other advanced industrial democracies, and it seems unlikely it will return to the record levels of the past. Contemporary publics are participating more in a wider range of political activities, however, which should empower them and increase their influence in the democratic process.

Lessons for the Political Parties

In 2008 one of the crucial strategies of the Obama campaign was to appeal to independents—especially to the young, better-educated independents that we have labeled as apartisans. The Obama campaign needed to expand the electorate to win the nomination from Hillary Clinton and then be victorious in the general election.[14] In terms of conventional wisdom, this seemed like a losing strategy, because the experts said that independents did not vote, especially in primary elections. But the Obama campaign targeted independents in those states that allowed independents to vote in the primaries and sought to attract independent voters in the general election. This strategy succeeded.

Obama's courtship of independents in 2008 was a key factor in his success, and he is trying hard to repeat this feat in 2012. On the one hand, the 2008 campaign reflected Obama's political style—to deemphasize the clash between red and blue states and emphasize the commonality Americans share. On the other hand, it also represented his campaign advisers' awareness that a growing number of independents are politically interested, concerned about the issues, and can be mobilized to vote under the right circumstances.

Awareness of the changing nature of partisans and independents should affect how candidates and parties relate to the public. Mobilizing the party's core is a necessary strategy if the Democrats or the Republicans expect to win elections. The calls for party loyalty that have worked well for voters in the past may still work for ritual partisans. This would yield campaign speeches laced with references to a party's heritage, its past leaders, and its traditional voter base.[15]

In contrast, apartisans expect a different campaign rhetoric. Apartisans favor a postpartisan style of discourse that emphasizes issues and non-ideological decision making. Apartisans must be converted from independence to supporting a party, even though they are skeptical of partisan politics. This would imply a campaign rhetoric that eschews partisan appeals while discussing issues that are attractive to different segments of the apartisan public. In other words, appealing to ritual partisans and apartisans requires different—and somewhat contradictory—styles of discourse. Even cognitive partisans will be more demanding of their party, because their vote is not predicated on loyalty alone.[16]

Thus, political parties now have to speak to an electorate fragmented into different groups, which makes it difficult to successfully run a one-dimensional campaign. These tensions between voter mobilization and conversion have always been present in elections, they have just become more difficult to manage in an electorate in which two-fifths of voters are independent of either party. And in the present media environment, where every campaign event is reported, it is difficult to say one thing to party voters in the primary and another to the general electorate in November. It is hard to offer one image of the campaign to a meeting of party donors in San Francisco, California, and another to a college audience in Bloomington, Indiana. If there are contrasts in the style of campaign rhetoric, the media and the opposing campaign will highlight these contrasts. All this makes for a more complex and difficult campaign process for political candidates.

This differentiated campaign message has been evident in several recent presidential elections, but there is another alternative that some party strategists (of both parties) may prefer that would have the party candidates following the old model of catering to the party's base. This strategy would mobilize partisans and might be successful in congressional/local districts and statewide races where one party holds a clear majority and doesn't need to convert some independent voters. Often this strategy might also seek to demobilize apartisans and apolitical independents so the voters will be drawn disproportionately from the party's base. However, this approach can be problematic in elections where the share of the independents nears a plurality, such as in presidential elections or competitive state elections.

The urge to cater to a party base may be even greater for party leaders in parliamentary systems, where proportional representation (PR) allows small parties to gain instant access to offices and possibly government coalitions. Thus, dealignment in PR systems has increased the number of parties competing in elections and winning offices (see chapter 9), and some of these parties seem more interested in mobilizing a narrow issue base than in converting a broader group of voters to their cause. Dealignment thus increases the potential for parties to use this strategy in the short term.

We expect that this fragmentation of the electorate and the changing composition of partisans and nonpartisans will challenge parties to deal with a more fluid and volatile electoral landscape for the foreseeable future. When these patterns first emerged, I was more tentative about stating whether a new stable partisan alignment would develop.[17] Now, after several decades of increasing electoral change and cross-national evidence of dealignment, I think a return to a stable, predictable, more partisan electoral system is unlikely.

Some politicians want to reform politics to reverse the dealignment trend. At least some of the proposed national electoral system reforms in recent years have had that goal in mind and have sought to restore public confidence in parties, rekindle party attachments, and reverse the trend of declining turnout. It is not likely that such reforms can increase partisanship. To the degree that cognitive mobilization and related processes of social modernization have produced dealignment, reforming the electoral system will not reverse dealignment and restore the old partisan order. Further evidence in support of this conclusion comes from the cross-national breadth of dealignment. Regardless of the structure of the electoral system, the parties running for office, or the context of campaigning, dealignment is a general pattern in established democracies. In short, parties cannot turn back the electoral clock and must deal with this new electoral reality.

DEALIGNMENT AND DEMOCRACY

The American Voter was truly a seminal study of American political behavior.[18] It defined a theoretical framework that still guides research today.

The concept of party identification is a central part of that framework and a potent factor in shaping citizens' behavior and the macro-level electoral process. Party ID remains a key element in our understanding of electoral behavior.

The evidence presented here, however, argues that the electorate described by Campbell and his colleagues no longer exists. They described the reality that existed over fifty years ago, but social modernization has gradually changed the composition of the American public and its political behavior. Expanding educational levels, increased access to political information, the growing role of government, and other factors have produced a process of cognitive mobilization that expands the political skills and resources of the average citizen. Consequently, fewer individuals must rely on party loyalties passed down from their parents and reinforced by habitual support for the same party. Instead, more Americans approach politics with a greater ability to judge the candidates and issues without reliance on habitual party loyalties. This process has increased the sophistication of many partisans as well.

While these findings mostly have positive implications for democracy, there are two obvious areas of concern. First, most troublesome is the persistence of apolitical independents as a share of the American electorate. Despite the process of cognitive mobilization, these apoliticals count for approximately the same share of the public as they did in the 1950s and 1960s. Moreover, as other parts of society have become more politically engaged, these apoliticals appear even more distant from politics than they were during the past. In an increasingly complex political world, it becomes harder for them to participate and to make reasonable electoral choices when they do. The significance of this is magnified when we realize that apolitical independents are also concentrated among the lower-income populations and new minorities in America—those who often need government assistance the most. Ironically, although democratic participation is expanding, the inequality of participation and democratic citizenship is also increasing.

Another uncertainty concerns how politicians and parties respond to the changes among the citizenry. A more engaged and sophisticated public can deepen the democratic process; citizenship norms strengthen, more people participate, and people make more meaningful voting choices. However, a more fluid public that is decoupled from habitual party cues can also open the door to exploitation and demagoguery by political elites. Flash parties that rapidly emerge on the political stage may be a legitimate expression of public interests, but they can also arise from exploitative political elites or short-term reactions to a dramatic issue or event.[19] Some politicians may try to engage dealigned voters; others may try to insulate their parties by further alienating these citizens from electoral politics. Electoral change creates opportunities, but these opportunities can be a boon or curse for democracy depending on how the political system responds.

In summary, cognitive mobilization has produced an electorate that is divided in its basis of mobilization, and our findings thus strongly argue for a disaggregated view of the American public. Compared to the 1950s, when ritual partisans accounted for a large majority of the electorate, all four mobilization groups described in this study now comprise sizeable proportions of the public. These four groups of citizens bring very different decision-making criteria into their electoral choices, and this carries over to other aspects of political behavior. These differences need to be integrated into models of electoral and political behavior, as a single, undifferentiated model of citizen choice appears to violate the reality of how people think and act. Apolitical independents and apartisans have different political images of the world and different decision making processes—even though both are nonpartisans—just as there are basic differences in how ritual partisans and cognitive partisans relate to the political world. Such heterogeneity within the electorate and the need for differentiated campaigns that recognize these differences should be elements of American elections for a considerable time to come.

I do not want to overstate these findings, because understanding the world of politics is still a difficult task for many voters. And yet, expanding cognitive mobilization has the potential to move the electoral process toward the ideal of democratic theory: voters making independent judgments on the candidates and issues of the day. The findings of this book suggest that cognitive mobilization has moved the electorate closer to this normative ideal.

ENDNOTES

CHAPTER 1

1. Angus Campbell, Philip Converse, Warren Miller, and Donald Stokes, *The American Voter* (New York: Wiley, 1960), chapter 6. For a more recent restatement of this position see Donald Green, Bradley Palmquist, and Eric Schickler, *Partisan Hearts and Minds: Political Parties and the Social Identities of Voters* (New Haven: Yale University Press, 2002).
2. Angus Campbell, Gerald Gurin, and Warren Miller, *The Voter Decides* (New York: Row Patterson, 1954).
3. Robert Hess and Judith Torney, *The Development of Political Attitudes in Children* (New York: Aldine, 1967); M. Kent Jennings and Richard Niemi, *The Political Character of Adolescence* (Princeton: Princeton University Press, 1974).
4. Herbert Weisberg and Steve Greene, "The Political Psychology of Party Identification," in *Electoral Democracy*, eds. Michael MacKuen and George Rabinowitz (Ann Arbor: University of Michigan Press, 2003), 115.
5. Russell Dalton, "The Decline of Party Identification," in *Parties without Partisans*, eds. Russell Dalton and Martin Wattenberg (Oxford: Oxford University Press, 2000), 20.
6. Campbell et al., *The American Voter*, 121.
7. Ole Borre and Daniel Katz, "Party Identification and Its Motivational Base in a Multiparty System," *Scandinavian Political Studies* 8 (1973): 69–111; Warren Miller, "The Cross-National Use of Party Identification as a Stimulus to Political Inquiry," in *Party Identification and Beyond*, eds. Ian Budge, Ivor Crewe, and Dennis Farlie (New York: Wiley, 1976); Martin Wattenberg, *The Decline of American Political Parties, 1952–1996* (Cambridge, MA: Harvard University Press, 1998).
8. Morris Fiorina, "Information and Rationality in Elections," in *Information and Democratic Processes*, eds. John Ferejohn and James Kuklinski (Urbana: University of Illinois Press, 1990).
9. Philip Converse, "The Normal Vote," in *Elections and the Political Order*, Angus Campbell et al. (New York: Wiley, 1966).
10. Sidney Verba, Kay Schlozman, and Henry Brady, *Voice and Equality: Civic Voluntarism in American Politics* (Cambridge, MA: Harvard University Press, 1995).
11. Herbert Weisberg, "A Multidimensional Conceptualization of Party Identification," *Political Behavior* 2 (1980): 33–60.
12. Sidney Verba, Norman Nie, and John Petrocik, *The Changing American Voter* (Chicago: University of Chicago Press, 1976); Wattenberg, *The Decline of American Political Parties;* Philip Converse, *The Dynamics of Party Support* (Beverly Hills: Sage, 1976).
13. Michael Lewis Beck et al., *The American Voter Revisited* (Ann Arbor: University of Michigan Press, 2008), chapter 6.
14. Bruce Keith et al., *The Myth of the Independent Voter* (Berkeley: University of California Press, 1992); also see Weisberg, "A Multidimensional Conceptualization of Party Identification."
15. David Magleby, Candice Nelson, and Mark Westlye, "The Myth of the Independent Voter Revisited," in *Facing the Challenge of Democracy: Explorations in the Analysis of Public Opinion and Political Participation*, eds. Paul Sniderman and Benjamin Highton (Princeton: Princeton University Press, 2011).
16. Karen Kaufmann, John Petrocik, and Daron Shaw, *Unconventional Wisdom: Facts and Myths about American Voters* (New York: Oxford University Press, 2008), chapter 2; Green, Palmquist, and

Schickler, *Partisan Hearts and Minds;* Warren Miller and J. Merrill Shanks, *The New American Voter* (Cambridge, MA:: Harvard University Press, 1996).

17.   Dalton, "The Decline of Party Identification"; Harold Clarke and Marianne Stewart, "The Decline of Parties in the Minds of Citizens, *Annual Review of Political Science* 1 (1998): 357–378; Paul Webb, "Conclusion: Political Parties and Democratic Control in Advanced Industrial Societies," in *Political Parties in Advanced Industrial Democracies*, eds. Paul Webb, David Farrell, and I. Holliday (Oxford: Oxford University Press, 2002).

18.   Campbell et al., *The American Voter*, 143–145.

19.   Nancy Rosenblum, *On the Side of Angels: An Appreciation of Parties and Partisanship* (Princeton: Princeton University Press, 2008).

20.   Bill Bishop, *The Big Sort: Why the Clustering of Like-minded Americans Is Tearing Us Apart* (New York: Houghton Mifflin Harcourt, 2008), 258.

21.   David Broder, "Why the Center Still Holds," *Washington Post*, April 12, 2009, A17.

22.   "Leaders Call for Cooperation, Not Polarization in National Politics," *USC Annenberg News,* June 20, 2007, http://annenberg.usc.edu/News%20and%20Events/News/070620CeaseFire.aspx.

23.   Barack Obama, *The Audacity of Hope: Thoughts on Reclaiming the American Dream* (New York: Crown, 2006), 9.

24.   Henry Goldman, "New York City Hosts 'No Labels' Political Group Countering 'Partisanship,'" *Bloomberg News*, December 13, 2010. Also see www.nolabels.org.

CHAPTER 2

1.   Angus Campbell, Gerald Gurin, and Warren Miller, *The Voter Decides* (New York: Row Patterson, 1954), 91–92.

2.   Anne Kornblut, "'Soul-Searching' Obama Aides: Democrats' Midterm Election Losses a Wake-Up Call," *Washington Post*, November 14, 2010.

3.   John Judis, "You've Got Them All Wrong, Mr. President: Obama's Misguided View of the Independent Voter," *New Republic*, November 18, 2010.

4.   Campbell, Gurin, and Miller, *The Voter Decides.*

5.   Philip Converse, *The Dynamics of Party Support* (Beverly Hills: Sage, 1976); Norman Nie, Sidney Verba, and John Petrocik, *The Changing American Voter* (Chicago: University of Chicago Press, 1976); Gerald Pomper, "The Decline of the Party in American Elections," *Political Science Quarterly* 92 (1977): 21–41; Martin Wattenberg, *The Decline of American Political Parties* (Cambridge, MA: Harvard University Press, 1984), chapter 3.

6.   Russell Dalton and Martin Wattenberg, eds., *Parties without Partisans: Political Change in Advanced Industrial Democracies* (Oxford: Oxford University Press, 2000); Harold Clarke and Marianne Stewart, "The Decline of Parties in the Minds of Citizens," *Annual Review of Political Science* 1 (1998): 357–378.

7.   Ronald Inglehart and Avram Hochstein, "Alignment and Dealignment of the Electorate in France and the United States," *Comparative Political Studies* 5 (1972): 343–372; Walter Dean Burnham, *Critical Elections and the Mainsprings of American Politics* (New York: Norton, 1970).

8.   As an introduction, see the discussions in Dalton and Wattenberg, eds., *Parties without Partisans;* Bruce Keith et al., *The Myth of the Independent Voter* (Berkeley: University of California Press, 1992).

9.   This was the primary explanation in Nie, Verba, and Petrocik, *The Changing American Voter.*

10.   Arthur Miller and Martin Wattenberg, "Measuring Party Identification: Independent or No Partisan Preference," *American Journal of Political Science* 27 (1983): 106–121; Marc Hetherington, "Resurgent Mass Partisanship: The Role of Elite Polarization," *American Political Science Review* 95 (2001): 619–639.

11.   Russell Dalton, "Mobilization and the Changing American Electorate," *Electoral Studies* 26 (2007): 274–286; Russell Dalton, "The Decline of Party Identification," in *Parties without Partisans: Political Change in Advanced Industrial Democracies*, eds. Russell Dalton and Martin Wattenberg (Oxford: Oxford University Press, 2000).

12. Keith et al., *The Myth of the Independent Voter*; also see Herbert Weisberg, "A Multidimensional Conceptualization of Party Identification," *Political Behavior* 2 (1980): 33–60.

13. Donald Green, Bradley Palmquist, and Eric Schickler, *Partisan Hearts and Minds: Political Parties and the Social Identities of Voters* (New Haven: Yale University Press, 2002), 51.

14. Karen Kaufmann, John Petrocik, and Daron Shaw, *Unconventional Wisdom: Facts and Myths about American Voters* (New York: Oxford University Press, 2008), 23.

15. David Magleby, Candice Nelson, and Mark Westlye, "The Myth of the Independent Voter Revisited," in *Facing the Challenge of Democracy: Explorations in the Analysis of Public Opinion and Political Participation*, eds. Paul Sniderman and Benjamin Highton (Princeton: Princeton University Press, 2011).

16. Campbell, Gurin, and Miller, *The Voter Decides*.

17. Our thanks to the American National Election Study and the Inter-university Consortium for Political and Social Research for providing access to these surveys. The project Web site (www.electionstudies .org) documents these surveys and their findings and provides access to the original survey materials.

18. The ANES methodology on coding partisanship has changed slightly over time, primarily with regards to the coding of apoliticals and missing data categories. I follow the methodology described in Matthew DeBell et al., "Clarification of 'Apolitical' Codes in the Party Identification Summary Variable on ANES Datasets," American National Election Studies, December 2009. This method essentially excludes apoliticals, "don't know" responses, and other missing data from the seven-point party identification scale. This has produced a lower level of nonpartisans in all years, especially in the early surveys when voter registration rules and social pressures led many African Americans into the apolitical category.

19. Warren Miller and Teresa Levetin, *Leadership and Change: Presidential Elections from 1952–1972* (Boston: Little Brown, 1976); Converse, *The Dynamics of Party Support*; Nie, Verba, and Petrocik, *The Changing American Voter*.

20. Keith et al., *The Myth of the Independent Voter*, chapter 2.

21. The Gallup Poll developed a separate measure of partisan attachments and did not use random-area probability samples until the 1960s. The typical Gallup question asks: "As of today, do you regard yourself as a Republican, a Democrat, or an Independent in politics?" This is generally viewed as closer to immediate party preferences than the ANES question, because the phrasing discusses politics "as of today" and lacks the implicit identity reference.

22. These data were obtained from the iPOLL database of the Roper Center at the University of Connecticut (http://www.ropercenter.uconn.edu/). In most months ABC polled about one thousand respondents. Several additional months in 2010–2011 came from the *Washington Post* poll that often is conducted with the ABC News poll. The percentage of independents includes those saying they are independent or giving an "other" or "don't know" response to the core party ID question.

23. The ABC/*Washington Post* polls may underestimate the percentage of independents because they conduct telephone interviews and have a shorter fieldwork period, which tends to lower survey response rates compared to the ANES and may overrepresent groups that are politically engaged.

24. M. Kent Jennings et al., *Youth-Parent Socialization Panel Study, 1965–1997: Four Waves Combined*, Interuniversity Consortium for Political and Social Research, study 4037 (www.icpsr.org).

25. John Petrocik, "Party Identification: Leaners Are Not Independents," *Electoral Studies* 28 (2009): 562–572; also see Keith et al., *The Myth of the Independent Voter*.

26. For additional time comparisons see Keith et al., *The Myth of the Independent Voter*, chapter 5. However, they draw a different conclusion from these patterns.

27. This comparison includes leaners, weak partisans, or strong partisans of the other party.

28. In two-thirds of these cases, the respondents retain a core identity as an independent but say they lean either toward the Democrats or the Republicans.

29. Warren Miller, "Party Identification Re-Examined: The Reagan Era," in *Where's the Party?* eds. Warren Miller and John Petrocik (Washington, DC: University Press of America, 1987), 24; similarly, Philip Converse and Roy Pierce assert that the follow-up question for independents taps current preferences rather than deeper partisan identities ("Measuring Partisanship," *Political Methodology* [1985] 11: 143). Also see Zoltan Hajnal and Taeku Lee, *Why Americans Don't Join the Party* (Princeton: Princeton University Press, 2011), chapter 8.

30. The 1972 statistics are from Michael Barone, *The Almanac of American Politics 1974* (Boston: Gambit, 1974); the 2004 statistics are from Martin Wattenberg, personal communication; the 2008 statistics are from Michael McDonald, "Partisan Registration Totals," *Huffington Post*, October 12, 2010.

31. I relied on the following sources: the California Secretary of State, http://www.sos.ca.gov/elections/elections-pub-res.htm; the Connecticut Secretary of State, http://www.ct.gov/sots/LIB/sots/ElectionServices/ElectionResults/statistics/enrolhst.pdf; the Florida Department of State, http://election.dos.state.fl.us/voter-registration/statistics/elections.shtml; the Iowa Secretary of State, http://www.sos.state.ia.us/elections/results/index.html; the Oregon Secretary of State, http://www.sos.state.or.us/elections/votreg/genlpty.htm; the Pennsylvania Department of State, http://www.portal.state.pa.us/portal/server.pt/community/voter_registration_statistics/12725; and the *Almanac of American Politics* (Boston: Gambit, various years).

32. California has a complex history of party registration. Until 1996 it had a closed primary system in which only individuals registered as partisans could vote in their respective party's primary. Proposition 198 created an open primary system in 1996, but it was ruled unconstitutional by the state supreme court in 2000. In 2001 a modified open primary was adopted, which allowed independents to vote in a chosen party primary if the party authorized open primary voting. The two major parties have authorized open voting in most subsequent elections.

33. Eric McGhee and Daniel Krimm, "Party Registration and the Geography of Party Polarization," *Polity* 41 (2009): 367.

34. In a few states the electoral rules allow nonpartisans to choose to vote in either party primary; if this option expands it might be one factor that encourages more people to register as independents.

35. After development by Campbell et al., the concept of party identification was soon exported to other democratic party systems. Researchers debated the applicability of this concept in parliamentary systems that lack some of the features that gave partisan identification its analytic power and conceptual basis in the United States. See Ian Budge, Ivor Crewe, and Dennis Farlie, eds., *Party Identification and Beyond* (New York: Wiley, 1976). Eventually, researchers accepted that the concept could be usefully applied in most democratic systems. Most voters approach elections with a standing party predisposition, even if the measurement of the predisposition differs according to the political and electoral context.

36. Bo Saarlvik and Ivor Crewe, *Decade of Dealignment* (Cambridge: Cambridge University Press, 1985); Harold Clarke et al., *Performance Politics and the British Voter* (New York: Cambridge University Press, 2009), chapter 7.

37. Sören Holmberg, "Party Identification Compared across the Atlantic," in *Elections at Home and Abroad*, eds. M. Kent Jennings and Thomas Mann (Ann Arbor: University of Michigan Press, 1994); Henrik Oscarsson and Sören Holmberg, *Swedish Voting Behavior*, Swedish Election Studies Program, Department of Political Science, University of Gothenburg, Sweden, June 2010, www.valforskning.pol.gu.se/digitalAssets/1309/1309446_swedish-voting-behavior-juni-2010.pdf.

38. Russell Dalton, *Democratic Challenges, Democratic Choices* (Oxford: Oxford University Press, 2004), chapter 2.

39. Clarke and Stewart, "The Decline of Parties in the Minds of Citizens."

40. Russell Dalton and Steve Weldon, "Public Images of Political Parties: A Necessary Evil?" *West European Politics* 28 (2005): 931–951.

41. The question read: "Do you consider yourself to be close to any particular party? <If yes> Do you feel yourself to be very close to this party, fairly close, or merely a sympathasizer?"

Figure 2.6 is based on the weighted sample pooling the nine nations for which data exist for this full period: Belgium, France, the Netherlands, Germany, Italy, Luxembourg, Denmark, Ireland, and Britain.

CHAPTER 3

1. Quoted in Nancy Rosenblum, *On the Side of Angels: An Appreciation of Parties and Partisanship* (Princeton: Princeton University Press, 2008), 5.

2. Rosenblum, *On the Side of Angels*.

3. Even Angus Campbell and his colleagues acknowledged this ideal: "The ideal of the Independent citizen, attentive to politics, concerned with the course of government, who weights the rival appeals of a campaign and reaches a judgment that is unswayed by partisan prejudice, has ... a vigorous history in the tradition of political reform." Angus Campbell, Philip Converse, Warren Miller, and Donald Stokes, *The American Voter* (New York: Wiley, 1961), 143. However, they argued that this normative ideal poorly fit independents.

4. Campbell et al., *The American Voter*; Bruce Keith et al., *The Myth of the Independent Voter* (Berkeley: University of California Press, 1992); Donald Green, Bradley Palmquist, and Eric Schickler, *Partisan Hearts and Minds: Political Parties and the Social Identities of Voters* (New Haven: Yale University Press, 2002).

5. Michael Kazin, "The Trouble with Independents," *The New Republic*, April 26, 2011, http://www.tnr .com/article/not-even-past/87379/republican-democrats-independents-dewey-lippmann.

6. Pew Center for People and the Press, "Independents Oppose Party in Power ... Again," September 23, 2010, http://people-press.org/report/ 658/.

7. Neil Nevitte, *The Decline of Deference* (Petersborough, Canada: Broadview, 1996).

8. Robert Putnam and David Campbell, *American Grace: How Religion Divides and Unites Us* (New York: Simon and Schuster, 2010); F. Mannering and C. Winston, "Brand Loyalty and the Decline of American Automobile Firms," *Brookings Papers on Economic Activity: Microeconomics* (1991): 67–114.

9. Robert Hess and Judith Tourney, *The Development of Political Attitudes in Children* (Chicago: Aldine, 1967).

10. M. Kent Jennings and Greg Markus, "Partisan Orientations over the Long Haul: Results from the Three-Wave Political Socialization Panel Study," *American Political Science Review* 78 (1984): 1000–1018.

11. The landmark study is M. Kent Jennings and Richard Niemi, *The Political Character of Adolescence: The Influence of Families and Schools* (Princeton: Princeton University Press, 1974); for a recent review of this literature, see M. Kent Jennings, "Political Socialization," in *The Oxford Handbook of Political Behavior*, eds. Russell Dalton and Hans-Dieter Klingemann (Oxford: Oxford University Press, 2007).

12. Combining both parents also shows a weakening of generational continuity. In the 1950s, the Multiple R of perceived mother's and father's partisanship predicting the respondent's party ID was .58, or 34 percent of the variance. By 1992 the Multiple R was reduced to .48, or 23% of the variance.

13. The share of those who said their mother was an independent rose from 6 percent in the 1950s to 14 percent in 1992; simultaneously, the percent who listed "other" or "apolitical" for their mother decreased from 13 to 4 percent. This is evidence of the politicization of women over the past half century, although a similar but weaker pattern is also apparent for fathers' partisanship.

14. Jennings and Niemi, *The Political Character of Adolescence;* M. Kent Jennings and Laura Stoker, "Study of Political Socialization: Parent-Child Pairs Based on Survey of Youth Panel and Their Offspring, 1997," Interuniversity Consortium for Political and Social Research, study 4037 (www.icpsr.org). Also see M. Kent Jennings, Laura Stoker, and Jake Bowers, "Politics across Generations: Family Transmission Reexamined," *Journal of Politics* 71 (2009): 782–799.

15. Martin Kroh and Peter Selb, "Inheritance and the Dynamics of Party Identification," *Political Behavior* 31 (1999): 559–574.

16. A part of these age patterns is due to generational effects: older citizens in the 1950s were not just older, they were also raised during a different historical period. The aging effects are demonstrated more clearly in Table 3.3.

17. See, for example, the discussion of these trends and their potential transformative effects in Richard Florida, *The Rise of the Creative Class* (New York: Basic Books, 2002), chapter 3; Russell Dalton, *The Good Citizen: How a Younger Generation Is Transforming American Politics*, rev. edition (Washington, DC: CQ Press, 2009), chapters 1–2.

18. Henry Milner, *Civic Literacy: How Informed Citizens Make Democracy Work* (Hanover, VT: University Press of New England, 2002); Norman Nie, Jane Junn, and Kenneth Stehlik-Barry, *Education and Democratic Citizenship in America* (Chicago: University of Chicago Press, 1996); Samuel Popkin, *The Reasoning Voter* (Chicago: University of Chicago Press, 1991).

19. Markus Prior, *Post-Broadcast Democracy: How Media Choice Increases Inequality in Political Involvement and Polarizes Elections* (New York: Cambridge University Press, 2007), chapter 5.

20. This argument is partially based on a functionalist model of partisanship developed by W. Philips Shively, "The Development of Party Identification among Adults," *American Political Science Review* 73 (1979): 1039–1054; also see Russell Dalton, "Cognitive Mobilization and Partisan Dealignment in Advanced Industrial Democracies," *Journal of Politics* 46 (1984): 264–84; Ronald Inglehart, *Culture Shift in Advanced Industrial Society* (Princeton: Princeton University Press, 1990), chapter 10.

21. Joseph Bafumi and Robert Shapiro, "A New Partisan Voter," *Journal of Politics* 71 (2009): 1–24; there are similar arguments in Warren Miller and Merrill Shanks, *The New American Voter* (Cambridge, MA: Harvard University Press, 1996).

22. For the critical perspective see Jeremy Albright, "Does Political Knowledge Erode Party Attachments? A Review of the Cognitive Mobilization Thesis," *Electoral Studies* 28 (2009): 248–260; Frode Berglund et al., "Party Identification and Party Choice," in *The European Voter*, ed. Jacques Thomassen (Oxford: Oxford University Press, 2005); Eric R. A. N. Smith, *The Unchanging American Voter* (Berkeley: University of California Press, 1989).

23. This typology is derived from Olof Peterson, "The 1976 Election: New Trends in the Swedish Electorate," *Scandinavian Political Studies* 1 (1978): 109–121; also see Dalton, "Cognitive Mobilization and Partisan Dealignment in Advanced Industrial Democracies."

24. Bafumi and Shapiro, "A New Partisan Voter."

25. The cognitive mobilization index is a simple additive combination of education and general interest in public affairs. The respondent – s educational level was coded as follows: 1) primary school or less, 2) high school diploma or less, 3) some college education, or 4) college degree or more. Interest in public affairs was coded as follows: 1) hardly at all, 2) only now and then, 3) some of the time, and 4) most of the time. These two questions were added together to yield a seven-point index (2–8).

    The index depends on the availability of questions. Ideally, we would want a general question on political engagement. A question on interest in the election is asked across the ANES elections, but this focuses too narrowly on elections. Therefore, we use the general interest in politics question even though it is available only starting with the 1964 ANES.

    The cutting point on the cognitive mobilization index is an analytic decision. I set a value of six or greater as high cognitive mobilization. Over the 1964–2008 period, this scores about 45 percent of the combined ANES samples as high on cognitive mobilization. Education levels have increased dramatically over time for the electorate as a whole. There is significant variability in political interest across elections, with a slight trend in more interest over this time series.

26. The question regarding interest in public affairs was first asked in 1960, but the response categories changed in 1964 and so I began the series in that year.

27. For instance, in 1952 a full 62 percent of the respondents had less than a high school education; this dropped to 45 percent by 1964. Political interest also grew over time; Russell Dalton, *Citizen Politics in Advanced Industrial Democracies*, 5th ed. (Washington, DC: CQ Press, 2009), chapter 2.

28. See, for example, the patterns of stability in partisanship in Figure 2.3 and how changing party preferences changes party attachments between elections in Figure 8.5.

29. The analyses are based on those who were 21–29 in either the 1964 or 1966 election.

30. Joseph Nye, Philip Zelikow, and David King, eds., *Why People Don't Trust Government* (Cambridge, MA: Harvard University Press, 1997); Russell Dalton, *Democratic Challenges, Democratic Choices: The Erosion of Political Support in Advanced Industrial Democracies* (Oxford: Oxford University Press, 2004); the Pew Center for People and the Press found trust in government in early 2010 was the lowest recorded over the previous half century. ("Distrust, Discontent, Anger and Partisan Rancor," April 18, 2010, http://people-press.org/files/legacy-pdf/606.pdf.)

31. The typical ANES question reads: "I'd like to talk about some of the different ideas about the government in Washington. These ideas don't refer to Democrats or Republicans in particular, but just to government in general. We want to see how you feel about these ideas. For example: How much of

the time do you think you can trust the government in Washington to do what is right—just about always, most of the time, only some of the time, or almost never?"

32. I came to that conclusion by comparing the correlation between trust and apolitical independence over time and the correlation between trust and being an apartisan. In Figure 3.5, for instance, the Pearson's *r* correlation for apolitical independents is .05, and the correlation for apartisans is .02. This ratio is about the same across most time periods. However, some other trust questions show a small difference between apolitical independents and apartisans.

33. Inglehart, *Culture Shift in Advanced Industrial Society;* Ronald Inglehart, *The Silent Revolution* (Princeton: Princeton University Press, 1977), 1–18, 339–340. This is similar to the definition of "engaged citizenship" in Dalton, *The Good Citizen.*

34. Dalton, "Cognitive Mobilization and Partisan Dealignment in Advanced Industrial Democracies," 275.

35. The postmaterial question was included in six surveys between 1972 and 1992, and the highest Pearson *r* correlation was .06.

36. The figure presents standardized regression coefficients (ß) for ease of comparison, but the unstandardized coefficients yield the same patterns. The regression used pairwise deletion of missing data since not all questions have been asked since 1964.

37. I also included several racial/ethnic categories as potential predictors, but there is little systematic variance after controlling for the other variables. The one consistent result is that African Americans are less likely to be independents because of their close ties to the Democratic Party. For additional research on partisanship across racial and ethnic groups see Zoltan Hajnal and Taeku Lee, *Why Americans Don't Join the Party* (Princeton: Princeton University Press, 2011).

CHAPTER 4

1. Available online at http://www.youtube.com/watch?v=ANTDkfkoBaI.

2. Norman Nie, Jane Junn, and Kenneth Stehlik-Barry, *Education for Democratic Citizenship* (Chicago: University of Chicago Press, 1996); Arthur Lupia, Mathew McCubbins, and Samuel Popkin, eds., *Elements of Reason* (New York: Cambridge University Press, 2000); Paul Sniderman, Richard Brody, and Philip Tetlock, *Reasoning and Choice: Explorations in Political Psychology* (New York: Cambridge University Press, 1991).

3. Angus Campbell, Philip Converse, Warren Miller, and Donald Stokes, *The American Voter* (New York: Wiley, 1963), chapter 6.

4. Arthur Lupia and Mathew McCubbins, *The Democratic Dilemma: Can Citizens Learn What They Need to Know?* (Cambridge: Cambridge University Press, 1998).

5. Michael Delli Carpini and Scott Keeter, *What Americans Know about Politics and Why It Matters* (New Haven: Yale University Press, 1996); Lupia and McCubbins, *The Democratic Dilemma.*

6. Nie, Junn, and Stehlik-Barry's *Education for Democratic Citizenship* provides an excellent analysis of the impact of education on participation and citizenship norms.

7. Philip Converse, "Change in the American Electorate," in *The Human Meaning of Social Change,* eds. Angus Campbell and Philip Converse (New York: Russell Sage Foundation, 1972), 324.

8. A partial validation for including both items in a cognitive mobilization index comes from predicting political knowledge. In a multivariate model predicting knowledge, both have substantial and equivalent independent impact, and their total impact is greater than that of either taken alone. A regression model predicting knowledge yields the following results (2000 ANES):

Variable	Betaweight
Education	.39
Interest	.39
Multiple R	.62

9. Nie, Junn, and Stehlik-Barry, *Education for Democratic Citizenship,* chapter 2. They also examined democratic participation, which is considered in the following chapter.

10. A typical question read: "How much attention did you pay to news on TV about the campaign for President—a great deal, quite a bit, some, very little, or none?" Figure 4.1 displays the percentage answering "a great deal" for each media source.

11. Delli Carpini, and Keeter, *What Americans Know about Politics and Why It Matters*; Martin Wattenberg, *Is Voting for Young People?* (New York: Longman, 2007), chapter 3.

12. At the time of the post-election survey, the correct answers were: Nancy Pelosi, Speaker of the U.S. House of Representatives; Dick Cheney, vice president of the United States; Gordon Brown, prime minister of England, and John Roberts, chief justice of the United States. I coded the knowledge scores since the ANES recoding was delayed until late 2011.

13. The item read: "Interviewer: R's general level of information about politics and public affairs seemed: Very high, fairly high, average, fairly low, or very low."

14. Nie, Junn, and Stehlik-Barry, *Education for Democratic Citizenship*, chapter 2.

15. Herbert McClosky and Alida Brill, *Dimensions of Tolerance: What Americans Believe about Civil Liberties* (New York: Russell Sage Foundation, 1983); Norman Nie, Jane Junn, and Kenneth Stehlik-Barry, *Education and Democratic Citizenship in America* (Chicago: University of Chicago Press, 1996); Lawrence Bobo and Frederick Licari, "Education and Political Tolerance: Testing the Effects of Cognitive Sophistication and Target Group Affect," *Public Opinion Quarterly* 53 (1989): 285–308.

16. The survey was conducted in 2005 by the Center for Democracy and Civil Society at Georgetown University. The project Web site is http://www.uscidsurvey.org/. The data and survey documentation are available through the Web site. The measure of tolerance is based on asking about the most disliked groups from a list of alternatives and then the willingness to allow members of the least-favored group to make public speeches, run for public office, or hold public rallies. See Russell Dalton, *The Good Citizen: How a Younger Generation Is Transforming American Politics*, rev. ed. (Washington, DC: CQ Press, 2009), 94–95.

17. Question Q99 presents a dozen items on various democratic principles. Factor analysis was used to create a summary index of democratic values, and the figure displays the percentage scoring above the national mean on this index.

18. Dalton, *The Good Citizen*, chapter 2.

19. Sniderman, Brody, and Tetlock, *Reasoning and Choice;* also see chapter 7 in this book.

20. The answers in Figure 4.4 might arise from a respondent's projection of desirable traits rather than actual behavior. Even if this is the case, the results indicate how cog-partisan groups vary in these projections. In addition, there is some validation for these differences in the interviewers' assessment of the overall intelligence of respondents (the percentage rated "very intelligent": apartisans 35 percent, cognitive partisans 32 percent, ritual partisans 11 percent, and apolitical independents 6 percent).

21. The question read: "Some people have opinions about almost everything; other people have opinions about just some things; and still other people have very few opinions. What about you? Would you say you have opinions about almost everything, about many things, about some things, or about very few things?"

22. The question read: "Some people like to have responsibility for handling situations that require a lot of thinking, and other people don't like to have responsibility for situations like that. What about you? Do you like having responsibility for handling situations that require a lot of thinking, do you dislike it, or do you neither like it nor dislike it?"

23. The question read: "Some people prefer to solve simple problems instead of complex ones, whereas other people prefer to solve more complex problems. Which type of problem do you prefer to solve: simple or complex?"

24. Nie, Junn, and Stehlik-Barry, *Education for Democratic Citizenship*; Henry Milner, *Civic Literacy: How Informed Citizens Make Democracy Work* (Hanover, NH: Tufts University Press, 2002).

CHAPTER 5

1. Angus Campbell, Philip Converse, Warren Miller, and Donald Stokes, *The American Voter* (New York: Wiley, 1961), 143.

2. Sidney Verba and Norman Nie, *Participation in America* (New York: Harper and Row, 1972), chapters 5 and 12; Stephen Rosenstone and John Hansen, *Mobilization, Participation and Democracy in America*

(New York: Macmillan, 1993); Sidney Verba, Kay Schlozman, and Henry Brady, *Voice and Equality: Civic Voluntarism in American Politics* (Cambridge, MA: Harvard University Press, 1995), chapter 12.

3. Martin Wattenberg, *Where Have All the Voters Gone?* (Cambridge, MA: Harvard University Press, 2002), 66.

4. Ibid.

5. Ibid. For a cautious statement on calculating this turnout decline, see Michael McDonald and Samuel Popkin, "The Myth of the Vanishing Voter," *American Political Science Review* 95 (2001): 963–974; and McDonald's Web site on voting: http://elections.gmu.edu/index.html.

6. Overreporting is, perhaps, increasing. See Michael McDonald, "On the Overreport Bias of the National Election Study Turnout Rate," *Political Analysis* 11 (2003): 180–186.

7. Also see Wattenberg, *Where Have All the Voters Gone?* chapter 3.

8. Since the political interest question is not available for 1952, I simply calculated the change in education levels and proportionately adjusted the 1964 voting statistics.

9. The nationally representative CID survey conducted in-person interviews with 1,001 respondents between May 16 and July 19, 2005. International Communications Research (ICR) did the interviews using a clustered area-probability sample of households and random selection of respondents. I appreciate the assistance of Marc Howard and the CDCS in providing access to these data. Additional information on the survey is available from the project Web site at www.uscidsurvey.org/.

10. I used a principal components analysis to determine scores, weighing each activity by its relationship with the underlying component. Five items were used in the ANES survey: tried to influence others, attended a campaign meeting, worked for campaign, displayed campaign material, or donated to a candidate or a party. The CID had fifteen different participation items. I used principal components to provide scores for four areas of participation that are examined in this chapter: electoral participation, direct contacting, protest, and internet activism. For more on these participation dimensions, see Miki Caul Kittilson and Russell Dalton, "Virtual Civil Society: The New Frontier of Social Capital?" *Political Behavior* 33 (2011): 625–644.

11. Rousseau states "The English people believes itself to be free; it is gravely mistaken; it is free only during election of members of parliament; as soon as the members are elected, the people is enslaved." See Jean-Jacques Rousseau, *The Social Contract: Book III*, chapter 15.

12. Russell Dalton, *The Good Citizen: How a Younger Generation Is Transforming American Politics*, rev. ed. (Washington, DC: CQ Press, 2009), chapter 4; Cliff Zukin et al., *A New Engagement? Political Participation, Civic Life, and the Changing American Citizen* (New York: Oxford University Press, 2006). For a contrasting view, see Robert Putnam, *Bowling Alone: The Collapse and Renewal of American Community* (New York: Simon and Schuster, 2000).

13. Verba, Schlozman, and Brady, *Voice and Equality,* chapter 12.

14. For addition information on this index, see note 11.

15. Pippa Norris, *The Democratic Phoenix: Reinventing Political Activism* (New York: Cambridge University Press, 2002); Russell Dalton, *Citizen Politics in Advanced Industrial Democracies,* 5th ed. (Washington, DC: CQ Press, 2008), chapter 3.

16. The protest score is based primarily on participation in legal demonstrations and illegal protests. See Kittilson and Dalton, "Virtual Civil Society."

17. Aaron Smith et al., *The Internet and Civic Engagement* (Washington, DC: Pew Internet and American Life Project, 2009), available online at http://www.pewinternet.org/Reports/2009/15--The-Internet-and-Civic-Engagement.aspx.

18. Pew Research Center for People and the Press, "Internet Gains on Television as Public's Main News Source," January 4, 2011, http://people-press.org/report/689/.

19. Kathy Zickuhr, *Generations 2010* (Washington, DC: Pew Internet and American Life Project, 2010), available online at http://www.pewinternet.org/Reports/2010/Generations-2010.aspx; Henry Milner, *The Internet Generation: Engaged Citizens or Political Dropouts* (Medford, MA: Tufts University Press, 2010); Kittilson and Dalton, "Virtual Civil Society."

20. This index is primarily based on three items: forwarding a political e-mail, visiting a political Web site, or other types of online activism. See Kittilson and Dalton, "Virtual Civil Society."

21. This is based on scores combining all the fifteen participation items in the CID that were presented in Figures 5.3–5.6 in the first principal axis dimension. The weighted scores of these activities produced the index in Figure 5.7.

22. I relied on the Cog-Partisan Index to simplify the presentation of relationships, but another method is to include both mobilization factors in a multivariate regression predicting each type of political activity. The standardized regression coefficients below show that both aspects of cognitive mobilization outweigh the strength of party identification as a predictor of participation:

	Electoral	Direct action	Protest	Internet	All activity
Political interest	.19	.26	.00	.16	.47
Education	.08	.21	.09	.23	.24
Strength of PID	.06	.08	-.06	-.03	.04
Multiple R	.24	.38	.11	.30	.58

This is similar to Verba et al.'s findings for the American public in 1990; Verba, Schlozman, and Brady, *Voice and Equality*, 351–354.

CHAPTER 6

1. Russell Dalton and Steve Weldon, "Public Images of Political Parties: A Necessary Evil?" *West European Politics* 28 (2005): 931–951.

2. John Aldrich, *Why Parties? The Origin and Transformation of Political Parties in America* (Chicago: University of Chicago Press, 1995); Russell Dalton and Martin Wattenberg, "Unthinkable Democracy," in *Parties without Partisans*, eds. Russell Dalton and Martin Wattenberg (Oxford: Oxford University Press, 2000).

3. Arthur Miller and Martin Wattenberg, "Measuring Party Identification: Independent or No Partisan Preference?" *American Journal of Political Science* 27 (1983): 106–121.

4. Martin Wattenberg, *The Decline of American Political Parties, 1952–1992* (Cambridge, MA: Harvard University Press, 1993); Similar patterns are also occurring in other established democracies. See Russell Dalton, Ian McAllister, and Martin Wattenberg, "The Consequences of Dealignment," in *Parties without Partisans*, eds. Russell Dalton and Martin Wattenberg (Oxford: Oxford University Press, 2000).

5. Aldrich, *Why Parties?*; Russell Dalton, David Farrell, and Ian McAllister, *Party Linkage and the Democratic Process* (Oxford: Oxford University Press, 2011).

6. The questions are worded as follows: "Is there anything in particular that you like about the Democratic Party? What is that? Anything else [you like about the Democratic Party]?" and "Is there anything in particular that you don't like about the Democratic Party? What is that? Anything else [you don't like about the Democratic Party]?" The project coded up to five responses for likes and an additional five for dislikes.

7. Because these are codings of open-ended responses, it's also possible that the first election studies pressed more forcefully for responses or were more generous in coding multiple responses. Even if we discount the first two elections, there is little clear trend in comments from 1960 until 2008. Because the ANES had not coded the open-ended questions on party likes/dislikes by the end of 2011, the 2008 data in this chapter were coded by the author.

8. Angus Campbell, Philip Converse, Warren Miller, and Donald Stokes, *The American Voter* (New York: Wiley, 1961), 143.

9. Wattenberg, *The Decline of American Political Parties*, chapter 10.

10. The beta correlations show this widening gap: 1964–1966, .37; 1968–1978, .37; 1980–1990, .42; 1992–2000, .43; 2002–2004, 39.

11. Dalton and Weldon, "Public Images of Political Parties"; Russell Dalton, *Democratic Challenges, Democratic Choices: The Erosion of Political Support in Advanced Industrial Democracies* (Oxford: Oxford University Press), chapter 2.

12. Logically, a fourth option is that more people have become positive toward both parties. I consider this option later in the chapter, but research consistently shows that only a small percentage of the public holds this opinion, and there is relatively little change in the size of this group over time.

13. Wattenberg, *The Decline of American Political Parties*, chapter 10.

14. Gary Jacobson, "Party Polarization in National Politics," in *Polarized Politics: Congress and the President in a Partisan Era*, eds. John Bond and R. Fleischer (Washington, DC: CQ Press, 2000); Keith Poole and Harold Rosenthal, "D-Nominate After Ten Years," *Legislative Studies Quarterly* 26 (2001): 5–29.

15. Bill Bishop, *The Big Sort: Why the Clustering of Like-Minded America is Tearing Us Apart* (Boston: Mariner Books, 2009). For a contrasting view, see Andrew Gelman, *Red State, Blue State, Rich State, Poor State: Why Americans Vote the Way They Do* (Princeton: Princeton University Press, 2009).

16. The following descriptions are paraphrased from David Berry, who maintains that these two stereotypes are excessively overdrawn by the media. Quoted in James Q. Wilson, "How Divided Are We?" *Commentary Magazine*, February 2006, http://www.commentarymagazine.com/article/how-divided-are-we/. Also see Morris Fiorina, *Culture War? The Myth of a Polarized America* (New York: Longman, 2004).

17. Marc Hetherington, "Resurgent Mass Partisanship: The Role of Elite Polarization," *American Political Science Review* 95 (2001): 619–632; also see Geoffrey Layman and Thomas Carsey, "Party Polarization and Conflict Extension in the American Electorate," *American Journal of Political Science* 46 (2002): 786–802.

18. Karen Kaufman, John Petrocik, and Daron Shaw, *Unconventional Wisdom: Facts and Myths about American Voters* (New York: Oxford University Press, 2008), 56–60. However, by relying on thermometer questions that began in 1980, their analyses do not show the long-term trend in which 1980 is a low point in party polarization.

19. See, for example, the contrasting interpretations of Norman Nie, Sidney Verba, and John Petrocik, *The Changing American Voter* (Chicago: University of Chicago Press, 1976); Wattenberg, *The Decline of American Political Parties*; Hetherington, "Resurgent Mass Partisanship."

20. I computed separate scores for the Democratic and Republican Parties as the difference between the numbers of responses for things liked about the party minus the number of disliked items. In theory the index could range from +5 (five likes and no dislikes) to -5 (five dislikes and no likes).

21. See Fiorina, *Culture War?*; Kaufman, Petrocik, and Shaw, *Unconventional Wisdom*, chapter 3; Matthew Levendusky, *The Partisan Sort: How Liberals Became Democrats and Conservatives Became Republicans* (Chicago: University of Chicago Press, 2009); Alan Abramowitz, *The Disappearing Center: Engaged Citizens, Polarization, and American Democracy* (New Haven: Yale University Press, 2010).

22. Since 1972 the ANES has asked respondents to place the two major parties, and later the presidential candidates, on a seven-point liberal/conservative scale.

23. Replicating these analyses with images of the presidential candidates does, however, show high levels of polarization starting with the 1984 election and continuing through 2004.

24. Wattenberg, *The Decline of American Political Parties*; Martin Wattenberg, *The Rise of Candidate-Centered Voting* (Cambridge, MA: Harvard University Press, 1992).

25. As partial support for this position, I compared the stability of party identification and party affect across the 1992–1996 ANES panel that included all the questions in both years. Party ID was highly stable over this four-year period (r=.77), while relative affect for Democrats minus Republicans was much less stable (r=.16). In addition, party identification was more strongly related to relative party affect in 1996 (r=. 25) than was party affect from 1992.

26. These analyses are based on the absolute gap between affect toward the Democratic Party and Republican Party as presented in Figure 6.4.

27. For the pooled period from 1972 until 2004, the liberal/conservative gap was: apolitical independents = 1.03, ritual partisans = 1.23, apartisans = 2.08, and cognitive partisans = 2.31. In addition, these differences generally widened over time between the two groups high in cognitive mobilization and the two less mobilized groups.

28. Miller and Wattenberg, "Measuring Party Identification"; Kaufman, Petrocik, and Shaw, *Unconventional Wisdom*, chapter 3.

CHAPTER 7

1. Philip Converse, "The Normal Vote," in *Elections and the Political Order*, Angus Campbell et al. (New York: Wiley, 1966).

2. Warren Miller and J. Merrill Shanks, *The New American Voter* (Cambridge, MA: Harvard University Press, 1996), 146–147.

3. Larry Bartels, "Partisanship and Voting Behavior," *American Journal of Political Science* 44 (2000): 44; Karen Kaufmann, John Petrocik, and Daron Shaw, *Unconventional Wisdom: Facts and Myths about American Voters* (New York: Oxford University Press, 2008).

4. Morris Fiorina, "Parties and Partisanship: A Forty-Year Retrospective," *Political Behavior* 24 (2002): 93–115.

5. Fiorina, "Parties and Partisanship"; Morris Fiorina, *Retrospective Voting in American National Elections* (New Haven: Yale University Press, 1981).

6. The question typically read: "Now I'd like to ask you about the good and bad points of the major candidates for President. Is there anything in particular about George W. Bush that might make you want to vote for him? Is there anything in particular about George W. Bush that might make you want to vote against him?" This same good and bad points question was then repeated for the major candidate of the other party. Up to five responses were coded for each of the four questions.

    Unfortunately, the ANES had not coded the open-ended questions on candidate good/bad points for the 2000 election even by the end of 2011. Consequently, this chapter focuses on the empirical results for the 2000 and 2004 presidential elections, with some illustrative quotes from the 2008 survey.

7. We use the 1998 election because this is the last ANES midterm election that included the good and bad points question for House candidates. In 1998 about one-fifth of the surveyed sample lived in districts where no Democrat was running for Congress (either for an uncontested seat or as a third-party rival to the Republican). About 6 percent of respondents were from districts without a Republican candidate. These two sets of districts were excluded from the respective analyses in the 1998 analyses presented here.

    For additional analyses of these questions for other congressional and senatorial elections, see Gary Jacobson, *The Politics of Congressional Elections*, 7th ed. (New York: Longman, 2009); Paul Gronke, *The Electorate, the Campaign, and the Office: A Unified Approach to Senate and House Elections* (Ann Arbor: University of Michigan Press, 2000).

8. For more extensive analyses of these questions, see Martin Wattenberg, *The Decline of American Political Parties*, 5th ed. (Cambridge, MA: Harvard University Press, 1998); Martin Wattenberg, *The Rise of Candidate Centered Politics* (Cambridge, MA: Harvard University Press, 1992).

9. Gronke, *The Electorate, the Campaign, and the Office*, chapter 6.

10. That is, ritual partisans do not differ substantially from apolitical independents, and cognitive partisans are not substantially more likely than apartisans to express candidate likes or dislikes.

11. Wattenberg, *The Rise of Candidate Centered Politics*; Ian McAllister, "The Personalization of Politics," in *Oxford Handbook of Political Behavior*, eds. Russell Dalton and Hans-Dieter Klingemann (Oxford: Oxford University Press, 2007); Kees Aarts, André Blais, and Hermann Schmitt, eds., *Political Leaders and Democratic Elections* (Oxford: Oxford University Press, 2011).

12. Jacobson, *The Politics of Congressional Elections*, chapter 5.

13. These categories are based on the ANES master codes: 200–399 candidate abilities, 400–499 personal qualities, 500–599 party references, 600–699 government management, 700–799 miscellaneous, 800–1199 policy and political philosophy, and 1200–1299 group ties.

14. There is some evidence that the candidates' abilities and personal qualities have decreased in salience over time for congressional elections, while policy and partisan factors have increased. See Jacobson, *The Politics of Congressional Elections*, chapter 6. There are also sharp differences between incumbents and challengers.

15. Although the ANES had not coded responses to these questions in 2008, they provided an online database of the responses that are quoted in this chapter.

16. Russell Dalton, "Partisan Mobilization, Cognitive Mobilization and the Changing American Electorate," *Electoral Studies* 26 (2007): 274–286.

17. Angus Campbell, Philip Converse, Warren Miller, and Donald Stokes, *The American Voter* (New York: Wiley, 1960), 136. However, *The American Voter* stressed the low number of sophisticated citizens and argued that these levels would not change dramatically.

18. We do not present the 1998 House results because the low number of comments on candidate images makes subgroup percentages less reliable.

19. Donald Stokes, "Some Dynamic Elements of Contests for the Presidency," *American Political Science Review* 60 (1966): 19–28; also see Russell Dalton, "Partisan Mobilization, Cognitive Mobilization and the Changing American Electorate."

20. For a more extensive discussion of these points see Wendy Rahn, "The Role of Stereotypes in Information Processing about Political Candidates," *American Journal of Political Science* 27 (1993): 472–496.

21. Paul Sniderman, Richard Brody, and Philip Tetlock, *Reasoning and Choice* (New York: Cambridge University Press, 1991).

22. Morris Fiorina, "Information and Rationality in Elections," in *Information and Democratic Processes*, eds. John Ferejohn and James Kuklinski (Urbana: University of Illinois Press, 1990); Joseph Bafumi and Robert Shapiro, "A New Partisan Voter," *Journal of Politics* 71 (2009): 1–24.

23. This two-variable regression model yields the following standardized coefficients:

Variable	Total	Independent	Apartisan	Ritual partisan	Cognitive partisan
Left/right	.18	.08	.34	.12	.18
Party therm.	.69	.41	.58	.78	.75
Multiple R	.81	.45	.75	.85	.88

24. These are all open-ended responses about Barack Obama in the 2008 ANES survey.

25. As noted earlier, there are limits in using the open-ended questions. People may favor a candidate for one reason ("he/she is from my party") but then rationalize this choice with their list of good and bad points. The depth of a person's understanding of the points he or she cites is difficult to judge from such open-ended responses. See, for example, Rahn, "The Role of Stereotypes in Information Processing about Political Candidates." The voting models in this chapter are quite simple compared to many other analyses of voting choice.

   Still, in my opinion the advantages of this method outweigh the negatives in answering the questions we are asking. This method allows people to use their own words in describing the candidates, and this is especially valuable in exploring how cog-partisan groups vary in their perceptions of the candidates. It also allows us to compare different elections where the same fixed choice issue questions might not be available or the issues have changed in salience between elections.

26. I followed a very direct measurement strategy. For example, for party cues I counted the number of times the respondent mentioned party criteria as something good about a candidate or bad about his or her opponent. Then the difference between the Democrat's and Republican's party criteria yielded an overall measure of whether party cues leaned more toward one candidate or the other. I repeated this procedure for the policy responses and the candidate abilities and qualities criteria. In principle, each scale is a count of the relative candidate advantage on each dimension, with a theoretical maximum of +10 (pro-Democrat) and a theoretical minimum of -10 (pro-Republican). For a similar analysis of the 2000 election, see Dalton, "Partisan Mobilization, Cognitive Mobilization and the Changing American Electorate."

27. The feeling thermometer asks respondents to evaluate candidates on a 0 to 100 scale, where 0 is very cold and 100 is very warm toward the candidate. Because of the lower visibility of House elections, many respondents lacked a thermometer score for one candidate—typically the challenger. When respondents said "don't know" or could not judge in the 1998 survey, I coded their scores for this candidate as the mean for the entire sample, which was approximately 56 degrees.

28. I counted the total number of times a person used each criterion in evaluating either the good or bad points of either the Democratic or Republican candidates; the resulting scales thus run from zero to a theoretical maximum of twenty (five possible mentions of good or bad points for two candidates).

CHAPTER 8

1. For example, on the heels of Bush's victory in 2000, John Judis and Ruy Teixeira published *The Emerging Democratic Majority* (New York: Scribner, 2002), in which they claimed that long-term demographic trends favored the Democratic Party. Similarly, several decades earlier Kevin Phillip predicted a new Republican era in the wake of Nixon's 1968 victory in *The Emerging Republican Majority* (New York: Anchor, 1970). Neither prediction has come to pass.

2. A significant part of this swing between 2008 and 2010 was a change in who voted. Turnout dropped from over 60 percent in 2008 to 40 percent in 2010 (http://elections.gmu.edu/voter_turnout.htm). The 2010 electorate was also older, whiter, and more conservative than that of 2008. With Obama back at the top of the ticket in 2012, the tide might shift back in the other direction.

3. Angus Campbell, Philip Converse, Warren Miller, and Donald Stokes, *The American Voter* (New York: Wiley, 1961), 142; see also Michael S. Lewis-Beck et al., *The American Voter Revisited* (Ann Arbor: University of Michigan Press, 2008).

4. During the stable state of electoral politics in the 1950s and 1960s, changes in congressional election results varied by relatively small percentages from election to election. Even swings in presidential election results occurred against a backdrop of broader stability in congressional and state election patterns.

5. See Russell Dalton, Ian McAllister, and Martin Wattenberg, "The Consequences of Partisan Dealignment," in *Parties without Partisans*, eds. Russell Dalton and Martin Wattenberg (Oxford: Oxford University Press, 2000) They showed this is a general trend in established democracies.

6. Some 2008 results are not presented in this chapter because the relevant ANES variables were not coded by late 2011.

7. The United States is one of the rare countries where the volatility of the legislative vote share has not increased over time. This deserves more research, but it may reflect the development of safe seats through redistricting and the increasing advantages of incumbency in the U.S. system.

8. This is based on presidential elections from 1964 until 2008. A stable pattern involves not voting in both adjacent elections or voting for the same party. The figure displays those who shifted from voting to nonvoting or shifted from one major party to the other.

9. David Magleby, Candice Nelson, and Mark Westlye, "The Myth of the Independent Voter Revisited," in *Facing the Challenge of Democracy: Explorations in the Analysis of Public Opinion and Political Participation*, eds. Paul Sniderman and Benjamin Highton (Princeton: Princeton University Press, 2011); John Petrocik, "Party Identification: Leaners Are Not Independents," *Electoral Studies* 28 (2009): 562–572; Donald Green, Bradley Palmquist, and Eric Schickler, *Partisan Hearts and Minds: Political Parties and the Social Identities of Voters* (New Haven: Yale University Press, 2002); Bruce Keith et al., *The Myth of the Independent Voter* (Berkeley: University of California Press, 1992).

10. The feeling thermometer measures the person's feelings toward the candidate on a 0 to 100 scale, with 100 being the most positive. I computed the simple difference between thermometer scores of the Democratic minus the Republican candidate in both elections. This yields a measure of relative candidate preference in both years. I then took the difference between the two elections to see if relative opinions in 2000 changed in 2004. If relative candidate opinions in 2004 were within +/- 10 degrees of those in 2000, this was coded as no change. If opinions shifted more than 10 degrees, this was coded as a change in relative opinions. I then compared the direction of change (pro-Democrat or pro-Republican) to the person's initial party leaning on the 2000 party identification question.

11. Because of the small size of the 2000–2004 panel, I combined the separate results for Republican and Democratic identifiers to provide a larger group size for comparisons. The groups in the figure range from 52 to 105 people.

12. The same patterns appear if we compare only those who changed absolute preferences from one party to another, but these comparisons are based on a small number of people.

13. Keith et al., *The Myth of the Independent Voter*, 93–95. Their interpretation of leaners has also been criticized by Zoltan Hajnal and Taeku Lee in chapter 8 of *Why Americans Don't Join the Party*

(Princeton: Princeton University Press, 2011). Hajnal and Lee present additional panel data on how the expressed partisanship of leaners follows their current voting preferences.

14. Howard Gold, "Third Party Voting in Presidential Elections: A Study of Perot, Anderson, and Wallace," *Political Research Quarterly* 48 (1995): 751–773.

15. Pew Center for People and the Press, "September 2010 Political Independents Survey," http://people-press.org/files/legacy-pdf/658.pdf.

16. Russell Dalton and Mark Gray, "Expanding the Electoral Marketplace," in *Democracy Transformed? Expanding Citizen Access in Advanced Industrial Democracies,* eds. Bruce Cain, Russell Dalton, and Susan Scarrow (Oxford: Oxford University Press, 2003).

17. Keith et al., *The Myth of the Independent Voter,* chapter 2.

18. The estimates in this paragraph are based on a linear regression predicting presidential-House vote splitting by the year of the survey. The estimates are based on the two-party comparisons (ignoring third-party presidential candidates). Over fifty years the unstandardized regression coefficient for the total sample describes a 5 percent increase in split-ticket voting (50*.001). For southern whites the regression coefficient is -.002, and for nonsouthern whites it is .002.

19. Nonvoters are included in the calculations of percentages to account for the different turnout rates across the cog-partisan groups and thus the likelihood a person in each group would vote and split his or her ticket.

20. Nonvoters in presidential elections are included in the calculations of these percentages to account for the different turnout rates across the cog-partisan groups. However, since turnout in state and local elections is generally much lower than in presidential elections, this substantially underrepresents the number of nonvoters. If a better measure of turnout were available, it should increase the differences across groups.

21. My colleague also pointed out that betting on U.S. elections is illegal in Nevada, so I would have to travel to London to place my bet.

CHAPTER 9

1. Ian Budge, Ivor Crewe, and Dennis Farlie, eds., *Party Identification and Beyond* (New York: Wiley, 1976); David Butler and Donald Stokes, *Political Change in Britain* (New York: St. Martin's, 1969); Franz Urban Pappi, "Parteiensystem und Sozialstruktur in der Bundesrepublik," *Politische Vierteljahresschrift* 14 (1973): 191–213; Jacques Thomassen, "Party Identification as a Cross-National Concept: Its Meaning in the Netherlands," in *Party Identification and Beyond,* eds. Ian Budge, Ivor Crewe, and Dennis Farlie (London: Wiley, 1976); Jacques Thomassen and Martin Rosema, "Party Identification Revisited," in *Party Identification, Social Identity and Political Experience,* eds. John Bartle and Paolo Bellucci (London: Routledge, 2009).

2. Sören Holmberg, "Party Identification Compared across the Atlantic," in *Elections at Home and Abroad,* eds. M. K. Jennings and T. Mann (Ann Arbor: University of Michigan Press, 1994); Donald Green, Bradley Palmquist, and Eric Schickler, *Partisan Hearts and Minds: Political Parties and the Social Identities of Voters* (New Haven: Yale University Press, 2002), chapter 7.

3. The question reads: "Many people in the Federal Republic lean toward a particular party for a long time, although they may occasionally vote for a different party. How about you: Do you in general lean toward a particular party? Which one?" It then goes on to ask about the strength of these party leanings.

4. Ivor Crewe and John Denver, eds., *Electoral Change* (Oxford: Oxford University Press, 1985); Russell Dalton, Scott Flanagan, and Paul Beck, eds., *Electoral Change in Advanced Industrial Democracies* (Princeton: Princeton University Press, 1984).

5. Russell Dalton and Martin Wattenberg, "Partisan Change and the Democratic Process," in *Parties without Partisans,* eds. Russell Dalton and Martin Wattenberg (Oxford: Oxford University Press, 2000), 266.

6. These data are available from the ESS Web site at www.cses.org. I do not include the Eastern European nations because I expect that partisan development follows a different course in these new democracies. The Comparative Study of Electoral Systems (CSES) asks a similar question on closeness, but it does not include a political interest question that we need for the cognitive mobilization index.

7. Samuel Barnes et al. extensively compared the traditional American party identification question and a party closeness question from the political action study. They found high correlations between both measures at two time points (r=.85 and .88) and general consistency in the patterns and correlates of both questions. Samuel Barnes et al., "Party Identification and Party Closeness in Comparative Perspective," *Political Behavior* 10 (1988): 215–231.

8. The nationally representative CID survey conducted in-person interviews with 1,001 respondents between May 16 and July 19, 2005. International Communications Research (ICR) did the interviews using a clustered, area-probability sample of households and random selection of respondents. Additional information on the survey is available from the project Web site at www.uscidsurvey.org/.

9. Russell Dalton and Steve Weldon, "Partisanship and Party System Institutionalization," *Party Politics* 13 (2007): 179–196. The difference between the two questions in the ANES may arise because prompting individuals with party labels in the ANES version may increase levels of expressed partisanship.

10. Frode Berglund, Sören Holmberg, Hermann Schmitt, and Jacques Thomassen, "Party Identification and Party Choice," in *The European Voter*, ed. Jacques Thomassen (Oxford: Oxford University Press, 2005); Russell Dalton, "The Decline of Party Identification," in *Parties without Partisans*, eds. Russell Dalton and Martin Wattenberg (Oxford: Oxford University Press, 2000); Harold Clarke and Marianne Stewart, "The Decline of Parties in the Minds of Citizens," *Annual Review of Political Science* 1 (1998): 357–378; Anders Todal Jenssen, "All That Is Solid Melts Into Air: Party Identification in Norway," *Scandinavian Political Studies* 22 (1999). 1–27, Günther Lengauer, "Austrian Electoral Behavior in International Comparison," in *The Changing Austrian Voter*, eds. Günter Bischof and Fritz Plasser (Piscataway, NJ: Transaction Press, 2008); Henrik Oscarsson and Sören Holmberg, *Swedish Voting Behavior*, Swedish Election Studies Program, Department of Political Science, University of Gothenburg, June 2010; Ian McAllister, *The Australian Voter: Fifty Years of Change* (Sydney: University of New South Wales Press, 2011), chapter 3.

11. For a review of this evidence see Russell Dalton and Steven Weldon, "Public Images of Parties: A Necessary Evil?" *West European Politics* 9 (2010): 9–23; Pippa Norris, *Democratic Deficit: Critical Citizens Revisited* (New York: Cambridge University Press, 2011), chapter 4.

12. Another possibility is that voters are expressing doubts about parties other than their own. In other words, most parties might be considered untrustworthy—except for the party that the respondent personally supports. It is likely that voters hold their own party as more trustworthy than that of the opposition—democracy functions on this premise—but it is also apparent that attachments to one's preferred party have also weakened.

13. Dalton's "The Decline of Party Identification" presents analyses for a larger set of nations, arguing that the consistency of dealignment undermines nation specific explanations for it. Just as Americans cite Watergate, Vietnam, and other unique events, experts in other nations have their own particular explanations. But it is highly unlikely that independent events coincided in this large set of nations to produce similar dealignment patterns.

14. Ronald Inglehart, *Culture Shift in Advanced Industrial Society* (Princeton: Princeton University Press, 1990), 366. See Figure 2.6 on partisanship trends in Europe.

15. The ESS cognitive mobilization index combines the education and political interest variables. The respondent's educational level is coded: 1) primary school or less, 2) secondary school or less, 3) some college education, or 4) college degree or more. Interest in politics is coded: 1) not at all interested, 2) hardly, 3) quite, and 4) very interested. These two questions were added together to yield a seven-point index (2–8). Those scoring 5 or higher are coded as high on cognitive mobilization.

16. Harold Clarke et al., *Political Choice in Britain* (Oxford: Oxford University Press, 2004), chapter 6.

17. The interpretation of age differences in one survey as generational change is inconclusive because age patterns reflect both generational and life cycle effects. However, Inglehart has shown persisting generational patterns among Europeans across more than a decade (Inglehart, *Culture Shift in Advanced Industrial Society*, 366).

18. I based this supposition on the fact that 24 percent of apolitical independents said "don't know" when asked their left/right position, compared to less than 10 percent of any other group.

19. Angus Campbell, Philip Converse, Warren Miller, and Donald Stokes, *The American Voter* (New York: Wiley, 1961), 143; Sidney Verba, Kay Schlozman, and Henry Brady, *Voice and Equality: Civic*

Voluntarism in American Politics (Cambridge, MA: Harvard University Press, 1995), chapter 12; Martin Wattenberg, *Where Have All the Voters Gone?* (Cambridge, MA: Harvard University Press, 2002).

20. Pippa Norris, *The Democratic Phoenix* (New York: Cambridge University Press, 1998); Charles Pattie, Patrick Seyd, and Paul Whiteley, *Citizenship in Britain: Values, Participation and Democracy* (New York: Cambridge University Press, 2004).

21. Ian Budge, *The New Challenge of Direct Democracy* (Oxford: Polity Press, 1996).

22. To simplify the figure I did not separate ritual and cognitive partisans. As we should expect, apartisan turnout (79 percent) was essentially the same as that of ritual partisans (83 percent), and cognitive partisans were more likely than either group to vote (90 percent) because they experience both partisan and cognitive mobilization.

23. Each index is constructed from a factor analysis, so the population average is zero. For additional discussion of these four indices and a list of items, see chapter 5. The ESS did not contain the additional questions on internet participation that were asked in the United States. I also recalculated the American participation measures in Figure 9.6 and excluded the Internet participation questions.

24. The ESS does not contain relevant questions, and the Comparative Study of Electoral Systems does not include a political interest question that is needed to measure cognitive mobilization. Hence, we turn to a set of national election surveys that include the necessary questions.

25. Russell Dalton, "Apartisans and the Changing German Electorate," *Electoral Studies* (forthcoming in 2012).

26. This figure overstates the pattern for apolitical independents because a larger percentage of this group does not vote (see Figure 9.5).

27. Independents also are changeable voters, but fewer of them actually vote. In addition, the specific patterns of vote switching suggest that independents' voting is less ideologically structured and varies across ideological lines, while vote switching among apartisans seems more ideologically consistent.

28. Bernhard Wessels, "Re-Mobilisierung, Floating oder Abwanderung? Wechselwähler 2002 und 2005 im Vergleich," in *Die Bundestagswahl 2005: Analysen des Wahlkampfes und der Wahlergebnisse*, eds. Frank Brettschneider, Oskar Niedermayer, and Bernhard Wessels (Weisbaden: Verlag für Sozialwissenschaften, 2009); Oscarsson and Holmberg, *Swedish Voting Behavior;* Russell Dalton, Ian McAllister, and Martin Wattenberg, "The Consequences of Dealignment," in *Parties without Partisans*, eds. Russell Dalton and Martin Wattenberg (Oxford: Oxford University Press, 2000).

29. Dalton, "Apartisans and the Changing German Electorate."

30. Philip Converse and Georges Dupeux, "Politicization of the Electorate in France and the United States," *Public Opinion Quarterly* 26 (1962): 1–23.

31. Dalton, McAllister, and Wattenberg, "The Consequences of Dealignment"; William Mayer, ed., *The Swing Voter in American Politics* (Washington: Brookings Press, 2007).

32. The volatility index is calculated as the total percentage-point gains for all the parties between the two adjacent elections. See Mogens Pedersen, "The Dynamics of European Party Systems," *European Journal of Political Research* 7 (1979): 1–26. The figure combines results from the following nineteen nations: Australia, Austria, Belgium, Canada, Denmark, Finland, France, Germany, Iceland, Ireland, Italy, Japan, the Netherlands, New Zealand, Norway, Sweden, Switzerland, the United Kingdom, and the United States.

33. The simple linear relationship is close to the value of the curvilinear model presented in Figure 9.9. If we exclude a handful of outlier elections, such as the Japanese realignment of the 1950s and the Italian realignment of the 1990s, the correlation increases.

34. For earlier national results, see Dalton, McAllister, and Wattenberg, "The Consequences of Dealignment," 41. I updated these trends through 2010 in Figure 9.9. The French case remains the one exception, with no trend from 1951 until 2007. The French pattern reflects the collapse of the Fourth Republic's party system in the late 1950s and the restructuring of the party system under the Fifth Republic. After the new party system was established in France, volatility has increased since the 1960s here as well.

35. See Laakso and Taagepera for the calculation of this statistic: Markku Laakso and Rein Taagepera, "Effective Number of Parties: A Measure with Applications to West Europe," *Comparative Political Studies* 12 (1979): 3–27. The analyses here update Dalton, McAllister, and Wattenberg, "The Consequences of Dealignment."

36. This figure is based on the same set of nations as Figure 9.9.

37. Dalton, "The Decline of Party Identification."

38. The earlier analyses included several European nations and were based on the Eurobarometer studies, but the Eurobarometer no longer regularly asks the party identification question.

39. In several nations the trends are even stronger if one factors in the strength of party identification. See Dalton, "The Decline of Party Identification."

40. Oscarsson and Holmberg, *Swedish Voting Behavior.*

41. Dalton, "The Decline of Party Identification."

CHAPTER 10

1. For two interesting studies of these changes, see Richard Florida, *The Rise of the Creative Class: How It's Transforming Work, Leisure, Community and Everyday Life* (New York: Perseus Books, 2002); Russell Dalton, *The Good Citizen: How a Younger Generation Is Transforming American Politics,* rev. ed. (Washington, DC: CQ Press, 2009).

2. Russell Dalton, Paul Beck, and Scott Flanagan, "Electoral Change in Advanced Industrial Democracies," in *Electoral Change in Advanced Industrial Democracies: Realignment or Dealignment,* eds. Russell Dalton, Paul Beck, and Scott Flanagan (Princeton: Princeton University Press, 1984), 14.

3. Ronald Inglehart and Avram Hochstein, "Alignment and Dealignment of the Electorate in France and the United States," *Comparative Political Studies* (1972) 5: 345. Italics are in original.

4. See Figure 2.3. Also see Pew Center for People and the Press, "Independents Oppose Party in Power . . . Again," September 23, 2010, http://people-press.org/files/legacy-pdf/658.pdf; Jeffrey M. Jones, "Democratic Party ID Drops in 2010, Tying 22-Year Low," Gallup, January 5, 2011, http://www.gallup.com/poll/145463/Democratic-Party-Drops-2010-Tying-Year-Low.aspx.

5. Zoltan Hajnal and Taeku Lee, *Why Americans Don't Join the Party* (Princeton: Princeton University Press, 2011).

6. Mark Hetherington, "Resurgent Mass Partisanship: The Role of Elite Polarization," *American Political Science Review* 95 (2001): 619–632.

7. Larry Bartels, "Partisanship and Voting Behavior," *American Journal of Political Science* 44 (2000): 35–50; Karen Kaufmann, John Petrocik, and Daron Shaw, *Unconventional Wisdom: Facts and Myths about American Voters* (New York: Oxford University Press, 2008), chapter 2; Warren Miller and J. Merrill Shanks, *The New American Voter* (Cambridge, MA: Harvard University Press, 1996).

8. Bruce Keith et al., *The Myth of the Independent Voter* (Berkeley: University of California Press, 1992); Donald Green, Bradley Palmquist, and Eric Schickler, *Partisan Hearts and Minds: Political Parties and the Social Identities of Voters* (New Haven: Yale University Press, 2002); David Magleby, Candice Nelson, and Mark Westlye, "The Myth of the Independent Voter Revisited," in *Facing the Challenge of Democracy: Explorations in the Analysis of Public Opinion and Political Participation,* eds. Paul Sniderman and Benjamin Highton (Princeton: Princeton University Press, 2011).

9. Warren Miller, "Party Identification Re-examined: The Reagan Era," in *Where's the Party?* eds. Warren Miller and John Petrocik (Washington, DC: Center for National Policy, 1987); Philip Converse and Roy Pierce, "Measuring Partisanship," *Political Methodology* 11 (1985): 143. Also see Hajnal and Taeku Lee, *Why Americans Don't Join the Party,* chapter 8.

10. Angus Campbell, Philip Converse, Warren Miller, and Donald Stokes, *The American Voter* (New York: Wiley, 1960) 143.

11. One of the surprising findings is that the processes of social modernization and cognitive mobilization have not significantly decreased the percentage of the American electorate that fits this category of traditional apolitical independents (see chapter 3).

12. Morris Fiorina, "Parties and Partisanship: A Forty Year Retrospective," *Political Behavior* 24 (2002): 93–115; Morris Fiorina, *Retrospective Voting in American National Elections* (New Haven: Yale University Press, 1981).

13. Associated Press, June 17, 2011.

14. David Plouffe, *The Audacity to Win* (New York: Viking, 2009).

15. Wattenberg showed that party references in the candidates' acceptance of the presidential nomination have decreased markedly over time. See Martin Wattenberg, *The Rise of Candidate-Centered Politics* (Cambridge, MA: Harvard University Press, 2002).

16. Also see Joseph Bafumi and Robert Shapiro, "A New Partisan Voter," *Journal of Politics* 71 (2009): 1–24.

17. Russell Dalton, Paul Beck, and Scott Flanagan, "Political Forces and Partisan Change," in *Electoral Change in Advanced Industrial Democracies: Realignment or Dealignment,* eds. Russell Dalton, Paul Beck, and Scott Flanagan (Princeton: Princeton University Press, 1984).

18. Campbell et al., *The American Voter.*

19. See discussion in Pippa Norris, *Radical Right: Voters and Parties in the Electoral Market* (New York: Cambridge University Press, 2005); Russell Dalton, Ian McAllister, and Martin Wattenberg, "The Consequences of Dealignment," in *Parties without Partisans,* eds. Russell Dalton and Martin Wattenberg (Oxford: Oxford University Press, 2000).

INDEX